PSYCHOLOGY
The Science of Mind and Behaviour
STUDY GUIDE

Richard D. Gross and Paul Humphreys

Hodder & Stoughton

A MEMBER OF THE HODDER HEADLINE GROUP

ACKNOWLEDGEMENTS

The authors would like to thank the following: Hugh Coolican for his very constructive criticism of the first draft and later comments on the schematic summaries, Tracy Cullis for her very helpful comments on the schematic summaries, Louise Tooms for her editing of the typescript, and Tim Gregson-Williams for his support, advice and all-round expertise throughout the course of this project. Finally, but by no means least, thanks to all those readers of **Psychology: The Science of Mind & Behaviour**, both students and teachers, who have pointed out the need for a Study Guide.

150/GRO

British Library Cataloguing in Publication Data

Gross, Richard D.
   Psychology: Science of Mind and
   Behaviour. – Study Guide
   I. Title II. Humphreys, Paul
   150

ISBN 0–340–58736–9

First published 1993

Impression number   10   9   8   7   6   5
Year   1998   1997   1996   1995   1994

Typeset by Wearset, Boldon, Tyne and Wear
Printed in Great Britain for Hodder & Stoughton Educational, a division of Hodder Headline Plc, 338 Euston Road, London NW1 3BH by Thomson Litho Ltd, East Kilbride, Scotland.

CONTENTS

To Jan, Tanya and Jo, with love from Richard

In these days of greater sensitivity to all matters relating to Equal Opportunities, Paul would like to record his thanks and love for Dee, Cathie and Hannah who gave him the necessary space and support to do what a writer (as opposed to a partner or a father) needs to do.

INTRODUCTION

This Study Guide is intended as a companion or supplement to
Psychology: The Science of Mind & Behaviour (2nd edition). Each
chapter in Part 1 relates to the corresponding chapter in the main text and
is designed to help you digest and consolidate the material. Nevertheless,
this book will be a valuable study/revision aid for all students of
Psychology, regardless of which textbook you are using.

How should this Study Guide be used?

Part 1 consists of 31 chapters. Each chapter follows the same format:

- multiple choice questions;
- self-assessment questions;
- key terms/concepts; and
- a schematic summary.

For the **multiple-choice questions**, you should choose one of the four
options (a–d). Some questions are deliberately more difficult than others
in that they require you to select the correct *combination* of terms or terms
in the correct *order*; more straightforward questions require you simply to
choose a single option. They are all designed to help you think about the
material: when checking your answers you may sometimes find that you
have to go back to the textbook to convince yourself. The answers are
provided at the end of the book but you must, of course, resist the
temptation to check your answers until you have completed all the
questions!

These sections should ideally be used immediately after you have first
read the chapter; they can then be used later on as a revision aid. It is
therefore advisable to write your answers on a separate sheet of paper and
not in the book itself.

The **self-assessment questions** also vary in terms of the amount of
information and the type/complexity of the answer required: sometimes a
single sentence definition is all that is being asked for (e.g. 'What is meant
by . . . ?'), sometimes a full-length essay (e.g. 'Critically evaluate . . .').
These instruction words reflect those you will find in any essay questions
set as part of your course and in your examinations (detailed help on this
can be found in Part 2 of the Study Guide). Compare these questions
with those actually set by looking back at past AEB A-level papers,
especially those from 1992 onwards.

The **schematic summaries** of each chapter not only reduce 30–40 pages
of text from the main book to a single page, but also make links with
other chapters and other topics. You may already be familiar with this
kind of summarizing technique: for example, you may use 'spider
diagrams' when taking notes in lectures or when reading textbooks.

Certainly, we recommend that you get into the habit of reducing large amounts of information in a way that allows you to revise the material effectively.

In some cases, you will notice that we have provided two schemas for a single chapter. This is because the sheer amount of material in those chapters could not be summarized in one schema without it becoming too crowded and complicated. You may find it useful to produce your own schemas, perhaps taking several topics from a single chapter and preparing one schema for each topic.

To get the most out of this Study Guide, you should make a point of referring back to the relevant section in the textbook after completing each set of exercises; this will help you forge ever-stronger links between the two books and help you improve your overview of the topics covered in the textbook.

Finally, we hope that you will find that using this Study Guide makes the task of becoming a successful student of Psychology at least a little bit easier and, therefore, more enjoyable.

RICHARD GROSS
PAUL HUMPHREYS

PART ONE

1 WHAT IS PSYCHOLOGY?

MULTIPLE-CHOICE QUESTIONS

1 The word 'psychology' literally means __ .

a) study of the brain
b) study of the mind
c) study of behaviour
d) study of the truth

2 The method used by the early psychologists to study the mind was __, which involves observing and analyzing one's own thoughts, feelings etc.

a) psychoanalysis
b) self-hypnosis
c) introspection
d) introversion

3 Watson condemned the study of the mind through introspection on the grounds that it is far too __, i.e. no one else can check out what we report about our thoughts etc.

a) personal
b) objective
c) subjective
d) time-consuming

4 Instead of the mind, Watson argued that an objective, scientific psychology should study __.

a) people's relationships
b) the physiology of the brain
c) observable behaviour
d) all of these

5 Major critics of Watson's Behaviourism were the __ psychologists, who rejected any attempt to break things down into their constituent parts.

a) cognitive

b) Gestalt
c) psychoanalytic
d) clinical

6 The central concept in Freud's Psychoanalytic theory is __.

a) operant conditioning
b) classical conditioning
c) the unconscious mind
d) behavioural analysis

7 'Cognitive processes' refer to all the ways in which we __.

a) learn to change other people's behaviour
b) come to attain, retain and regain information
c) attend, perceive, remember, solve problems, use language and 'think'
d) b and c

8 Regarding people as information processors is the distinguishing feature of __ psychologists.

a) cognitive
b) Gestalt
c) psychoanalytic
d) clinical

9 A distinction, which is sometimes made, is that between the academic and the applied psychologist, which corresponds to that between __.

a) psychoanalysis and behaviourism
b) educational and clinical psychologists
c) the psychologist as scientist/investigator and as practitioner
d) psychology and psychiatry

10 Research carried out largely for its own sake is known as __, while that which is carried out in order to solve a problem is known as __.

a) intrinsic, extrinsic
b) academic, applied
c) applied, pure
d) pure, applied

11 The __ approach focuses on the processes or mechanisms underlying behaviour, while the __ approach focuses more directly on the person.

a) pure, applied
b) process, person
c) psychoanalytic, behaviourist
d) person, process

12 The study of animal behaviour (animal or comparative psychology) was inspired by Darwin's __.

a) conditioning theory
b) psychoanalytic theory
c) laboratory studies of animals
d) theory of evolution

13 Those zoologists who study animal behaviour in its natural habitat are called __.

a) behaviourists
b) ethologists
c) nativists
d) all of these

14 Lorenz is best known for his study of __ in goslings.

a) conditioning
b) unconscious wishes
c) imprinting
d) egg-rolling

15 Social psychology is concerned with __.

a) social facilitation, leadership, conformity and obedience
b) interpersonal perception and attraction
c) attitudes, attitude change, prejudice, pro- and anti-social behaviour
d) all of these

16 Study of the physical, intellectual, social and emotional changes which take place in people over time is the concern of __.

a) social psychology
b) ethology
c) cognitive psychology
d) developmental psychology

17 The lifespan approach sees development as taking place __.

a) throughout the life-cycle
b) from cradle to grave
c) during adulthood as well as in childhood and adolescence
d) all of these

18 Individual differences includes the study of __.

a) learning and conditioning
b) personality, both normal and abnormal
c) intelligence
d) b and c

19 The trait and type approach to personality is closely related to __, which means __ and which uses standardized tests to compare individuals and groups of individuals.

a) psychometrics, mental measurement
b) biometrics, mental measurement
c) paediatrics, assessment of children's development
d) psychometrics, behavioural measurement

20 Freud, Jung and Adler all represent the __ approach to the study of personality.

a) social learning
b) cognitive
c) psychodynamic
d) humanistic

21 The humanistic approach is associated mainly with __.

a) Freud, Jung and Adler
b) Mischell
c) Kelly
d) Maslow and Rogers

22 Educational psychologists __.

a) are trained in the use of psychological tests, particularly intelligence tests
b) are involved in the planning of remedial and other kinds of special education
c) usually work for the Local Education Authority in child guidance clinics, schools or residential children's homes
d) all of these

23 Clinical psychologists __.

a) are trained to assess the mentally handicapped and assess brain damage
b) devise rehabilitation programmes for long-term psychiatric patients
c) plan and implement behaviour therapy/modification
d) all of these

24 Psychotherapy may be carried out by clinical psychologists, but is more likely to be performed by __, who are doctors specializing in psychological illness, or by __, who may have come from a variety of professional backgrounds before receiving a special training in psychotherapy.

a) psychiatrists, psychotherapists
b) psychoanalysts, psychiatrists
c) psychiatric social workers, behaviour therapists
d) paediatricians, psychotherapists

25 Industrial or occupational psychologists __.

a) administer aptitude tests and tests of interest as part of the selection of people for jobs and vocational guidance
b) design training schemes to help workers adapt to new technology and production methods
c) design equipment and machinery and the work environment generally
d) all of these

26 The computer analogy is a way of trying to __.

a) understand how computers work by comparing them with human cognitive processes
b) understand how the brain/human cognitive processes work by comparing them with how computer programs work
c) compare different computers with each other in terms of the size of their memories
d) all of these

27 The major function of a theory is to __.

a) describe the facts/observed phenomena
b) explain the facts/observed phenomena
c) account for the facts/observed phenomena
d) b and c

28 A testable statement about the relationship between two or more variables is a definition of __.

a) a theory
b) a model
c) science
d) a hypothesis

29 We are all psychologists in the sense that __.

a) we all have psychological problems from time to time
b) we inevitably try to make sense of our own and other people's behaviour
c) we carry out experiments and publish the results
d) all of these

30 In its formal/scientific role, psychology should aim to __.

a) confirm common sense
b) contradict common sense
c) provide understanding, prediction and control above the levels of common sense
d) all of these

SELF-ASSESSMENT QUESTIONS

1 What was different about Wundt's approach to studying the mind compared with previous approaches?

2 How have definitions of psychology changed during the 110 years or so of psychology's history?

3 Outline Watson's objections to the study of the mind through introspection. How was behaviourism meant to meet these objections?

4 Compare and contrast the process and person approaches, giving examples of each approach.

5 Choose one area of applied psychology and describe in detail the role(s) performed by the psychologists concerned.

6 What is the relationship between psychology and other sciences/social sciences? In particular, how is psychology related to cognitive science?

7 Compare and contrast any two major schools of thought/theoretical approaches in terms of how they see the nature of human beings, psychological normality and abnormality, methods of treatment and goals of treatment, development and preferred methods of study.

8 Define the following: hypothetical construct; computer analogy; theory; hypothesis; model.

9 Explain the difference between formal and informal psychology and how they are related.

KEY TERMS/CONCEPTS

academic/applied branches
animal psychology
artificial intelligence
behaviour modification
behaviour therapy
behaviourist/behaviourism
biological bases of
  behaviour
British Psychological
  Society
chartered psychologist
classical/operant
  conditioning
clinical psychology
cognitive development
cognitive learning
cognitive processes
cognitive science
common sense/informal
  psychology
comparative psychology

computer analogy
conscious thought/mental
  life
controlled conditions
developmental psychology
educational psychology
ergonomics/human
  engineering
ethologist/ethology
forensic/legal psychologist
genetics
Gestalt psychology
heredity–environment/
  nature–nurture issue
higher-order mental
  activities
hypothesis
hypothetical constructs
imprinting
individual differences
industrial/occupational

  psychologist
inference
information processor
insight learning
introspection(-ism)
investigator (scientist)/
  practitioner roles
learning
learning theory
lifespan approach
mental maps
mind–body issue
model
neurophysiological
  psychologists
observational learning
  (modelling)
ontogeny
organizational psychology
personality
phylogeny

process and person
  approaches
psychiatrist
psychoanalytic theory
psychopathology/
  abnormal psychology
psychotherapy/
  psychotherapist
pure and applied research
reductionism
schools of thought/
  theoretical approaches
social cognition
social learning theory
social psychology
sociobiology
stimulus–response (S–R)
structuralism
theories of learning
theory
unconscious mind

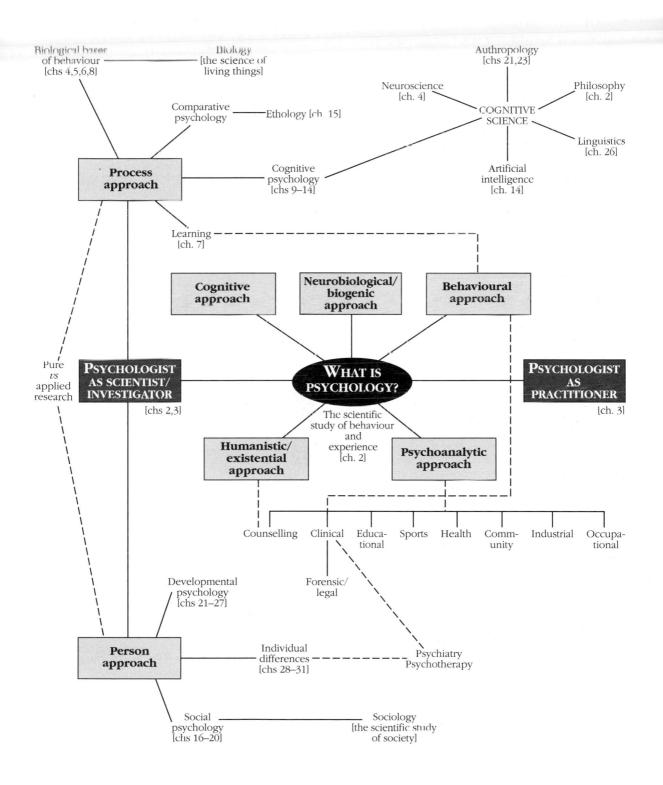

2 IS PSYCHOLOGY A SCIENCE?

MULTIPLE-CHOICE QUESTIONS

1 In order to understand the development of psychology as a separate discipline, we need to trace its __ roots, in particular __ and __.

a) scientific, experimentation, observation
b) philosophical, empiricism, nativism
c) philosophical, empiricism, positivism
d) philosophical, existentialism, realism

2 According to the empiricists, __.

a) the only source of true knowledge is what comes through our senses
b) knowledge of the world is largely inborn
c) both (a) and (b)
d) none of these

3 The extreme environmentalism of Locke's theory is built into the __ view of learning, whereby the child can be made into anything the environment wants it to become.

a) humanistic
b) psychoanalytic
c) behaviourist
d) cognitive

4 The word 'empirical' is often used to mean __ and implies the use of __ and __ as methods of establishing the truth.

a) psychological, introspection, self-observation
b) theoretical, reasoning, argument
c) scientific, observation measurement
d) logical, observation, measurement

5 Emphasis on the use of experiments and other scientific methods to collect data corresponds to __, while belief in the importance of the environment in shaping behaviour and the mind as a blank slate corresponds to __.

a) methodological behaviourism, philosophical behaviourism
b) operant conditioning, classical conditioning
c) philosophical behaviourism, methodological behaviourism
d) experimental psychology, humanistic psychology

6 Among the criteria of a science is __.

a) a definable subject-matter
b) theory construction and hypothesis testing
c) use of empirical methods to collect data
d) all of these

7 The classic picture of how science takes place is __ according to which __.

a) deduction; facts are discovered through rational argument
b) induction; facts are discovered through rational argument
c) deduction; general conclusions are drawn from a number of separate observations
d) induction; general conclusions are drawn from a number of separate observations

8 The problem with induction is that __.

a) there is no such thing as an unbiased or unprejudiced observation
b) however many observations we make,

we can never be certain about the conclusions we draw from them
c) observation is always related, more or less directly, to a theory
d) all of these

9 According to Kuhn's concept of a paradigm, __.

a) theory is absolutely central to the definition of a science
b) a majority of workers in the field must share a common theory or perspective for it to be called a science
c) where no common theory exists, a state of pre-science exists
d) all of these

10 The various theoretical approaches within psychology can each be thought of as a separate __, so that psychology as a whole is still in the stage of __.

a) science, normal science
b) discipline, normal science
c) paradigm, normal science
d) paradigm, pre-science

11 The importance of theories is that __.

a) they perform the heuristic function of guiding research
b) they help select from all the possible experiments which could be carried out
c) they provide explanations of the world around us
d) all of these

12 The falsifiability criterion of a theory __.

a) is also known as refutability
b) states that it must be possible to show the theory to be false
c) is meant to distinguish between scientific and non-scientific theories which the principle of verification cannot do
d) all of these

13 The idiographic approach refers to __, while the nomothetic approach refers to __.

a) the study of people, the study of animals
b) the study of groups, the study of individuals
c) the study of abnormality, the study of normality
d) the study of individuals, the study of groups

14 The three main aims of a science are usually taken to be __.

a) understanding, prediction and control
b) understanding, explanation and control
c) understanding, explanation and prediction
d) self-understanding, self-control and prediction

15 In the case of psychology, George Miller believes that __.

a) understanding and prediction are more appropriate aims than control
b) understanding, including self-understanding, is the primary aim
c) a major role is to change our conception of what we are like as human beings
d) all of these

16 The experiment is usually regarded as the most scientific of all the methods used by psychologists because __.

a) it is replicable
b) it tells us about cause and effect
c) it allows the highest degree of control and objectivity
d) all of these

17 Statistics are used to __.

a) describe the data, making it easier to understand
b) tell us about the probability of the results having occurred by chance alone
c) tell us about the significance of the results
d) all of these

18 Replication of other researchers' results illustrates the very ___ nature of scientific activity, whereby there are internationally agreed ___ about how to report one's findings so that others may check them for themselves.

a) objective, criteria
b) private, conventions
c) social, conventions
d) systematic, rules

19 It is the ___ of people, compared with inanimate objects, which makes human subjects much ___ of people in general.

a) variability, more representative
b) homogeneity, less representative
c) heterogeneity, more representative
d) variability, less representative

20 Experiments are of two major kinds, ___ and ___. This distinction demonstrates that an experiment is *not* defined by ___ it takes place but by ___ it is conducted.

a) laboratory, field, where, how
b) laboratory, field, how, where
c) artificial, realistic, how, where
d) laboratory, field, where, whom

21 A major argument in favour of using animals as subjects is that ___.

a) there is an underlying evolutionary continuity between humans and other species
b) there are only quantitative differences between humans and other species (i.e. differences of degree)
c) humans are merely more complex than other species
d) all of these

22 The mistake of trying to explain human behaviour in terms of how rats perform in Skinner boxes is called ___, while ___ is the mistake of attributing human characteristics to non-human animals or objects.

a) ratomorphism, egocentrism
b) anthropomorphism, ratomorphism

c) ratomorphism, anthropomorphism
d) ethnocentrism, animism

23 A fundamental feature of the psychological experiment which makes it less than completely objective is that ___.

a) it is a social situation
b) the subject engages in a form of problem-solving behaviour, trying to work out how he/she should behave
c) the experimenter unconsciously conveys to the subject how he/she should behave
d) all of these

24 The double-blind technique ___.

a) is a way of trying to reduce experimenter bias
b) involves making sure that the experimenter who tests subjects' performance does not know who is being tested under which condition of the experiment
c) is a way of trying to study perceptual bias or set
d) a and b

25 Reductionism refers to any attempt to explain ___.

a) a complex whole in terms of its basic units
b) something by comparison with something else
c) some phenomenon by studying it on a smaller scale
d) a complex whole in terms of something even more complex

26 According to 'soft determinism' ___.

a) an act may be considered free as long as it is free from coercion or compulsion
b) free acts may be caused by conscious mental life
c) whether or not an act is free depends on the nature of the cause rather than the presence or absence of one
d) all of these

SELF-ASSESSMENT QUESTIONS

1 In what ways did empiricism and positivism contribute to the development of psychology as a separate discipline?

2 What is the difference between philosophical and methodological behaviourism?

3 Outline the main criteria of a science.

4 Describe the differences between the inductive and hypothetico-deductive methods.

5 Describe Kuhn's concept of a paradigm. How useful is it in assessing the scientific status of psychology?

6 What is meant by the falsifiability/ refutability criterion of a theory? How does it differ from the principle of verification?

7 What is the difference between the idiographic and nomothetic approaches to the study of behaviour?

8 What are the three main aims of science? How appropriate are they as applied to psychology?

9 Why is the experiment the 'method of choice'?

10 Outline some of the arguments put forward for the use of animal studies in psychology.

11 In what ways is the psychology experiment a fundamentally social situation?

12 Define the term 'reductionism'. Using examples, discuss some of the criticisms of the attempt to reduce psychological phenomena to neurophysiological ones.

13 Briefly describe three theories of the relationship between the mind and the body (or the mind and brain).

14 Does belief in free-will necessarily exclude a belief in (some form of) determinism?

KEY TERMS/CONCEPTS

actions versus movements
animal experiments
anthropomorphism
artificiality (of laboratory
  experiments)
association
cause and effect
computational theory of
  mind (CTM)
conscious mental life
  (CML)
data collection
demand characteristics
descriptive statistics
double-aspect theory
double-blind technique
dualism
empirical methods
empiricists/empiricism/
  empirical
environmentalism
epiphenomenalism
experiment as method of
  choice
experimental control
experimental design
experimenter bias
fertility criterion (of a

theory)
field experiments
freedom as an illusion
  (Skinner)
free-will versus
  determinism
general laws/principles
heuristic function (of
  theories)
hierarchy of levels of
  explanation
hypothesis testing
hypothetical construct
hypothetico-deductive
  method
idealism
identity theory
idiographic
independent and
  dependent variables
induction
interactionism
internal consistency (of a
  theory)
isomorphism
law of parsimony/Occam's
  razor
logical behaviourism

logical positivists
materialism
methodological
  behaviourism
mind–body problem/
  problem of mind and
  brain
monism
nativists
naturalistic functionalism
nomothetic
objectivity
paradigm
paradigm shift
personal construct theory
philosophical
  behaviourism
positivism
pre-science/normal
  science/revolution
probability
problem-solving behaviour
  (of subjects)
psychology experiment as
  a social situation
psychophysical parallelism
quantitative versus
  qualitative differences

rationalists
ratomorphism
reductionism
reflexive/reflexivity
refutability/falsifiability
replicability (repeatability)
responsibility/moral
  responsibility
rule following
science
self-understanding
single-blind technique
situational variables
soft determinism
software versus hardware
statistical tests of
  significance
stimulus–response units
subject variables
tabula rasa
theory construction
truth value
understanding, prediction
  and control
universe of discourse
verification

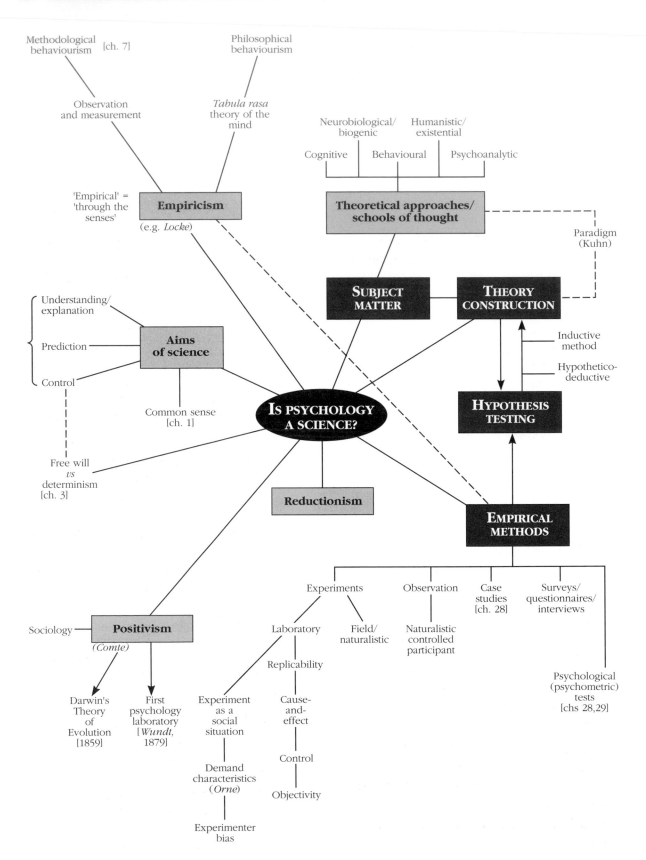

Methodological behaviourism [ch. 7]

Philosophical behaviourism

Observation and measurement

Tabula rasa theory of the mind

'Empirical' = 'through the senses'

Empiricism
(e.g. *Locke*)

Neurobiological/ biogenic

Humanistic/ existential

Cognitive   Behavioural   Psychoanalytic

Theoretical approaches/ schools of thought

Paradigm (Kuhn)

Understanding/ explanation

Prediction

Control

Aims of science

Common sense [ch. 1]

SUBJECT MATTER

THEORY CONSTRUCTION

Inductive method

Hypothetico-deductive

IS PSYCHOLOGY A SCIENCE?

HYPOTHESIS TESTING

Free will *vs* determinism [ch. 3]

Reductionism

EMPIRICAL METHODS

Sociology

Positivism
(*Comte*)

Experiments

Observation

Case studies [ch. 28]

Surveys/ questionnaires/ interviews

Darwin's Theory of Evolution [1859]

First psychology laboratory [*Wundt*, 1879]

Laboratory

Field/ naturalistic

Naturalistic controlled participant

Replicability

Experiment as a social situation

Cause-and-effect

Psychological (psychometric) tests [chs 28,29]

Demand characteristics (*Orne*)

Control

Objectivity

Experimenter bias

3 PSYCHOLOGY AND ETHICS

MULTIPLE-CHOICE QUESTIONS

1 An important distinction is that between __ and __, the latter role relating to practical and clinical situations where people's behaviour may undergo change.

a) psychologists as investigators, psychologists as scientists
b) psychologists as scientists, psychologists as practitioners
c) psychologists as investigators, psychologists as practitioners
d) b and c

2 Only if subjects are informed of the true purpose of the investigation can they give their __.

a) consent
b) permission
c) informed consent
d) all of these

3 Children and those with the mental age of children are unable to give consent and so __.

a) cannot participate in psychological research
b) can only be involved in observational studies
c) fall outside the ethical guidelines
d) require consent to be given on their behalf by parents and those in loco parentis

4 A basic right of subjects is that they should not be exposed to harm, unusual discomfort or other negative consequences for their future lives __.

a) unless their parents/guardians have agreed to it

b) unless they have given informed, real consent
c) unless there is very good reason for doing so
d) unless the investigation is concerned with masochism

5 Baumrind criticized Milgram for __.

a) not taking adequate steps to protect subjects' welfare
b) exposing subjects to unacceptably high levels of stress and emotional conflict
c) failing to select a representative sample
d) a and b

6 Even if Milgram did not expect/intend his subjects to experience so much stress, he still __, telling them it was a study of __.

a) believed it was justified, people's ability to tolerate conflict
b) deceived them as to the true purpose of the experiment, the effects of punishment on learning
c) defended his right to carry out any research he saw fit, conformity
d) deceived them as to the true purpose of the experiment, conformity and obedience

7 In the Prison Simulation Experiment, __.

a) there was much distress among prisoner subjects but no deception was involved
b) both prisoners and prison guards suffered much distress but no deception was involved
c) the study was ended earlier than

planned due to the distress of the
prisoners, but there was no deception
involved

d) a and c

8 Related to the giving of consent/informed
consent is the subject's right to __.

a) withdraw from the investigation at any
time
b) have his/her data destroyed
c) withdraw at any time regardless of any
payment received
d) all of these

9 Deception is most likely to have harmful
effects __.

a) in situations where subjects learn
something about themselves as a person
b) in situations that most resemble real
life, as in social psychology
c) when the subject's self-image is affected
d) all of these

10 In field experiments, such as the Piliavin
et al study of bystander intervention,
staged in the New York subway __.

a) subjects were unaware that an
experiment was taking place
b) subjects were unable to give either
consent or informed consent
c) subjects were unprotected from a range
of emotional responses to the staged
collapse (e.g. fear, guilt, distress)
d) all of these

11 At best, deception may only be justified if
__.

a) it is necessary that subjects believe they
are in a real-life situation
b) the behaviour being studied is of
general social significance
c) the psychologist believes that the
subjects will not suffer in any way
d) a and b

12 In addition to protecting the subject from
mental harm, the psychologist is obliged
to protect him/her from __ harm, a
principle which was blatantly breached in

the case of __, in whom a __ was
deliberately induced.

a) physical, Little Albert, fear of a white
rat
b) physical, Little Hans, fear of a horse
c) psychological, Little Peter, fear of food
d) physical, Little Hans, fear of his father

13 The risk of physical or mental harm
should be __ in the subject's normal
everyday life.

a) at least as great as
b) no greater than
c) considerably less than
d) significantly greater than

14 Debriefing may sometimes involve a
discussion with the experimenter
immediately after the experiment is over,
but it may also __.

a) be carried out over a much longer
period of time
b) involve follow-up questionnaires and
discussions
c) be thought of as a form of post-
experimental therapy
d) all of these

15 The principle of confidentiality may be
contravened __.

a) where there is a clear/direct risk to
human life
b) where the subject is a prisoner or
psychiatric patient
c) where the subject is a child
d) all of these

16 Psychologists are obliged to __.

a) report their results in a way which
enables others to test the hypothesis for
themselves
b) acknowledge all those who were
involved in the research
c) report their results fully and honestly
d) all of these

17 The two most common arguments in
defence of animal experiments are __.

a) the pursuit of scientific knowledge; the wish to control the numbers of certain species
b) the advancement of medicine; the wish to control the numbers of certain species
c) the pursuit of scientific knowledge; the advancement of medicine
d) b and c

18 Where the degree of suffering is extreme, as in the Executive Monkey experiment, ___.

a) even the combination of the medical and scientific arguments is insufficient to justify continuation of the research
b) the medical argument is strong enough to justify continuation of the research
c) the scientific argument is strong enough to justify continuation of the research
d) extra care must be taken in generalizing the results to human beings

19 Any use of deprivation, electric shock or other kind of aversive stimulation ___.

a) is illegal unless the experimenter holds a Home Office licence and relevant certificates
b) must only proceed if there are no alternative ways of conducting the research
c) may only be conducted with non-endangered species
d) a and b

20 Gray believes that ___.

a) speciesism is justified
b) we have a moral duty to give preference to members of our own species
c) helping to prevent human suffering is the exception to the general ethical principle that it is wrong to inflict pain
d) all of these

21 The first loyalty of psychologists as practitioners is to ___.

a) their colleagues
b) the head of the institution
c) the employing authority
d) their clients

22 According to Fairbairn and Fairbairn, ethics has received relatively little attention in psychology, compared with other caring professions, because ___.

a) it is believed that psychology is a value-free science
b) it is believed that therapists should be value-neutral/non-directive
c) psychologists tend to be less moral than the others
d) a and b

23 According to the scientist–practitioner model of clinical psychology ___.

a) clinical psychology is guided by/operates within the framework of general scientific method
b) clinical psychologists cannot be both scientists and practitioners
c) clinical psychologists are primarily scientists and are helpers only in a secondary sense
d) clinical psychologists are primarily helpers and are scientists only in a secondary sense

24 Two major criticisms of scientific behaviour therapy/modification are that ___.

a) it dehumanizes its clients by treating them as if they were organisms rather than agents
b) clients come to see themselves as abnormal, helpless, worthless and passive organisms
c) it is ineffective
d) a and b

25 A basic ethical principle involved in psychologists' attempts to bring about change is ___.

a) respect for individuals as persons
b) helping clients to make responsible decisions about their lives
c) helping clients to take (some degree of) control of their lives
d) all of these

SELF-ASSESSMENT QUESTIONS

1 Why is it important to have codes of conduct/ethical guidelines at all in psychology?

2 What is the difference between consent and informed consent? Are there particular groups of subjects for whom consent is specially important as an ethical principle?

3 Briefly outline Milgram's obedience experiment. How were his subjects prevented from giving informed consent and from exercising their right to withdraw?

4 Describe one of Milgram's arguments in defence of his experiment. To what extent do you consider this to be a valid argument?

5 What is meant by debriefing? What is its function?

6 Can deception ever be justified as part of psychological research?

7 What particular ethical problems are faced by psychologists conducting naturalistic observations and field experiments?

8 Briefly describe the Executive Monkey experiments and explain why they are ethically unsound.

9 What are some of the safeguards taken to protect animals from aversive stimulation?

10 Define the term speciesism. To what extent do you agree with speciesism as an argument in support of animal experimentation?

11 Why should the belief in psychology as a value-free science make psychologists less likely to consider ethical issues than others working in the caring professions?

12 Outline some of the ethical criticisms of scientific behaviour therapy/modification.

13 What problems are involved in regarding therapists as value-neutral and non-directive?

14 What are the fundamental obligations of therapists and clinical psychologists to their clients?

KEY TERMS/CONCEPTS

advancement of medicine argument (for using animal subjects)

American Psychological Association

animal suffering

autonomy

behaviour therapy/ modification

British Psychological Society

Burt's Twin Studies data

case of Little Albert

Cayo Santiago

clinical (and other) psychologists as agents of psychological change

codes of conduct/ethical guidelines

confidentiality

consent

consent given by parents/ those in loco parentis

debriefing

deception

exceptions to the rule of confidentiality

Executive Monkey Experiments

field versus laboratory experiments

food deprivation and electric shock as most objected-to treatments

free-feeding (ad lib) body weight

'giving psychology away' to the people

helping clients take responsibility for/control of their own lives

importance of acknowledging all those who contribute to a research project

informed/real consent

involuntary participation (in naturalistic observation/field experiments)

loyalty to clients by clinical psychologists

Milgram's obedience experiments

need for Home Office licence

need to disturb wild animals as little as possible

need to report data fully and honestly

need to understand species differences

participants versus subjects

protection of subjects from both mental and physical harm

psychologist as practitioner

psychologist as scientist/ investigator

psychology as value-free

science

replication

respect for clients as persons

right to withdraw from the investigation

role of ethical committees

scientific knowledge argument (for using animal subjects)

scientist–practitioner model (of clinical psychology)

speciesism (as argument for animal research)

the role of stooges/ confederates

therapists as value-neutral and non-directive

ultimate goal of human betterment

Zimbardo et al's Prison Simulation Experiment

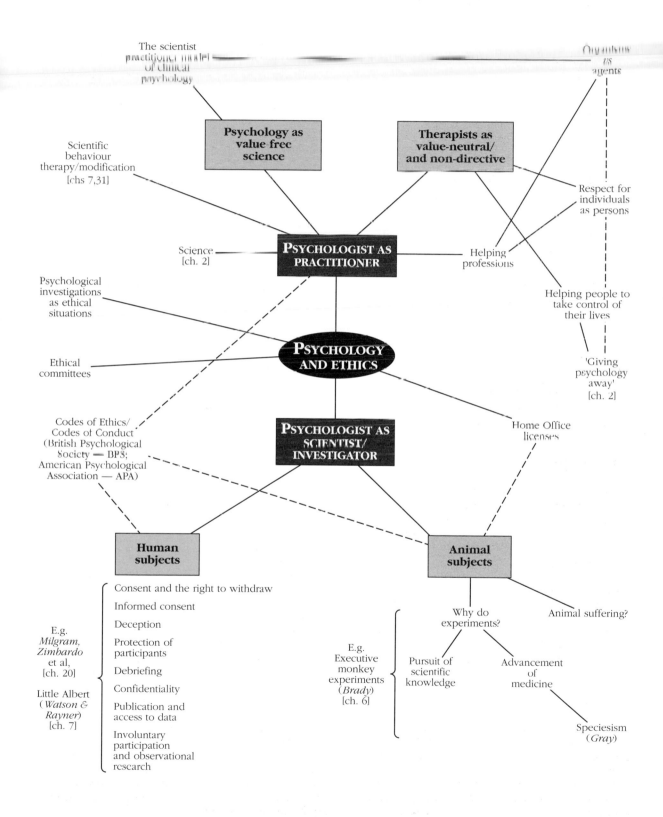

4 THE NERVOUS SYSTEM

MULTIPLE-CHOICE QUESTIONS

1 Neurons or nerve cells __.

a) are the only kind of cell in the nervous system
b) are the basic structural units/building blocks of the nervous system
c) are most numerous in the brain, particularly the cerebral cortex
d) b and c

2 There are __ main types of neuron, __.

a) two, central and peripheral
b) three, central, connector and peripheral
c) two, sensory and motor
d) three, sensory, motor and interneuron/connector

3 Information is passed from neuron to neuron in the form of __ which are received by the __ and then travel down the __ away from the cell body/soma.

a) electrochemical impulses, nucleus, dendrites
b) magnetic waves, dendrites, axon
c) electrochemical impulses, dendrites, axon
d) electrochemical impulses, nucleus, axon

4 The synaptic cleft (or gap) refers to the __.

a) point at which two terminal buttons touch
b) area of the terminal button containing the neurotransmitter
c) minute gap between the pre-synaptic and the post-synaptic membranes
d) none of these

5 The electrochemical signal which passes down the axon is called __.

a) the sodium-potassium pump
b) a potential action
c) a neurotransmitter
d) an action potential

6 When an action potential occurs, __.

a) the inside of the neuron changes very briefly from negative to positive
b) the sodium channels are opened
c) the neuron becomes permeable to sodium ions
d) all of these

7 __ pairs of __ nerves leave the brain through holes in the skull, while __ pairs of __ nerves leave the spinal cord through the vertebrae.

a) 31, spinal, 12, cranial
b) 12, spinal, 31, cranial
c) 12, cranial, 31, spinal
d) 31, cranial, 12, spinal

8 Neurotransmitters __.

a) are what determine whether a synapse is either excitatory or inhibitory
b) are localized in specific groups of neurons and pathways
c) have a fairly direct influence on receiving neurons, unlike neuromodulators
d) all of these

9 Neuromodulators __.

a) prepare neurons for stimulation by neurotransmitters
b) include the encephaline and the endorphins (also known as optoids)
c) stimulate neurons directly, just as neurotransmitters do
d) a and b

10 Tricyclics and monoamine oxidase (MAO) inhibitors are both types of __.

a) amphetamines
b) tranquillizers
c) hallucinogens
d) antidepressants

11 The minor tranquillizers are also known as __ and work by affecting the neurotransmitter __.

a) benzodiazepines, GABA
b) anxiolytic sedatives, dopamine
c) anxiolytic sedatives, GABA
d) a and c

12 The need for ever larger amounts of a drug in order to produce the same effect is called __ which soon gives way to __.

a) addiction, tolerance/dependence
b) dependence, tolerance/addiction
c) tolerance, dependence/addiction
d) craving, dependence/addiction

13 The nervous system as a whole is subdivided into the __ and the __ nervous systems, the latter subdividing into the __ and __ nervous systems.

a) central, peripheral, sympathetic, parasympathetic
b) central, peripheral, autonomic, somatic
c) central, autonomic, sympathetic, parasympathetic
d) central, somatic, peripheral, autonomic

14 The sympathetic and parasympathetic are the two branches of the __.

a) central nervous system
b) peripheral nervous system
c) automatic nervous system
d) autonomic nervous system

15 The electroencephalogram (EEG)

a) involves attaching electrodes to the scalp
b) records the action potentials of large groups of neurons
c) has been used extensively in the study of sleep and other states of consciousness
d) all of these

16 The brain is usually subdivided into __.

a) the cerebral hemispheres and the sub-cortical areas
b) the neo-cortex and the 'old mammalian brain'
c) the forebrain, midbrain and hindbrain
d) the frontal, temporal, parietal and occipital lobes

17 The frontal, parietal, occipital and temporal lobes are the locations of the cortex, __ cortex, __ cortex and __ cortex respectively.

a) motor, somatosensory, visual, auditory
b) motor, visual, auditory, somatosensory
c) visual, auditory, motor, somatosensory
d) auditory, visual, somatosensory, motor

18 The hypothalamus __.

a) comprises seven distinct structural and functional areas
b) represents a crucial link between the central and autonomic nervous systems
c) plays a crucial role in homeostasis and motivation
d) all of these

19 Together, the thalamus, hypothalamus, amygdala, olfactory bulb (plus other structures) comprise the functional area called the __.
a) basal ganglia
b) midbrain
c) limbic system
d) hindbrain

20 The midbrain, pons and medulla oblongata together make up __.

a) the limbic system
b) the reticular activating system
c) the brain stem
d) the peripheral nervous system

21 The cerebellum __.

a) plays a vital role in the co-ordination of voluntary muscle activity
b) plays a crucial role in the performance of well-learned, 'automatic', behaviour, such as walking
c) is crucially involved in motivation and emotion
d) a and b

22 The spinal reflex arc (e.g. the knee-jerk reflex) is the basic __ unit of the nervous system and consists of just __ neurons, linked by a __ synapse.

a) structural, two, single
b) functional, two, single
c) functional, three, simple
d) physical, two, single

23 According to the __, corresponding parts of the brain are able to take over the function of the area which has been damaged.

a) law of mass action
b) all-or-none rule
c) law of parsimony
d) law of equipotentiality

24 If, in a split-brain experiment, 'key' is flashed onto the screen such that only the *right* hemisphere 'sees' the word, the subject __.

a) can select the key from a pile of objects using the left hand
b) is unable to say what word appeared on the screen
c) cannot say why he/she chose that object
d) all of these

25 Based largely on split-brain studies, Sperry and others have argued that each hemisphere __.

a) has its own separate perceptions, thoughts etc.
b) is specialized for different kinds of ability
c) constitutes a separate mind/sphere of consciousness
d) all of these

26 The left hemisphere is commonly seen as specialized for __ thinking, processing information in a __ way and using a __ mode of operation.

a) synthetic, diffuse, holistic
b) analytic, sequential, linear
c) logical, diffuse, holistic
d) analytic, logical, holistic

27 The autonomic nervous system

a) is part of the peripheral nervous system
b) controls the internal organs over which we have little, if any, voluntary control
c) comprises two branches, the sympathetic and parasympathetic
d) all of these

28 The sympathetic branch takes over __.

a) in emergency, 'fight or flight' situations
b) under catabolic conditions
c) under anabolic conditions
d) a and b

29 The endocrine system is controlled by the __ gland, which is found in the brain, close to the __ but is not __ part of the nervous system.

a) pituitary, thalamus, functionally
b) adrenal, hypothalamus, structurally
c) pituitary, hypothalamus, functionally
d) thyroid, thalamus, functionally

30 The adrenal medulla secretes __ and __ which are the neurotransmitters for the __ branch of the autonomic nervous system.

a) adrenaline, noradrenaline, sympathetic
b) adrenaline, noradrenaline, parasympathetic
c) ACTH, adrenaline, sympathetic
d) ACTH, noradrenaline, sympathetic

SELF-ASSESSMENT QUESTIONS

1 Describe the basic structure of a neuron. What are the different functions performed by different kinds of neuron?

2 Outline the process by which information is passed between neurons in the form of electrochemical impulses.

3 Name four neurotransmitters and describe their effects on the receiving neuron and associated behaviour.

4 Name three kinds of psychoactive drugs and describe their effects on neurotransmitters and on physiology, mood and behaviour.

5 What are the major subdivisions of the nervous system? How are the central and autonomic nervous systems related?

6 Describe and evaluate some of the methods used to investigate the brain.

7 Outline the major changes which occur in the brain during the post-natal period.

8 Describe the structure and function of the cerebral hemispheres.

9 Describe a typical split-brain study. How valid are the conclusions regarding the characteristics of the two cerebral hemispheres which have been drawn from such studies?

10 Explain the role of the hypothalamus as a link between the central and autonomic nervous systems.

11 What are the major differences between the sympathetic and parasympathetic branches of the autonomic nervous system?

12 Describe the role of the pituitary gland in relation to the endocrine system as a whole. How are the pituitary and the hypothalamus related?

KEY TERMS/CONCEPTS

ablation
absolute refractory period
acetylcholine (ACh)/ noradrenaline/dopamine/ serotonin/GABA
action potential
adrenal glands-medulla and cortex
all-or-none-rule
amphetamines/ antidepressants/L-dopa/ major tranquillizers (phenothiazines)/minor tranquillizers (benzodiazepines)/ hallucinogens
anatomical studies/post-mortems
ANS-sympathetic/ parasympathetic branches
average evoked potentials (AEPs)
axon
basal ganglia
bilateral representation
brain stem/midbrain/ pons/medulla oblongata
Broca's area
central nervous system (CNS)/brain and spinal

cord
cerebellum
cerebral cortex
cerebral hemispheres (cerebrum)
chemical stimulation electrical stimulation and recording
clinical studies
commissurotomy
contralateral control
corpus callosum
corticospinal decussation
cranial/spinal nerves
cytoplasm
dendrites
dorsal/ventral root (of spinal nerves)
electrochemical impulses
electroencephalogram (EEG)
endocrine (hormonal) system
excitatory/inhibitory synapses
frontal/parietal/occipital/ temporal lobes
glial ('glue') cell
habituation
homeostasis
hypothalamus

Lashley's laws of mass action and equipotentiality
lesion
limbic system
localization of brain function/functional lateralization
medulla oblongata
motor (expressive) aphasia
motor/somatosensory/ visual/auditory/ association cortex
neuromodulators
neuron/nerve cell
neurotransmitters
orienting reflex
peripheral nervous system (PNS)–somatic nervous system (SNS)/autonomic nervous system (ANS)
phylogenetic-evolutionary scale
pituitary gland-anterior and posterior
placebos ('dummy drugs')
pons
presynaptic/postsynaptic membrane
principle of multiple control

psychoactive drugs
radioactive labelling/CAT scan/PET scan/NMR or MRI
receptive aphasia
relative refractory period
resting potential
reticular activating system (RAS)/ascending RAS (ARAS)
sensory (afferent)/motor (efferent)/inter (connector) neurons
spinal reflex arc (e.g. knee-jerk reflex)
split-brain patients/studies
summation
synaptic cleft/gap
synaptic vesicle
terminal button/bouton/ synaptic knob
thalamus-ventrobasal complex/lateral geniculate body (LGB)/ medial geniculate body (MGB)
threshold of response
Wernicke's area

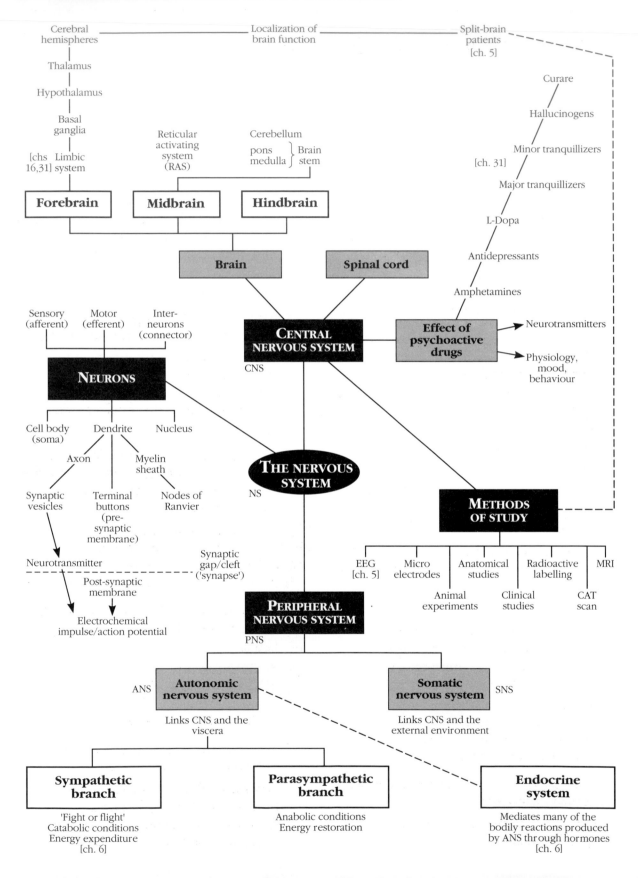

5 STATES OF CONSCIOUSNESS

MULTIPLE-CHOICE QUESTIONS

1 According to Freud, consciousness comprises three levels: __.

a) conscious, subconscious, unconscious
b) conscious, preconscious, collective unconscious
c) conscious, preconscious, unconscious
d) conscience, preconscious, unconscious

2 The fairly predictable changes in daytime alertness are controlled by a(n) __ rhythm, while night-time (sleep-related) changes are controlled by a(n) __ rhythm.

a) diurnal, ultradian
b) ultradian, diurnal
c) diurnal, biological
d) none of these

3 Short-term changes in arousal involve changes in __ alertness. Two important components of this are __ and __.

a) tonic, orienting response, habituation
b) phasic, orienting response, habituation
c) phasic, habituation, adaptation
d) tonic, orienting response, adaptation

4 The experimental study of attention represents a way of 'pinning down' __. An important distinction is that between __ and __ attention or awareness.

a) consciousness, focal, peripheral
b) arousal, focal, tonic
c) consciousness, focal, phasic
d) arousal, tonic, phasic

5 Ornstein and others believe that the two cerebral hemispheres __.

a) are both dominant in relation to specific functions

b) do not easily substitute for each other (even though they are complementary and we alternate between them)
c) represent two distinct forms of consciousness
d) all of these

6 Compared with the right, the left hemisphere may be more involved in __.

a) highly conscious processes
b) processes requiring intentional behaviour
c) behaviour requiring focal attention
d) all of these

7 The electroencephalogram records the electrical output of __, which is amplified __ times and appears as rows of oscillating waves.

a) single neurons, one million
b) single neurons, one thousand
c) large groups of neurons, one million
d) small groups of neurons, one thousand

8 'Circadian' means '__' but the natural, internal, body clock is set for about __ hours.

a) about one day, 24
b) about one day, 25
c) about half a day, 13
d) about once per day, 24

9 The internal or biological clock is thought to be the __, situated in the __.

a) corpus callosum, forebrain
b) association cortex, forebrain
c) suprachiasmatic nucleus, hypothalamus
d) suprachiasmatic nucleus, thalamus

10 While the circadian rhythm is largely a(n) __ property, the crucial environmental cue of darkness is registered by the __, situated at the top of the __.

a) internal, suprachiasmatic nucleus, brain stem
b) external, pineal gland, limbic system
c) internal, pineal gland, brain stem
d) external, suprachiasmatic nucleus, brain stem

11 The pineal gland secretes __, a hormone which in turn acts on neurons which produce __, a sleep-related neurotransmitter.

a) melatonin, dopamine
b) oestrogen, serotonin
c) melatonin, serotonin
d) testosterone, melatonin

12 Collectively, stages 1 to 4 are known as __.

a) rapid eye movement (REM) sleep
b) non-rapid eye movement (NREM) sleep
c) the S-state
d) b and c

13 Compared with stages 1 and 2, in stages 3 and 4 __.
a) sleep is deeper and it is more difficult to wake the sleeper
b) there is a much larger proportion of long, slow, delta waves
c) heart rate, blood pressure and body temperature are all dropping
d) all of these

14 While the EEGs in REM sleep resemble those of someone who is awake, __.

a) it is relatively easy to wake the sleeper in REM sleep
b) it is even more difficult to wake the sleeper in REM sleep than someone who is in the deep stage 4 sleep
c) the arm and leg muscles are paralyzed
d) b and c

15 With each 90 minute cycle __.

a) the duration of REM sleep increases
b) the duration of NREM sleep decreases
c) the proportion of REM sleep increases relative to NREM
d) all of these

16 If subjects are woken during REM sleep (as opposed to NREM sleep), __.

a) they are about five times more likely to report that they have been dreaming
b) their reported dreams tend to be shorter, less vivid and less visual
c) they are more likely to report having been 'thinking' than dreaming
d) all of these

17 If subjects are deprived of two hours of REM sleep (but otherwise allowed to sleep normally), the following night __.

a) an increase in their REM sleep occurs
b) a decrease in their REM sleep occurs
c) the REM rebound occurs
d) a and c

18 According to the original (1966) version of Oswald's Restoration theory of sleep, __.

a) both REM and NREM sleep help to restore bodily processes/tissue
b) both REM and NREM sleep help to restore brain processes
c) NREM sleep helps to restore bodily processes and REM sleep helps to restore brain processes
d) REM sleep helps to restore bodily processes and NREM sleep helps to restore brain processes

19 Consistent with Oswald's theory are the findings that __.

a) patients who survive drug overdoses experience six to eight weeks of increased REM sleep
b) about half the brain's protein is replaced within about six weeks
c) stage 4 sleep is needed for the nocturnal secretion of growth hormone (producing bodily protein synthesis)
d) all of these

20 According to the Evolutionary theory of sleep, __.

a) sleep is an advantage because it keeps the animal immobilized for long periods
b) being immobilized makes the animal less conspicuous to would-be predators
c) the safer the animal from predators, the longer it is likely to sleep
d) all of these

21 According to the Activation-Synthesis model, __.

a) the brain is very active during REM sleep, although very little stimulation is provided by external sources
b) stimulation is spontaneously provided by the pontine brain stem and by the motor cortex
c) dreams are a conscious interpretation of all this activity
d) all of these

22 An extension of the Activation-Synthesis model claims that __.

a) the cortex consists of richly interconnected neuronal networks
b) network systems malfunction when faced with overload of incoming information
c) REM sleep and dreaming represent a mechanism for 'cleaning up' the network so as to prevent overload and allow new learning to take place
d) all of these

23 __ is sometimes defined as an __ and sometimes as a state of increased __.

a) biofeedback, altered state of consciousness, suggestibility
b) meditation, altered state of awareness, conformity
c) hypnosis, altered state of consciousness, role-playing
d) hypnosis, altered state of consciousness, suggestibility

24 As measured by EEGs, the hypnotic state __.

a) is identical to REM sleep
b) is very similar to stage 4 NREM sleep
c) is a sleep state but distinct from other sleep states
d) is not a state of sleep

25 Critics of hypnosis claim that __.

a) experienced hypnotists cannot distinguish subjects trained to act as if hypnotized from those who are actually hypnotized
b) the hypnotized person is simply highly motivated to co-operate with the hypnotist's suggestions
c) the only distinctive change produced by hypnosis is relaxation
d) all of these

26 The separation between different aspects of consciousness and the presence of a 'hidden observer' are central features of __.

a) Freud's psychoanalytic theory
b) Erikson's neo-Freudian theory
c) Hilgard's neo-dissociation theory
d) Jung's free-association theory

27 The crucial feature of meditation seems to be a __ state, in which the body's __ is greatly slowed down.
a) dream-like, activity
b) sleep-like, metabolism
c) trance-like, movement
d) trance-like, metabolism

28 Through __, individuals are provided with __ about specific physiological responses, such as __, which they learn to control __.

a) hypnosis, information, blood pressure and GSR, consciously
b) meditation, feedback, blood pressure and metabolism, deliberately
c) biofeedback, information, blood pressure and GSR, consciously
d) biofeedback, suggestions, blood pressure and EEG, consciously

SELF-ASSESSMENT QUESTIONS

1 Give some examples of (a) the different uses of the word 'consciousness' in everyday language and (b) the different ways in which psychologists have used the term.

2 Explain the relationship between consciousness, arousal, alertness and attention.

3 What is involved in the electroencephalogram (EEG)? How has it (together with other physiological measurements) helped psychologists to understand different states of consciousness, in particular, sleep?

4 Explain what is meant by the term 'circadian rhythm'. How does sleep form a part of that rhythm?

5 Outline the neurophysiological processes involved in sleep. How have psychologists studied sleep in the laboratory? What conclusions have they reached regarding different kinds of sleep?

6 What is the relationship between sleeping and dreaming?

7 Describe and evaluate one theory of sleep.

8 Outline and evaluate one theory of dreaming.

9 Describe some of the effects of sleep deprivation.

10 How do dreams differ from waking consciousness?

11 Consider the evidence that the hypnotic state is a distinct, qualitatively different state of consciousness.

12 What is involved in meditation? How might it have its effect upon physiological processes?

13 What is involved in biofeedback? Does the evidence support the claim that it can effectively bring autonomic processes under voluntary control?

KEY TERMS/CONCEPTS

activation-synthesis model of dreaming/cleaning up the neuronal networks
arousal and alertness
autonomic responses and operant conditioning
biofeedback
circadian rhythm
consciousness and problem-solving
consciousness
delta/theta/alpha/beta waves
dreams as the reorganization of schemas
elaborations (SCEs) (secondary cognitive)
electroencephalogram (EEG)

electromyogram (EMG)
electrooculogram (EOG)
evolutionary theory of sleep
factor S
focal and peripheral attention
frequency and amplitude (of waves)
Freud's theory: conscious/ preconscious/ unconscious (repression)
hibernation theory of sleep
hidden observer
hypnogogic period
hypnosis
internal/biological clock
locus coeruleus
meditation
melatonin

neo-dissociation theory of hypnosis
non-rapid-eye-movement (NREM) sleep (stages 1 to 4 (S-state))
personal and collective unconscious (Jung)
phasic alertness: orienting response and habituation
pontine brainstem
primary visual experiences (PVEs)
protein synthesis
raphe nuclei
rapid-eye-movement (REM) sleep (D-state)
REM rebound
restoration theory of sleep
reticular activating system (RAS)

right and left hemisphere consciousness
self-consciousness
serotonin
sleep as a primary drive
sleep deprivation (gradual/ abrupt)
Stanford Hypnotic Susceptibility Scales
suprachiasmatic nucleus (SN)
symbolism in dreams
tonic alertness: diurnal and ultradian rhythms

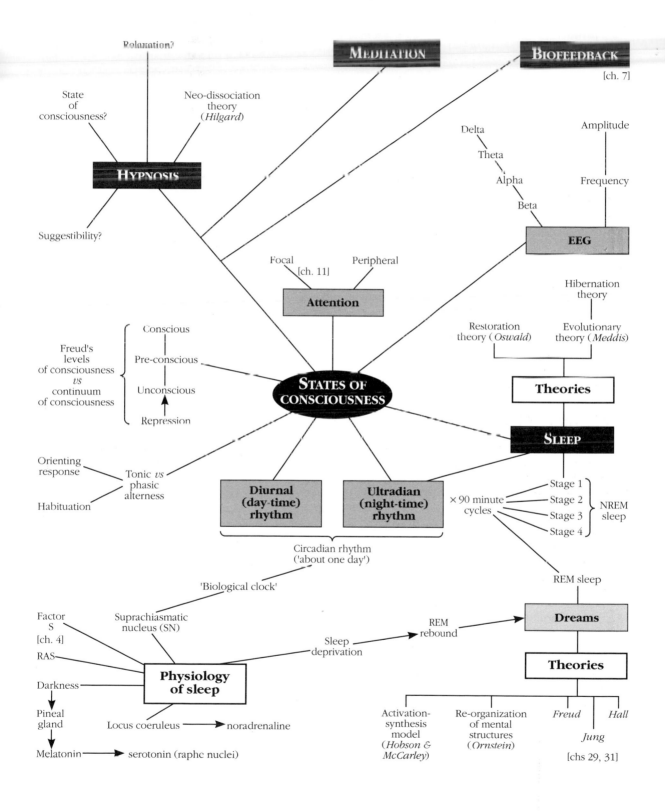

6 MOTIVATION, EMOTION AND STRESS

MULTIPLE-CHOICE QUESTIONS

1 The theories of both __ and __ can be seen as based upon the principles of hedonism.

a) Maslow, Freud
b) Freud, Darwin
c) Skinner, Darwin
d) Freud, Skinner

2 The concept of a homeostatic drive refers to __.

a) tissue-needs which can only be satisfied through voluntary behaviour
b) what motivates the animal to engage in some appropriate behaviour
c) voluntary and discontinuous behaviours, such as eating and drinking
d) all of these

3 Opposed to Cannon's belief that the hunger drive is caused by stomach contractions is the finding that __.

a) people without stomachs still feel hungry
b) a full stomach doesn't prevent feelings of hunger if the passage to the small intestine is blocked
c) the duodenum is probably more important than the stomach in affecting feelings of hunger
d) all of these

4 Two major areas of the hypothalamus involved in eating behaviour are the __.

a) ventro-medial nucleus (VMH), lateral geniculate body (LGB)
b) lateral hypothalamus (LH), limbic system

c) corpus callosum, lateral hypothalamus (LH)
d) ventro-medial nucleus (VMH), lateral hypothalamus (LH)

5 In rats, lesions in the __ cause __, i.e. the rat will carry on eating until it becomes grotesquely fat.

a) VMH, hyperphagia
b) VMH, aphagia
c) LH, aphagia
d) LH, hyperphagia

6 Thirst seems to be a much __ drive than hunger. As with aphagia, a lesion in the __ causes __, a prolonged refusal to drink.

a) less powerful, VMH, adipsia
b) more powerful, VMH, adipsia
c) more powerful, LH, hyperphagia
d) more powerful, LH, adipsia

7 Two important mechanisms involved in bringing drinking to an end are __.

a) stomach distention, the osmoreceptors
b) the mouth-metering mechanism, salt-concentration cells
c) stomach distention, the mouth-metering mechanism
d) the osmoreceptors, salt-concentration cells

8 Hull's drive-reduction theory was meant to explain the principle of __, which can either be __ (the presentation of a stimulus) or __ (the removal/avoidance of a stimulus).

a) repression, positive, negative

b) reinforcement, negative, positive
c) reinforcement, primary, secondary
d) reinforcement, positive, negative

9 Hull believed that all human and animal behaviour stems from the satisfaction of the __ drives, which include __.

a) primary, hunger, thirst, sleep and cognitive consistency
b) homeostatic, hunger, thirst, sleep, defecation and urination
c) primary, air, avoiding injury, activity and reproduction
d) b and c

10 A major example of a non-primary/homeostatic drive in animals is __, the main reward site for which is thought to be the __.

a) electrical self-stimulation of the brain, LH
b) ESB, median forebrain bundle
c) electrical self-stimulation of the brain, MFB
d) b and c

11 __ is the capacity to deal effectively with the environment. Unlike the hunger drive, competence motives often involve the __, as in __ and __.

a) self-actualization, search for excitement, sport, drug-taking
b) competence, search for stimulation, curiosity, exploration
c) intelligence, search for problems, play, problem solving
d) competence, search for excitement, sport, sexual activity

12 According to optimal-level/arousal theories, __.

a) curiosity, exploration and manipulation are based on an in-built tendency to seek an optimum level of stimulation
b) if the unfamiliar is too discrepant from what we are used to, arousal will rise above the optimum level
c) if the unfamiliar is not different enough from what we are used to, arousal will fall below the optimum level
d) all of these

13 Achievement motivation or __ is one of Murray's __ motives which he contrasted with __ motives.

a) need for achievement, psychogenic, viscerogenic
b) nAch, psychological, physiological
c) nAch, psychogenic, viscerogenic
d) all of these

14 According to the James-Lange theory of emotion, __.

a) we react emotionally to something which then produces certain bodily and/or behavioural changes
b) our emotional experience is an inference made from feedback from our bodily changes
c) we see a bear, run away and infer that we must be frightened
d) b and c

15 The Valins study involving false feedback of heart-rate responses to semi-nude females and the Laird study of facial expressions and cartoon slides both strongly suggest that __.

a) overt behaviour may serve as a cause of emotional experience
b) physiological arousal is not sufficient to account for emotional experience
c) physiological arousal may not even be necessary and cognitive factors may be sufficient
d) all of these

16 What makes the Cannon-Bard theory different from the James-Lange theory is the claim that __.

a) the subjective emotion is quite independent of the physiological changes
b) physiological changes precede the experience of emotion
c) the experience of emotion depends both on physiological changes and the interpretation of those changes
d) all of these

17 According to __, physiological arousal is necessary for emotional experience, but __.

a) the Cannon-Bard theory, labelling the arousal is equally necessary for emotional experience
b) Schachter's cognitive labelling theory, labelling the arousal is also necessary for emotional experience
c) the James-Lange theory, it may also be sufficient, depending on the intensity of the arousal
d) Schachter's cognitive labelling theory, it may also be sufficient, depending on the intensity of the arousal

18 The Speisman et al 'Subincision in the Arunta' experiment shows __.

a) the importance of puberty rites in non-Western cultures
b) the impact of physiological arousal in emotional experience
c) how stress may be reduced by changing people's cognitive appraisal of the situation
d) the irrelevance of cognitive factors in emotion

19 The three models of stress identified by Cox are __.

a) the engineering, psychological and transactional
b) the engineering, physiological and psychoanalytic
c) the physiological, transactional and psychoanalytic
d) the engineering, physiological and transactional

20 Disruption of circadian rhythms as a source of stress __.

a) involves the internal desynchronization of the body's functions
b) often produces insomnia, digestive problems and irritability

c) is particularly harmful if produced by a weekly rotation of shifts
d) all of these

21 A major variable, which interacts with life changes in making them stressful and harmful, is __.

a) whether anything like them has happened before
b) how controllable they are perceived to be
c) how expected and predictable they are seen to be
d) b and c

22 Compared with the Type B personality, the Type A personality __.

a) has a chronic sense of time urgency
b) is excessively competitive and suffers from 'hurry sickness'
c) is at risk from high blood pressure and coronary heart disease
d) all of these

23 The __, according to Selye, represents the body's defence against stress, regardless of the __.

a) General Anxiety Syndrome, source of the stress
b) General Arousal Syndrome, personality of the victim
c) General Adaptation Syndrome, source of the stress
d) General Adaptation Syndrome, personality of the victim

24 A major way in which stress may result in disease is through its influence on __, which tends to be depleted following traumatic events, such as __.

a) the ANS, a period of illness
b) the body's immune system, the death of a loved one
c) the CNS, the death of a loved one
d) all of these

SELF-ASSESSMENT QUESTIONS

1 Explain how the concept of motivation has been used in psychology, including the related concepts of instinct and drive.

2 What is meant by the term 'homeostasis'? Outline the physiological mechanisms involved in either hunger or thirst.

3 Describe and evaluate Hull's drive reduction theory.

4 What is meant by 'competence motives'?

5 To what extent can play be regarded as a form of motivation?

6 What attempts have been made by psychologists to classify human emotions?

7 Compare and contrast any two theories of emotion.

8 Outline and evaluate cognitive labelling theory.

9 Briefly describe the three major models of stress. How are they related to each other?

10 Explain how disruption of the circadian rhythm can be stressful and how such stress may be reduced/prevented.

11 Evaluate the claim that mental and physical ill health are related to life changes.

12 Outline the three stages of the General Adaptation Syndrome.

13 Describe some of the ways in which people cope with stress.

14 What is the relationship between stress, personality and disease?

KEY TERMS/CONCEPTS

adipsia
angiotensin
anti-diuretic hormone (ADH)
anxiety (a secondary drive)
aphagia
approach: approach/ avoidance: avoidance/ approach: avoidance conflict
augmenters versus reducers
avoidance learning
beta-endorphins
Cannon-Bard theory of emotion
cognitive appraisal/ interpretation (and subliminal perception)
cognitive behaviourism/ latent learning (Tolman)
cognitive control
cognitive motives cognitive consistency/ achievement motivation (need for achievement or nAch)
competence ('the master reinforcer')
controllability of life events
coping mechanisms

disruption of circadian rhythms
drive
ego defence mechanisms
electrical self-stimulation of the brain (ESB)
everyday hassles and uplifts
Executive Monkey Experiments
fear of failure/fear of success
General Adaptation Syndrome (GAS) (Selye)
hedonism
homeostasis
homeostatic drive theory (Cannon)
Hull's drive-reduction theory
hyperphagia
informational control
internal desynchronization (of bodily functions)
internal versus external locus of control (Rotter)
James-Lange theory of emotion
jet-lag
lateral hypothalamus (LH) ('feeding centre')

learned helplessness
Life-Change Units (LCUs)
median forebrain bundle (MFB)
motivation
motives: survival/ physiological/ competence/cognitive/ social/self-actualization
motives as instincts
mouth-metering mechanism
need for control
needs versus drives
optimal-level (arousal) theories
osmoreceptors
peptides
play (Piaget)
primary/homeostatic versus secondary/ acquired/non- homeostatic drives
psychoimmunology
psychological reactance
rationalism
reinforcement: positive and negative
Schachter's cognitive labelling theory of emotion

search for stimulation: curiosity/exploration/ manipulation
sensory deprivation experiments
sensory overload
shift work
Social Readjustment Rating Scale (SRRS)
stomach distention
Thematic Apperception Test (TAT)
three components of emotion: subjective experience/physiological changes/behaviour
three models of stress: engineering/ physiological/ transactional
tissue-needs (physiological/ homeostatic needs)
Type A and Type B personality
ventro-medial nucleus (VMH) (of hypothalamus) ('satiety centre')

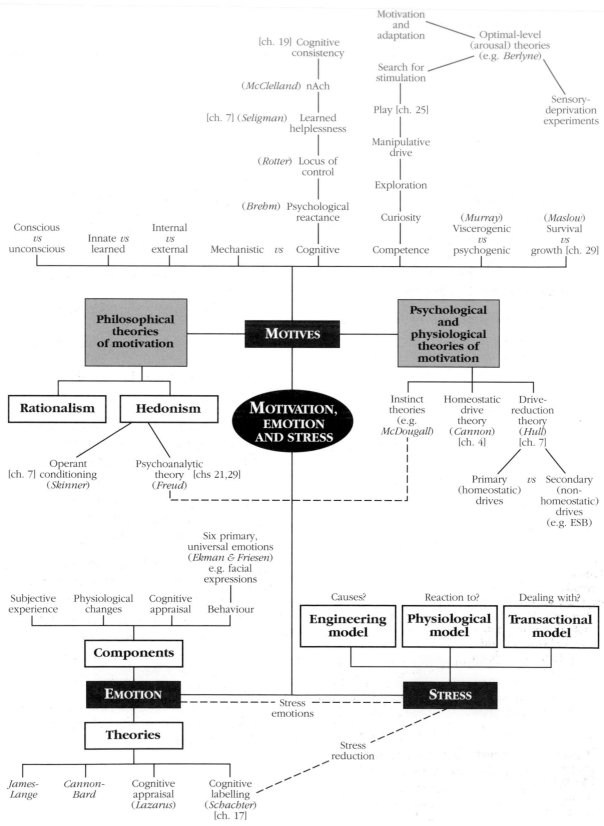

7 LEARNING

MULTIPLE-CHOICE QUESTIONS

1 A relatively permanent change in behaviour due to __ is how __ is usually defined.

a) maturational processes, learning
b) past experience, development
c) maturational processes, development
d) past experience, learning

2 In Pavlov's experiments with dogs, the food is referred to as the ___ and the salivation produced by the food as the __.

a) unconditioned stimulus (UCS), unconditioned response (UCR)
b) unconditioned response (UCR), unconditioned stimulus (UCS)
c) conditioned stimulus (CS), conditioned response (CR)
d) unconditioned stimulus (UCS), conditioned response (CR)

3 In the example of a dentist's drill hitting a nerve, the UCS is __ and the resulting pain/fear is the __.

a) the drill hitting the nerve, UCR
b) the sound of the drill, UCR
c) the drill hitting the nerve, CR
d) the sound of the drill, CS

4 If fear of the sound of the dentist's drill transfers to the sound of other kinds of drill, __ is said to have taken place. However, only being afraid of the dentist's drill illustrates the process of __.

a) discrimination, generalization
b) generalization, extinction
c) discrimination, extinction
d) generalization, discrimination

5 Following the learning of a conditioned salivation response to a bell, Pavlov's dogs __ if the bell was repeatedly presented without food. They were displaying the process of __.

a) carried on salivating quite happily, generalization
b) gradually stopped responding, discrimination
c) sometimes responded and sometimes didn't, extinction
d) gradually stopped responding, extinction

6 Following extinction, if the bell was re-presented, the __ would reappear, demonstrating the process of __.

a) CR, experimental neurosis
b) UCR, spontaneous recovery
c) CR, spontaneous recovery
d) CR, operant conditioning

7 Classical conditioning deals only with __ behaviour, while operant or instrumental conditioning __.

a) respondent, looks at how animals operate on their environment
b) involuntary, looks at how behaviour is instrumental in bringing about certain consequences
c) reflex, regards most animal and human behaviour as essentially voluntary
d) all of these

8 __ reinforcement involves presenting __, while __ reinforcement involves __.

a) positive, something the animal likes, negative, removal or avoidance of something aversive
b) positive, something the animal likes, primary, something the animal dislikes
c) negative, something aversive, secondary, something the animal learns to like
d) none of these

9 Money, trading stamps and tokens are all examples of __. They are also known as __, since they acquire their reinforcing values through association with primary reinforcers via __ conditioning.

a) secondary reinforcers, conditioned reinforcers, operant
b) positive reinforcers, secondary reinforcers, classical
c) secondary reinforcers, negative reinforcers, operant
d) secondary reinforcers, conditioned reinforcers, classical

10 Schedules of reinforcement can be analyzed in terms of __, with a __ schedule typically showing the greatest resistance to extinction.

a) pattern and rate of responding, variable ratio (VR)
b) resistance to extinction, variable interval (VI)
c) resistance to extinction, variable ratio (VR)
d) a and c

11 __ is defined as the reinforcement of __ to the desired or target behaviour.

a) generalization, systematic approximations
b) discrimination, successive approximations
c) shaping, successive approximations
d) shaping, systematic approximations

12 In avoidance learning __.

a) an anticipatory anxiety response to the warning signal is first learned, through classical conditioning
b) the avoidance response itself is learnt through negative reinforcement
c) anxiety is reduced by, say, jumping a barrier before the electric shock is switched on
d) all of these

13 Perhaps the most effective use of punishment is when __.

a) it is very intense
b) the behaviour which is punished is incompatible with some other behaviour which is positively reinforced
c) it is combined with negative reinforcement
d) all of these

14 What makes taste-aversion studies different from most conditioning experiments is that __.

a) the CS and the UCS are not contiguous
b) the time lapse between tasting the saccharine solution and onset of the drug-induced nausea varies from 5 to 180 minutes
c) the CS and UCS become associated despite not being presented close together in time
d) all of these

15 The finding that rats very quickly learn to press a lever for food but will not easily do so to avoid shock suggests that __.

a) food is a more powerful incentive than avoidance of shock
b) avoidance learning is more difficult than other kinds of learning
c) positive reinforcement is more effective than negative reinforcement
d) there are definite biological limitations on an animal's ability to learn specific responses

16 Preparedness in humans has been studied mainly __.

a) by seeing how easily conditioned fear responses can be induced by different kinds of stimuli

b) by finding out whether some naturally-occurring phobias are more common than others

c) in relation to individual differences in proneness to phobias

d) a and b

17 Pavlov implied that conditioning involves cognitive processes by stating that __.

a) the CS is a signal for the UCS

b) the relationship between the CS and the UCS is that of 'stimulus substitution'

c) the CR is an 'anticipatory' response, implying that his dogs were expecting the UCS to follow the CS

d) all of these

18 Tolman and Honzik's experiment with rats showed that __.

a) reinforcement is irrelevant to either initial learning or demonstration of that learning

b) initial learning does not require reinforcement

c) learning which takes place without reinforcement is latent or 'behaviourally silent'

d) b and c

19 Programmed instruction is based on the principles of __. Breaking the material up into very small steps ensures that __ and a __ schedule of reinforcement is used.

a) classical conditioning, very few errors are made, continuous

b) operant conditioning, the learner, doesn't get bored, fixed interval

c) operant conditioning, very few errors are made, continuous

d) Pavlovian conditioning, very few errors are made, fixed ratio

20 In contrast with orthodox learning theorists, such as Bandura, a leading social learning theorist, emphasises the role of __ ,

a) Pavlov, observational learning

b) Skinner, modelling

c) Watson, learning by observing the behaviour of others

d) all of these

21 A crucial difference between social learning theory and orthodox learning theory is the former's emphasis on the role of __. Examples of these are __.

a) animal experiments, attention, memory coding, motivation

b) cognitive factors, memory permanence, motivation

c) cognitive factors, attention, accurate reproduction of the observed behaviour

d) b and c

22 According to __, insight learning involves __ and contrasts it with the __ learning involved in operant conditioning.

a) Köhler, a sudden perceptual restructuring of the situation, trial and error

b) Tolman, the formation of cognitive maps, trial and error

c) Köhler, the formation of cognitive maps, stimulus–response

d) Bandura, the reproduction of other people's behaviour, random

23 According to Harlow, __ (or 'learning to learn') represent an intervening process between __ and __ learning.

a) learning sets, S–R, insight

b) insight learning, stimulus, response

c) learning sets, respondent, operant

d) concept learning, conditioning, cognitive

SELF-ASSESSMENT QUESTIONS

1 Define the term 'learning' and outline some of the differences in the way the term is used by different psychologists.

2 Describe the basic procedure involved in classical conditioning, using examples from both animal and human behaviour.

3 Describe the basic procedure involved in operant conditioning, using examples from both animal and human behaviour.

4 Explain the difference between positive and negative reinforcement and between primary and secondary reinforcers.

5 Describe the major schedules of reinforcement. How do they differ with respect to a) pattern and rate of responding and b) resistance to extinction?

6 Compare and contrast classical and operant conditioning.

7 Explain what is involved in avoidance learning. How are classical and operant processes both involved?

8 What are the effects of punishment on behaviour?

9 To what extent can a) taste aversion studies and b) the concept of biological preparedness help us to understand the basic process of conditioning?

10 Give some examples of the role of cognitive factors in conditioning.

11 What is meant by latent learning? Explain how it relates to the distinction between learning and performance.

12 How does programmed learning apply the principles of operant conditioning?

13 Outline the basic features of social learning theory. How is it related to orthodox learning theory?

14 What is meant by insight learning? How does it differ from trial and error learning?

15 Are S–R and cognitive theories of learning necessarily opposed?

16 How does the concept of a learning set bridge the gap between S–R and insight learning?

KEY TERMS/CONCEPTS

antecedents
backward conditioning
behaviour modification
behaviour therapy
biofeedback
biological preparedness
blocking
chain response/reflex theory
classical (respondent/ Pavlovian) conditioning
cognitive maps
computer-assisted instruction (CAI)
conditioned response (CR)
conditioned stimulus (CS)
conditioned suppression/ inhibition
consequences (of behaviour)
delayed/forward conditioning
discrimination

discriminative stimulus
experimental neurosis
extinction
Gagnés hierarchy of learning
generalization
Gestalt psychology
higher order conditioning
insight learning
interference
involuntary/automatic/ reflex/respondent behaviour
latent learning
law of contiguity
learned helplessness
learning
learning set ('learning to learn')
learning versus performance
linear versus branching programmes

negative reinforcement: escape and avoidance learning
negative transfer
observational learning/ modelling
operant (instrumental/ Skinnerian) conditioning
positive reinforcement
positive transfer
primary reinforcers
programmed learning/ instruction
punishment
reinforcer versus reinforcement
ripeness
role of cognitive factors
schedules of reinforcement
secondary reinforcers
shaping: reinforcement of successive approximations

sign learning theory (place learning)
simultaneous conditioning
Skinner box
social learning theory
spontaneous recovery
stimulus control
superstitious behaviour
systematic desensitization
taste aversion studies
teaching machines
Thorndike's law of effect
trace conditioning
transfer of learning/ training
trial and error learning
unconditioned response (UCR)
unconditioned stimulus (UCS)
voluntary operant behaviour

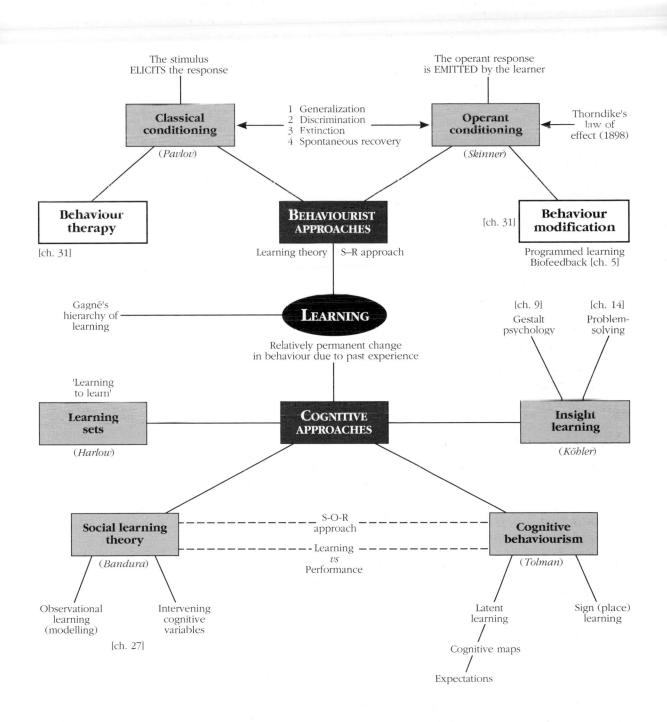

The stimulus
ELICITS the response

The operant response
is EMITTED by the learner

Classical conditioning (*Pavlov*)

1 Generalization
2 Discrimination
3 Extinction
4 Spontaneous recovery

Operant conditioning (*Skinner*)

Thorndike's
law of
effect (1898)

Behaviour therapy
[ch. 31]

BEHAVIOURIST APPROACHES
Learning theory   S–R approach

[ch. 31]

Behaviour modification
Programmed learning
Biofeedback [ch. 5]

Gagné's
hierarchy of
learning

LEARNING

Relatively permanent change
in behaviour due to past experience

[ch. 9]
Gestalt
psychology

[ch. 14]
Problem-
solving

'Learning
to learn'

Learning sets (*Harlow*)

COGNITIVE APPROACHES

Insight learning (*Köhler*)

Social learning theory (*Bandura*)

S-O-R
approach

Learning
vs
Performance

Cognitive behaviourism (*Tolman*)

Observational
learning
(modelling)

Intervening
cognitive
variables

[ch. 27]

Latent
learning

Cognitive maps

Expectations

Sign (place)
learning

8 SENSORY PROCESSES

MULTIPLE-CHOICE QUESTIONS

1 Each of our sensory systems __.

a) is only sensitive to a particular kind of physical stimulation
b) functions as a data reduction system
c) helps to discard irrelevant information so that we are not overwhelmed by the world as it really is
d) all of these

2 The visible spectrum __.

a) is that tiny portion of the entire spectrum which ranges from 380 to 780 nanometres
b) is that portion of the entire spectrum which we call light
c) is part of the spectrum of electromagnetic radiation
d) all of these

3 The five 'traditional' senses are __ and collectively they are referred to as the __.

a) vision, audition, olfaction, gustation, cutaneous senses, interoceptors
b) sight, hearing, smell, taste, touch, exteroceptors
c) vision, audition, olfaction, gustation, cutaneous senses, exteroceptors
d) b and c

4 Sense receptors are also known as __ and their function is to __.

a) transducers, convert the sense-data into electrical nerve impulses
b) accessory structures, act as the initial point of arrival for the sensory information
c) transducers, act as the initial point of arrival for the sensory information

d) accessory structures, convert the sense-data into electrical nerve impulses

5 The minimum amount of stimulation necessary to discriminate between two stimuli is the __.

a) difference threshold
b) absolute threshold
c) just noticeable difference (j.n.d.)
d) a and c

6 The Weber-Fechner law states that __.

a) the j.n.d. is a constant value
b) large increases in the intensity of a stimulus produce smaller, proportional, increases in the perceived intensity
c) the greater the intensity of the stimulus, the greater its perceived intensity
d) absolute thresholds vary between individuals

7 In __ light, the pupil __ to reduce the amount of light entering the eye, while in __ light, it __ in order to increase the amount of light entering the eye.

a) bright, contracts, dim, dilates
b) bright, dilates, dim, contracts
c) dim, contracts, bright, dilates
d) dim, dilates, bright, contracts

8 In __, the lens __ when focusing on __ objects and becomes __ when viewing more __ objects.

a) assimilation, thickens, nearby, flatter, distant
b) accommodation, thickens, distant, flatter, nearby

c) accommodation, thickens, nearby, flatter, distant
d) adaptation, thickens, nearby, flatter, distant

9 The central or __ visual field represents a small portion of the total optic array and is sampled with __ visual acuity compared with the much larger __ visual field.

a) foveal, high, peripheral
b) focal, high, peripheral
c) peripheral, high, foveal
d) peripheral, low, focal

10 While a TV camera transmits a stream of pictures to a TV set, __.

a) the optic nerve transmits pictures to the brain
b) the optic nerve transmits information about the pattern of light reaching the eye
c) the information reaching the brain from the optic nerve must be interpreted by the brain
d) b and c

11 The sense receptors of the visual system are the __, which __.

a) rods and cones, form the rear layer of the retina
b) rods and cones, are photosensitive cells which convert light energy into electrical nerve impulses
c) ganglion cells, connect rods and cones to bipolar cells
d) a and b

12 The rods are __.

a) distributed fairly evenly around the periphery of the retina,
b) specialized for vision in dim light
c) concentrated in the fovea
d) a and b

13 The rods contain __, a photosensitive chemical which changes structure in low levels of illumination. They help us see __ colour, also known as __ vision.

a) rhodopsin, achromatic, scotopic
b) iodopsin, chromatic, photopic
c) rhodopsin, chromatic, photopic
d) iodopsin, achromatic, scotopic

14 In the periphery of the retina, the degree of summation is __ than in the fovea, thereby providing __.

a) much greater, only very general visual information
b) much greater, very detailed visual information
c) much smaller, only very general visual information
d) much smaller, very detailed visual information

15 A __ is a usually circular region of the __, stimulation of which affects the firing rate of the __ cell to which it corresponds.

a) visual field, retina, ganglion
b) receptive field, retina, horizontal
c) receptive field, retina, ganglion
d) receptive field, retina, bipolar

16 The pathways from the half of each retina closest to the nose cross at the __ and travel to the __ hemisphere. Those furthest from the nose travel to the __ hemisphere and are called __ pathways.

a) optic chiasma, opposite, same side, uncrossed
b) lateral geniculate nucleus (LGN), opposite, same side, uncrossed
c) optic chiasma, same side, opposite, uncrossed
d) optic chasm, same side, opposite, crossed

17 Axons of LGN cells project to the __ lobe, specifically to the __ cortex. This pathway is called the __.

a) occipital, visual, geniculostriate path
b) occipital, striate, geniculostriate path
c) temporal, visual, retinotectal path
d) a and b

18 In humans, the __ is essential for __. People who suffer damage to their visual cortex will report complete blindness, although they can locate or even identify objects; this is called __.

a) geniculostriate path, conscious visual experience, blindsight
b) geniculostriate path, conscious visual experience, hindsight
c) geniculostriate path, depth perception, blindsight
d) retinotectal path, colour perception, figural identity

19 __ cells respond only to straight lines, edges and slits in particular __. For __ cells, only __ is important.

a) simple, orientations, complex, orientation
b) simple, locations, complex, orientation
c) complex, orientations, simple, location
d) a and b

20 Apart from the __ cortex, many regions of the __ cortex can be considered 'visual areas'. They are located in the __ lobes.

a) striate, extrastriate, occipital, temporal
b) striate, prestriate, temporal, parietal
c) prestriate, striate, occipital, frontal
d) a and b

21 According to the Young-Helmholtz __ theory, __.

a) trichromatic, colour is mediated by three different kinds of cone
b) trichromatic, colour is determined by the ratio of short, medium and long wavelengths of light
c) opponent colour, blue-sensitive cones are most responsive to short wavelengths
d) a and b

22 According to Hering's __ theory, __.

a) opponent colour, colour analysis depends on the action of two types of detector, each having two modes of response

b) opponent colour, one type of detector signals red or green, the other signals yellow or blue
c) trichromatic, one type of detector signals red or blue, the other signals green or yellow
d) a and b

23 Sounds are caused by __. They vary in __ and are initially 'trapped' by the __.

a) changes in air pressure, frequency, pinna
b) changes in electromagnetic radiation, intensity, eardrum
c) changes in air pressure, intensity, pinna
d) a and c

24 The eardrum (or __) is linked to the __, the first of three small bones (the others being the incus and stapes), which are collectively known as the __.

a) tympanum, malleus, ossicles
b) tympanum, cochlea, ossicles
c) tympanic membrane, malleus, ossicles
d) a and c

25 Pressure changes in the cochlear fluid causes the __ to vibrate. This causes bending of the __, which are the __ of the auditory system.

a) basilar membrane, hair cells of the organ of corti, sense receptors
b) tectoral membrane, hair cells of the organ of corti, sense organ
c) basilar membrane, hair cells of the organ of corti, transducers
d) a and c

26 The auditory nerve travels through the __ en route to the upper part of the __ lobe. Impulses from the auditory nerve at one side of the head pass up to __ hemisphere(s).

a) LGN, occipital, the same side
b) MGB, temporal, both
c) MGB, temporal, opposite side
d) LGN, occipital, both

SELF-ASSESSMENT QUESTIONS

1 Briefly explain the relationship between sensation and perception.

2 How are sensory systems classified?

3 What are the basic characteristics shared by all sensory systems?

4 Explain what is meant by psychophysics.

5 Briefly explain the difference between a) Weber's law and the Weber-Fechner law and b) the Weber-Fechner law and signal detection theory.

6 Outline the structure and function of the human eye.

7 To what extent can the eye be considered a camera?

8 Outline the structure and function of the retina.

9 How is information passed from the retina to the brain?

10 What is known about the role of the cortex in the processing of visual information?

11 Outline and evaluate one theory of colour vision.

12 Briefly outline Land's retinex theory of colour constancy.

13 Outline the structure and function of the human ear.

14 How is information passed from the ear to the brain?

15 Explain how psychological aspects of sound are processed.

KEY TERMS/CONCEPTS

absolute threshold
accommodation
achromatic colour
aggregate field
amacrine cells
ambient optic array
anterior chamber
aqueous humour
auditory canal
basilar membrane
bipolar cells
blindsight
brightness
choroid coat
chromatic colour
ciliary muscles
cochlea
colour constancy
cones
conjunctiva
convergence
cornea
corticotectal path
dark adaptation
data-reduction systems
difference threshold/just noticeable difference (jnd)
eardrum (tympanum/ tympanic membrane)
exteroceptors/ exteroception
extrastriate (prestriate) cortex
ganglion cells
geniculostriate path
hair cells of organ of corti
Hering's opponent colour theory
horizontal cells
hue
hypercolumns
inner ear
intensity differences
inter-aural time difference
interoceptors/ interoception
iodopsin
iris
Land's retinex theory
lateral geniculate nucleus (LGN)
lens
malleus (hammer)/incus (anvil)/stapes (stirrup) ossicles
medial geniculate body (MGB)
middle ear
monochromatic vision
ocular dominance
optic chiasma
outer/external ear
oval window
perception
peripheral/central (foveal) visual field
phase differences
photopic vision
pinna
pitch/loudness/timbre/ location
posterior chamber
proprioceptors/ proprioception- kinaesthetic sense/ vestibular sense
psychophysics
pupil
pursuit movements
receptive field
retinotectal path
rhodopsin
rods
saccades
saturation
sclerotic coat
scotopic vision
sensation/sense-data
sense organ (accessory structure)
sense receptor (transducer)
sensory system/modality
signal detection theory
signal-to-noise ratio
simple/complex/ hypercomplex cells
sound frequency
sound intensity
spectrum of electromagnetic radiation
summation
superior colliculi
suspensory ligaments
tapetum lucidium
tectoral membrane
trichromatic vision
visible spectrum
visual acuity
visual/striate cortex
vitreous humour
Weber-Fechner law
Weber's law
Young-Helmholtz trichromatic theory (of colour)

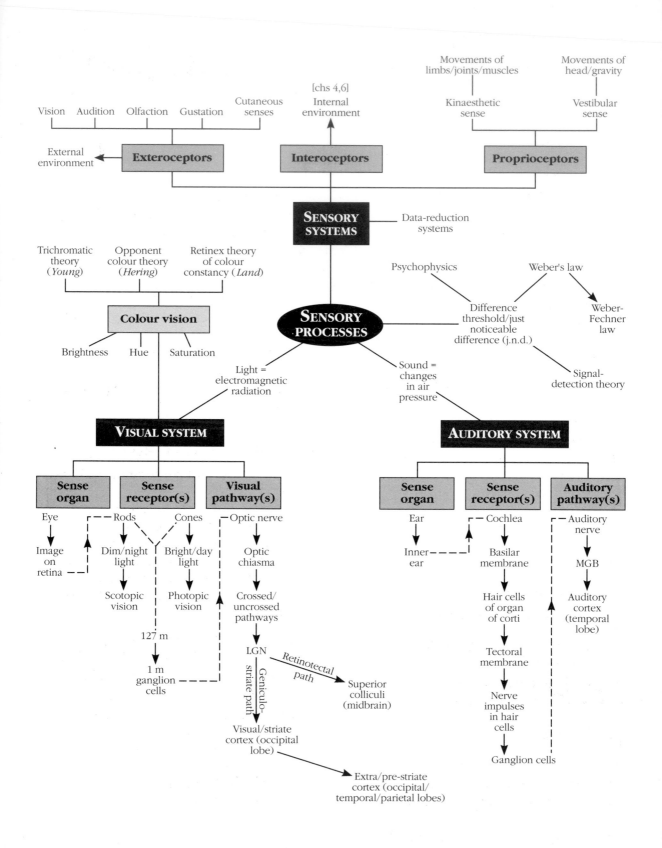

9 PERCEPTION

MULTIPLE-CHOICE QUESTIONS

1 Sensation and perception are related in that __.

a) they refer to the same basic process
b) sensation provides the 'raw material' for perception
c) perception provides the 'raw material' for sensation
d) sensation describes, while perception explains, our awareness of the world of objects

2 Theories which take a __ approach claim that __.

a) 'bottom-up', our awareness of the world is determined largely by the information presented to the sensory receptors
b) 'bottom-up', we perceive things in a fairly direct way
c) 'top-down', perception is determined by sensory information
d) a and b

3 Perceptual constancy involves __.

a) supplementing the available sensory stimulation
b) going beyond the immediately given evidence of the senses
c) making inferences about the shape/size/colour/location/brightness/of objects and people
d) all of these

4 Location constancy involves __.

a) the inhibition of the perception of movement when we move our heads around
b) the integration of kinaesthetic feedback from the muscles/organs of balance in the ear with the changing retinal stimulation
c) the perception of objects 'staying in their place'
d) all of these

5 Illusions may be classified as __.

a) distortions, e.g. the Müller-Lyer and Circle illusions
b) ambiguous figures, e.g. the Ponzo illusion
c) paradoxical figures, e.g. the Penrose impossible triangle
d) a and c

6 According to Gregory, illusions __.

a) reveal how normal, accurate, veridical, perception works
b) demonstrate the active nature of perception, whereby perceptual hypotheses are formulated and tested
c) involve the inappropriate interpretation of a stimulus figure based on our experience with real, everyday, objects
d) all of these

7 Since, in the Müller-Lyer illusion, the retinal images produced by the two shafts are equal, if one shaft is taken to be further away than the other, __.

a) through size constancy it will be perceived as longer
b) through constancy scaling it will appear longer
c) it must be longer in order to produce the same sized image
d) all of these

8 A succession of stationary images projected onto a screen sufficiently quickly to produce an illusion of continuous movement is called __.

a) the phi phenomenon
b) the autokinetic effect
c) stroboscopic motion
d) induced movement

9 Compared with Gregory, Gibson's theory of direct perception __.

a) sees retinal images as being much richer, typically including several objects, background, the horizon etc.
b) sees moving around in the world as playing a much greater role
c) emphasizes the role of 'top-down' processes
d) a and b

10 For Gibson, the correct starting point in trying to explain perception is __.

a) the retinal image
b) a pattern of light containing all the visual information from the environment striking the eye
c) the optical array
d) b and c

11 The invariant, unchanging features of the __ to which Gibson attached so much importance are __.

a) visual field, ecological optics
b) optic array, optic flow patterns (OFPs), affordances
c) optic array, texture gradient
d) b and c

12 The Ames Distorted Room is a demonstration used by the __ to show that __.

a) Transactionalists, perception is 'seeing as'
b) Gestalt psychologists, the whole is greater than the sum of its parts
c) Transactionalists, we interpret ambiguous sensory data in terms of past perceptions
d) a and c

13 Both Gregory and Gibson believe that __.

a) visual perception is mediated by light reflected from surfaces and objects
b) some kind of physiological system is needed to perceive
c) perceptual experience can be influenced by learning
d) all of these

14 Gregory's __ approach may be most applicable __.

a) bottom-up, under optimal viewing conditions
b) top-down, under optimal viewing conditions
c) bottom-up, when stimuli are presented very briefly
d) top-down, when stimuli are ambiguous.

15 Neisser's __ model sees perception as __.

a) Synthesis-by-Analysis, an interactive process
b) Analysis-by-Synthesis, involving bottom-up feature analysis
c) Analysis-by-Synthesis, involving top-down schemata and expectations
d) b and c

16 According to the Gestalt psychologists, __.

a) we perceive objects as combinations of isolated sensations
b) we perceive objects as organized wholes/patterns
c) we perceive objects in as good a way as possible
d) b and c

17 Proximity, closure, continuity and symmetry, similarity, Figure-Ground and the part-whole relationship can all be included under the more general __.

a) law of parsimony
b) law of Prägnanz
c) all-or-none rule
d) ecological optics

18 If subjects are presented visually with global letters composed of several smaller local letters, __.

a) they can more quickly identify a letter presented auditorily if it matches the global letter
b) they will identify more slowly a letter presented auditorily if it is different from the global letter
c) they will tend to ignore the local letters
d) all of these

19 For Marr, the __ is finding out how to extract useful information about a scene from __ of that scene.

a) problem of perception, incomplete descriptions
b) process of perception, images
c) 'vision problem', images
d) 'vision problem', incomplete descriptions

20 Without knowing what the task of the visual system is (i.e. the __), Marr believes that we shall never adequately understand the biology of the visual system (i.e. the __).

a) computational theory, hardware implementation
b) computational theory, algorithm
c) algorithm, image/grey-level description
d) 3-D model representation, hardware implementation

21 A perceptual bias or tendency to notice certain aspects of a stimulus and not others refers to the concept of __. This works as __ and is an important part of the __ approach to perception.

a) set, a selector, top-down
b) set, an interpreter, bottom-up
c) set, interpreter, top-down
d) a and c

22 The term __ refers to laboratory findings that subliminally perceived words with unpleasant emotional connotations __ than neutral words.

a) perceptual accentuation, register at a conscious level more quickly
b) perceptual defence, take longer to perceive consciously
c) perceptual defence, take less time to perceive consciously
d) perceptual sensitization, take longer to perceive consciously

23 Assigning meaning to visual input by identifying the objects in the visual field is a definition of __.

a) perceptual set
b) perceptual defence
c) perceptual organization
d) pattern recognition

24 According to __, pattern recognition involves a comparison between incoming stimulus information and stored __ of previously presented patterns/objects.

a) the template matching hypothesis, internal representations
b) prototype theories, templates
c) feature detection theories, internal representations
d) none of these

25 A criticism made of most feature detection theories is that they usually assume a __ form of processing. A major exception to this rule is __, which sees PR as involving __ processing.

a) parallel, Gibson's ecological optics, serial
b) serial, Selfridge's Pandemonium, parallel
c) parallel, Selfridge's Pandemonium, serial
d) serial, Hubel and Wiesel's cortical cell theory, parallel

SELF-ASSESSMENT QUESTIONS

1 Outline briefly the difference between sensation and perception.

2 What is perceptual constancy? How does it demonstrate the role of inference in perception?

3 Give some examples of visual illusions and explain how they demonstrate the indirect nature of perception.

4 Outline and evaluate Gregory's explanation of the Müller-Lyer illusion.

5 Describe some of the mechanisms involved in the perception of movement.

6 Explain briefly what Gibson means by a) the optical array b) optic flow patterns c) texture gradient d) affordances.

7 Explain the difference between a) seeing and b) seeing as. How useful is this distinction for evaluating Gibson's theory of direct perception?

8 Outline some of the Gestalt principles of perceptual organization and evaluate the evidence relating to them.

9 Describe Marr's 'vision problem'.

10 Briefly describe each of the stages or modules of Marr's computational theory of vision.

11 Give some examples of how set influences perception.

12 How are subliminal perception and perceptual defence related?

13 Assess the claim that perceptual defence is a truly perceptual phenomenon.

14 Describe four pictorial depth cues and all three non-pictorial depth cues.

15 Give a definition of pattern recognition. How is it related to perception as a whole?

16 Outline and evaluate one theory of pattern recognition.

17 Explain the difference between data-driven and conceptually-driven processing.

KEY TERMS/CONCEPTS

affordances
Ames Distorted Room
analysis by synthesis (Neisser)
binocular-non-pictorial depth cues (retinal disparity/stereoscopic vision/convergence)
bottom-up processing
catalogue of 3-D models
computational theory/ algorithm/hardware implementation
computational theory of vision (Marr) the image (grey-level description)/ primal sketch/$2\frac{1}{2}$-D sketch/3-D
conceptually-driven (top-down) processing
configuration change
constancy scaling
data-driven (bottom-up) processing

ecological optics (Gibson)
empiricism
feature detection theories
generalized cylinders
Gestalt psychology
hallucinations
Hochberg's 'minimum principle'
illusions of movement (apparent movement/ motion)
inference/'going beyond the evidence'
Law of Prägnanz (Koffka)
model representation
monocular-non-pictorial depth cues (accommodation)
monocular/pictorial depth cues
nativism
nature–nurture
optic flow patterns
optical array

optimal/sub-optimal viewing conditions
Pandemonium (Selfridge)
pattern recognition
perceiver (organismic) variables
'perception as hypotheses' (Gregory)
perceptual accentuation/ sensitization
perceptual constancy
perceptual defence
perceptual organization
perceptual set
probabilistic functionalism (Brunswick)
prototype theories
proximity/closure/ continuity and symmetry/Figure-Ground/part-whole relationship
schema/schemata
serial versus parallel

processing
set as selector/interpreter
stabilized retinal images
stick-figure representations
stimulus (situational) variables
subliminal perception
template matching hypothesis
seeing versus seeing as
top-down processing
transactionalists (e.g. Ames)
veridical perception/false (non-veridical) perception
veridical perception of movement
'vision problem'
visual illusions: distortions/ambiguous figures/paradoxical figures/fictions

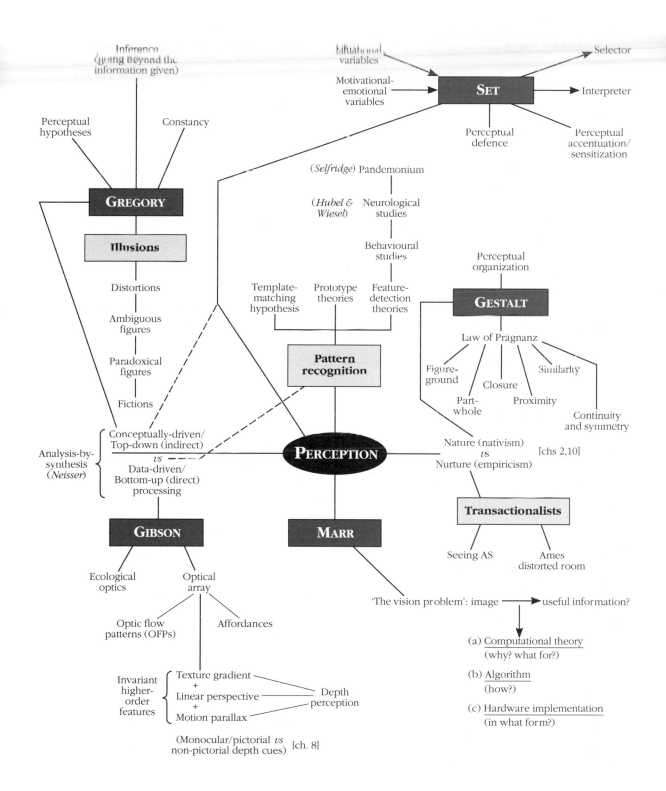

10 PERCEPTION: THE NATURE–NURTURE DEBATE

MULTIPLE-CHOICE QUESTIONS

1 Most present-day psychologists would consider themselves __, believing that __.

a) nativists, both biological and environmental influences are involved in the development of perceptual abilities
b) interactionists, perceptual abilities develop largely through the process of maturation
c) empiricists, learning and experience are the crucial influences on the development of perceptual abilities
d) interactionists, both biological and environmental influences are involved in the development of perceptual abilities

2 While most of the evidence as a whole supports the interactionist position, there is also reason to believe that __.

a) relatively simple abilities are largely under genetic control
b) relatively simple abilities are more immune to environmental influences
c) relatively complex abilities are largely under genetic control
d) a and b

3 The ability to distinguish Figure from Ground, fixate objects, scan them and follow moving objects with the eyes __.

a) are all features of figural unity
b) are all demonstrated by cataract patients before any opportunity for learning has arisen
c) are all features of figural identity
d) a and b

4 The abilities which cataract patients initially lack are __.

a) identifying through sight alone objects already familiar through touch
b) distinguishing geometrical shapes through sight alone
c) perceptual constancy
d) all of these

5 We cannot be sure, on the basis of cataract patients alone, that more complex abilities require learning because __.

a) preference for using touch may prevent the use of visual abilities
b) the emotional distress following surgery may interfere with the display of visual abilities
c) these patients may have suffered physical deterioration to their visual system through the years of blindness
d) all of these

6 The very limited visual abilities of chimps reared from birth in total darkness may show only that __.

a) perception is largely the product of experience
b) perception is largely biologically determined
c) a certain amount of light is physically necessary to maintain the visual system and to allow normal maturation
d) none of these

7 If kittens are exposed only to horizontal stripes from birth and then tested at five months with a vertical pointer, __.

a) they display 'behavioural blindness'
b) they display 'physiological blindness'
c) they respond to it as they would to a horizontal pointer
d) a and b

8 Held and Hein's famous __ apparatus shows that only by __ will normal sensory-motor co-ordination develop.

a) visual cliff, showing fear of the 'deep' side
b) kitten carousel, moving about in a visually rich environment
c) visual cliff, exposure to patterned light
d) kitten carousel, exposure to patterned light

9 Apart from the ethical objections, a major problem with animal experiments is that __.

a) animals cannot tell us about their perceptual experience
b) we can only infer what animals perceive from their behaviour and their physiological responses
c) unless an animal's abilities have become linked to its behaviour, we cannot be sure they exist
d) all of these

10 Perceptual adaptation/readjustment studies strongly support the __ position, by showing that even when the perceptual world is drastically altered, __.

a) empiricist, people are able to adapt to it
b) empiricist, people learn how to adjust to the changes
c) nativist, people are able to adapt to it
d) a and b

11 What subjects who participate in perceptual adaptation readjustment studies seem to be learning is __.

a) a new set of body movements

appropriate to their changed visual world
b) how to match their vision with signals reported by the rest of their body
c) how to see 'normally'
d) a and b

12 If we find consistent differences between different cultural groups in their response to the same visual stimuli, __.

a) we must conclude that how we in Western culture perceive is not universal
b) we must infer that environmental factors at least partly determine how we perceive
c) we may infer that social customs/ ecology/language and/or other cultural/ environmental influences are involved in perception
d) all of these

13 According to the 'carpentered world' hypothesis, __.

a) we tend to perceive 2-D illusion figures in keeping with our past experience
b) if we live in an environment in which right angles are commonplace, we add depth to drawings
c) our cultural experience tells us what the illusion figure could represent
d) all of these

14 Hudson's pictures of hunting scenes are usually taken as evidence that __.

a) both children and adults from many different African tribes cannot perceive depth in drawings
b) interpreting pictures is an inborn ability
c) members of non-Western cultures are less intelligent than members of Western culture
d) all of these

15 Presenting members of the Me'en tribe with pictures of animals on familiar cloth shows that __.

a) immediate recognition may be possible,

even though a picture has never been seen before
b) recognition may occur through the process of stimulus generalization
c) even with distracting cues removed, recognition is not achieved
d) a and b

16 If newborns don't display a particular ability, __.

a) that ability must depend on learning
b) it could develop later through maturation
c) it could be because it needs time to develop and mature
d) b and c

17 Preferential looking or __ allows the investigator to infer that the baby __.

a) the spontaneous visual preference technique, can tell the difference between two stimuli
b) the spontaneous visual perception test, has normal visual acuity
c) the spontaneous visual preference technique, prefers the stimulus it spends longer looking at
d) a and c

18 If an external stimulus and a mental representation of that stimulus match, then __.

a) the baby 'knows' the stimulus and so there is no reason for it to continue responding
b) habituation will take place
c) the baby's attention continues to be held
d) a and b

19 Evidence suggests that newborns discriminate shapes based on __. By about three months, a more true kind of form perception begins, where the baby responds to __.

a) lower order variables, higher order variables
b) variables such as orientation, contrast, the configuration or gestalt
c) particular features, the overall pattern or form
d) all of these

20 The claim that the human face has special, species-specific visual significance for the baby from birth onwards is supported by evidence that babies __.

a) very quickly learn to recognize and to prefer their mother's face
b) less than an hour old visually follow a face-like stimulus in preference to a 'scrambled face'
c) two to three months old prefer slides of 'attractive' female faces
d) all of these

21 An alternative to crawling as a measure of depth perception using the 'visual cliff' is to measure changes in the baby's __. A(n) __ in this indicates __ and if this only occurs on the __ side, depth perception may be inferred.

a) heart rate, decrease, interest, deep
b) heart rate, increase, interest, deep
c) breathing rate, decrease, fear, deep
d) heart rate, increase, fear, deep

22 According to __, visual constancy is __ so that babies are likely to be influenced by the __.

a) empiricists, learned, the retinal images projected by objects
b) nativists, innate, true size of an object regardless of the retinal image produced by the object
c) empiricists, innate, true size of an object regardless of the retinal image produced by the object
d) a and b

SELF-ASSESSMENT QUESTIONS

1 What do nativists and empiricists believe about what influences the development of perceptual abilities?

2 Briefly outline the major sources of evidence relevant to the nature–nurture debate in perception.

3 Explain the difference between figural unity and figural identity.

4 Consider some of the problems involved in interpreting the findings from studies of human cataract patients.

5 Describe two animal deprivation experiments and show how they have helped to explain the role of environmental factors in perceptual development.

6 Describe two perceptual adaptation/readjustment studies and explain exactly what is being learned by the subjects in each case.

7 Explain briefly what is involved in cross-cultural studies of perception and say why they are important.

8 What is the 'carpentered world' hypothesis? Summarize the evidence on which it is based.

9 What evidence is there to suggest that factors other than ecology are responsible for cultural differences in perception?

10 To what extent is the 'reading' of pictures and drawings a skill, influenced by cultural factors?

11 Outline three methods used to study the perceptual abilities of human infants.

12 What is the evidence that babies have an inborn ability to recognize the human face?

13 Consider the evidence that depth perception is an inborn ability.

14 What general conclusions can be drawn about the relative influence of genetic and environmental factors on the development of perceptual abilities?

KEY TERMS/CONCEPTS

accommodation
after-images/effects
animal deprivation
  experiments
areas of greatest contrast
behavioural blindness
'carpentered world
  hypothesis' (Segall et al)
conditioned head rotation
convergence
cross-cultural studies
cross-modal transfer
depth and distance cues:
  relative size/
  superimposition
  (overlap)/linear
  perspective/binocular
  disparity/motion
  parallax/texture gradient
  (gradient of density)/
  aerial perspective
distorting goggles/lenses/
  prisms
empiricists

facedness
figural identity (Hebb)
figural unity
Gestalt principle of closure
Gestalt psychology
habituation
heart and breathing rate
horizontal-vertical illusion
Hudson's drawings of
  hunting scenes
human cataract patients
integrated avoidance
  response
interactionists
kitten carousel (Held and
  Hein)
lower-order/higher-order
  variables
maturation
Müller-Lyer illusion
myelination (of optic
  nerve)
nativists
ocular dominance

columns
optokinetic reflex (optic
  nystagmus)
patterned/unpatterned
  light
perception of brightness
perception of colour
perception of depth
perception of movement
perception of pattern or
  form
perception of solid, 3-D
  objects
perceptual adaptation/
  readjustment studies
physiological blindness
preference for complexity
  (as a function of age)
'reading' 2-D
  representations of the
  3-D world
reflecting light on the
  cornea
rotating trapezoid illusion

scanning
'split'/'developed'/'chain-
  type' drawings
spontaneous visual
  preference technique
  (preferential looking)
studies of human infants
stylistic/artistic preference
sucking rate
the face as a supernormal
  stimulus (Rheingold)
transactionalists
translucent goggles
visual acuity
visual constancies: size/
  shape/feature/identity/
  existence (object
  permanence: Piaget)
object concept
'visual cliff' apparatus
  (Gibson and Walk)
visual saccades

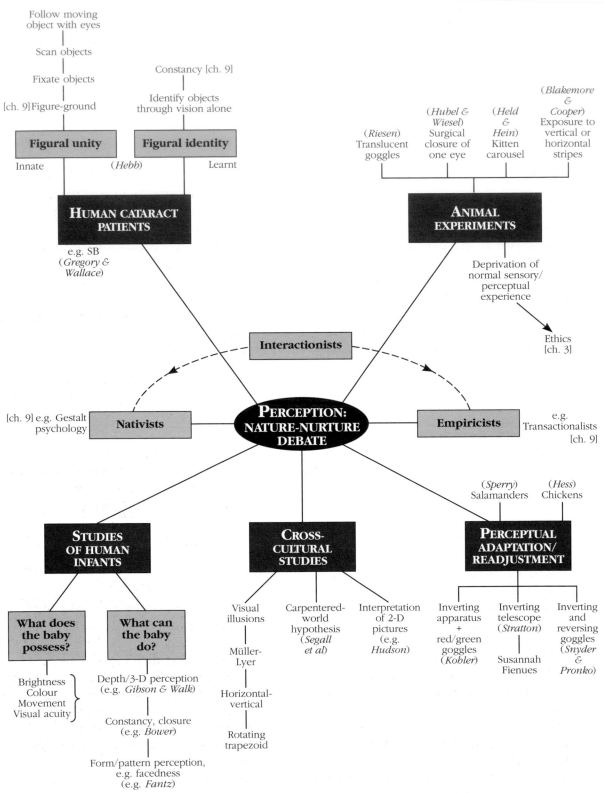

11 ATTENTION

MULTIPLE-CHOICE QUESTIONS

1 Perception and attention are related in that __.

a) they are both concerned with what we become aware of in our environment (although perception is not always conscious)
b) perception is studied by assuming that subjects are attending to the stimuli presented to them
c) attention is studied by assuming that subjects are perceiving the stimuli presented to them
d) a and b

2 The mechanisms which reject certain information and not others are referred to as __; the upper limit to how much information can be processed at one time is called __.

a) selective or focused attention, capacity or divided attention
b) capacity or divided attention, selective or focused attention
c) selective or divided attention, capacity or focused attention
d) capacity or focused attention, selective or divided attention

3 In the __ technique, __.

a) shadowing, the subject is asked to attend to and respond to both messages/ tasks
b) dual-task, the subject's attention is deliberately divided between two (or more) tasks
c) dual-task, the subject is asked to attend to and respond to both messages/tasks
d) b and c

4 Theories of selective attention __.

a) maintain that there is a 'bottleneck' or filter where the attended message is passed on for further processing
b) maintain that there is a 'bottleneck' or filter where the non-attended message is either filtered out or processed only to a limited degree
c) differ basically over the position of the filter
d) all of these

5 According to Broadbent's __ model, the bottleneck occurs very __ in processing and is based on the __ of the incoming stimuli.

a) filter, early, meaning
b) attenuator, early, physical properties
c) filter, early, physical properties
d) pertinence, late, meaning

6 If subjects hear 'crept out of . . . . flowers' as the shadowed message and 'brightly coloured . . . . the swamp' as the non-shadowed message, __.

a) according to the filter model they should report 'crept out of the swamp'
b) their ability to report 'crept out of the swamp' shows their capacity to switch attention rapidly from channel to channel
c) their ability to report 'crept out of the swamp' shows that familiarity with the grammatical and semantic aspects of language override instructions to attend only to one ear
d) b and c

7 The filter model sees input as attended to or not attended to, i.e. __.

a) the filter or bottleneck is very flexible
b) it is an all-or-none model
c) either input is allowed through or is filtered out
d) b and c

8 The role of the attenuator in Treisman's model is to __.

a) act as a 'perceptual filter'
b) 'turn down' the volume of irrelevant messages so that they are still available for higher level processing
c) ensure that any irrelevant messages do not 'get through'
d) a and b

9 Compared with the filter model, Treisman's attenuator model __.

a) can account for the 'cocktail party situation'
b) can account for how we attend to the meaning of the non-attended message and not just its physical characteristics
c) sees input analysis as being a hierarchical process
d) all of these

10 According to the __ model of Deutsch and Deutsch and Norman, the bottleneck is much __ the response end of the processing system, so that the decision regarding the __ of a message occurs much __ than in Treisman's model.

a) pertinence, nearer, relevance, earlier
b) attenuator, nearer, pertinence, later
c) pertinence, nearer, pertinence, earlier
d) a and c

11 A limitation of all models of selective attention is that __.

a) they either under or overestimate what subjects are able to report about the non-attended message;
b) they assume a single, general purpose, limited capacity, central processor

c) they are based on experimental research
d) a and b

12 In a fairly typical __ experiment, the subject hears a message presented to one ear while being asked to perform a second, __ task.

a) divided attention, concurrent
b) selective attention, interfering
c) dual-task, concurrent
d) a and c

13 If performance on two tasks performed together is worse than performance on either task performed separately, then we may conclude that __.

a) performing them together makes no difference
b) there is interference between the tasks
c) both tasks require some degree of conscious processing
d) b and c

14 When subjects try to shadow passages of prose while learning auditorily presented words, __.

a) their recognition memory of the words is as good as when the words are presented without a shadowing task
b) their recognition memory of the words is no better than chance
c) there is considerable interference between the tasks
d) b and c

15 Two tasks interfere to the extent that __.

a) they involve the same stimulus modality
b) use the same stages of processing
c) rely on related memory codes
d) all of these

16 Apart from task similarity, practice affects performance in dual-task experiments by __.

a) helping subjects develop new strategies so as to reduce interference
b) reducing the demands the task makes on attention or other central resources

c) producing a more economical use of processing resources
d) all of these

17 An important difference between studies of divided attention which reveal people's remarkable capacities to do two things at once, and studies of selective attention, is that __.

a) in the latter, the two messages are very similar
b) in the former, the subjects are often highly skilled in one of the tasks
c) in the former, the tasks are more difficult
d) a and b

18 Automatic processes __.

a) are fast and do not reduce the capacity for performing other tasks
b) make no demands on the person's attention
c) are not available to consciousness and are unavoidable
d) all of these

19 __ is demonstrated by __.

a) automatic processing, the skilled pianist
b) automaticity, the Stroop effect
c) controlled processing, learning to drive a car
d) all of these

20 The disadvantage of automatic processes, compared with controlled, is that __.

a) they are fast
b) they are inflexible
c) they can disrupt performance through the automatic response to to-be-ignored stimuli;
d) b and c

21 Tasks which require a lot of mental effort __.

a) require our conscious/focused attention
b) make heavy demands on the central processor
c) can be performed automatically
d) a and b

22 According to Kahneman's theory of attention, we can attend to more than one thing at a time as long as __.

a) we are motivated, aroused and alert
b) the total mental effort required doesn't exceed the total capacity available
c) the mental effort demanded by any one task doesn't use up most/all of the available capacity
d) all of these

23 According to Kahneman, the central processor adopts a(n) __, the function of which is to __.

a) central allocation policy, constantly evaluate the level of demand
b) central allocation policy, decide which tasks should receive more attention if total level of demand becomes excessive
c) executive resources allocation policy, maximize the number of tasks which can be performed at the same time
d) a and b

24 According to Baddeley's model of working memory, __.

a) a central capacity processor is at the top of a hierarchy
b) the central processor co-ordinates and controls the processing mechanisms lower down in the hierarchy, such as the articulatory loop and visuospatial scratch pad
c) lower-level processing mechanisms tend to operate in a modular fashion and fairly automatically
d) all of these

SELF-ASSESSMENT QUESTIONS

1 Explain the difference between a) selective or focused attention and b) capacity or divided attention.

2 Briefly explain how the concepts of attention and perception are related.

3 Outline the major experimental techniques used to study a) selective and b) divided attention.

4 Describe and evaluate two theories of selective attention.

5 Briefly explain what it is that all single channel models (of selective attention) have in common and how they differ.

6 Describe in detail two studies of selective attention and explain how the results support one particular model.

7 Describe in detail one study of divided attention and explain what the results tell us about the influence of either a) task similarity or b) task difficulty or c) practice on dual-task performance.

8 Explain the difference between a) controlled and b) automatic processing.

9 Briefly explain how practice can increase automaticity.

10 Describe Kahneman's theory of attention.

11 What is the connection between Baddeley's model of 'working memory' and the concept of attention?

KEY TERMS/CONCEPTS

articulatory loop
attenuator model (Treisman)
automatic processing/ automaticity
bottleneck or filter
capacity or divided attention
central allocation policy
central processor
'cocktail party' situation

controlled processing
dichotic listening
dual-task situation
filter model (Broadbent)
interference
Kahneman's theory of attention
mental effort
model of working memory (Baddeley)
perception

pertinence model (Deutsch and Deutsch/ Norman)
practice
resource allocation
selection
selective or focused attention
shadowing
single channel models
split-span procedure

Stroop effect
task difficulty
task similarity
theories of selective attention
three levels of functioning (Shallice): fully automatic/partially automatic processing/ deliberate control
visuo-spatial scratch pad

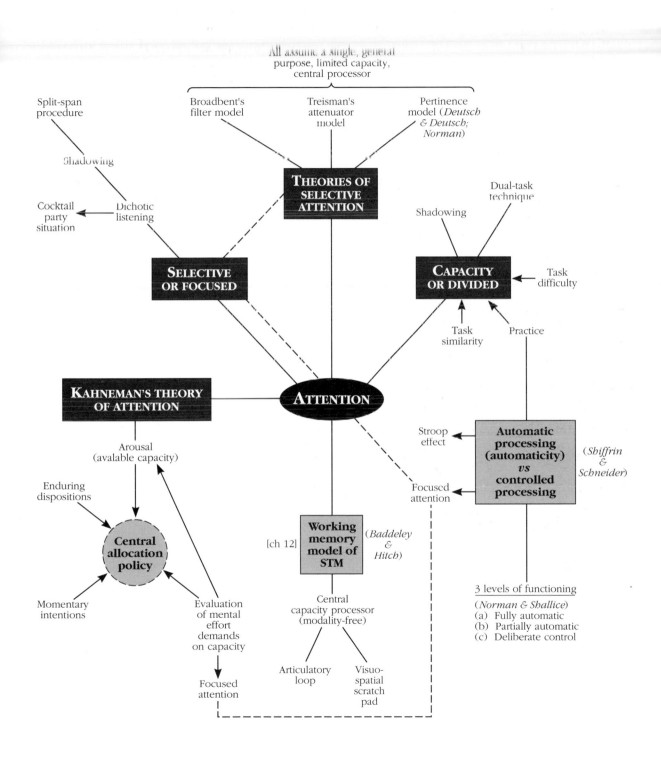

All assume a single, general purpose, limited capacity, central processor

Split-span procedure

Shadowing

Cocktail party situation

Dichotic listening

Broadbent's filter model

Treisman's attenuator model

Pertinence model (*Deutsch & Deutsch; Norman*)

THEORIES OF SELECTIVE ATTENTION

Shadowing

Dual-task technique

SELECTIVE OR FOCUSED

CAPACITY OR DIVIDED

Task difficulty

Task similarity

Practice

KAHNEMAN'S THEORY OF ATTENTION

ATTENTION

Stroop effect

Automatic processing (automaticity) *vs* controlled processing (*Shiffrin & Schneider*)

Arousal (avalable capacity)

Focused attention

Enduring dispositions

Central allocation policy

Momentary intentions

Evaluation of mental effort demands on capacity

Focused attention

[ch 12]

Working memory model of STM (*Baddeley & Hitch*)

Central capacity processor (modality-free)

Articulatory loop

Visuo-spatial scratch pad

3 levels of functioning

(*Norman & Shallice*)
(a) Fully automatic
(b) Partially automatic
(c) Deliberate control

12 MEMORY

MULTIPLE-CHOICE QUESTIONS

1 Whether or not information has been stored refers to the question of __, while __ refers to the question of whether or not the stored information can be retrieved.

a) accessibility, retrievability
b) accessibility, availability
c) availability, accessibility
d) assimilation, accommodation

2 According to Miller, the capacity of short-term memory is __ bits of information.

a) seventeen, plus or minus ten
b) seven, plus or minus two
c) seven
d) seventy, plus or minus twenty

3 The limited capacity of short-term memory can be increased through __.

a) practice
b) rehearsal
c) chunking
d) all of these

4 The capacity of long-term memory is __. It includes __.

a) unlimited, knowledge of the physical properties of objects
b) unlimited, knowledge of the social world, including ourselves
c) very large but limited, our knowledge of language
d) a and b

5 According to Atkinson and Shiffrin's __.

a) multi-store model, short-term and long-term memory are permanent

structural components of the memory system
b) dual memory theory, the memory system comprises relatively transient control processes
c) multi-store model, rehearsal is a major control process which keeps sensory information within short-term memory and transfers it to long-term memory
d) all of these

6 In a serial position curve, the __ effect reflects retrieval from __, while the __ effect reflects retrieval from __.

a) recency, short-term memory, primacy, long-term memory
b) recency, long-term memory, primacy, short-term memory
c) primacy, secondary memory, recency, primary memory
d) a and c

7 Rapid loss of information from memory when __ is prevented is usually taken as evidence for __ and hence for the __ model.

a) rehearsal, short-term memory, levels of processing
b) rehearsal, short-term memory, multi-store
c) chunking, long-term, multi-store
d) repeating it over and over, short-term memory, levels of processing

8 An important distinction is that between __ and __ rehearsal. Studies of __ in which subjects are able to remember material despite not expecting to be tested, suggests that __.

a) maintenance, elaborative, incidental learning, maintenance rehearsal is not necessary for storage
b) rote, elaborative, incidental learning, rote rehearsal is not necessary for storage
c) short-term, long-term, rote learning, rote rehearsal is not necessary for retrieval
d) a and b

9 The chunking involved in reading and understanding speech, and our long-term remembering of voices, melodies and faces, strongly suggests that __.

a) an acoustic code is not the only one used by short-term memory
b) long-term memory uses an acoustic code
c) no simple distinction in terms of coding can be made between short- and long-term memory
d) all of these

10 The kind of amnesic syndrome displayed by both H. M. and Clive Wearing __.

a) is not a general deterioration of memory function
b) involves the severe impairment of certain abilities, such as learning new information
c) does not involve an impairment of short-term remembering
d) all of these

11 If amnesic patients really do have an intact short-term memory, on a serial position curve based on dual-component tasks, compared with normal subjects, they should show __.

a) a similar recency effect but a different primacy effect
b) a similar primacy effect but a different recency effect
c) poorer recall for items earlier in the list
d) a and c

12 __ memory is a kind of long-term memory concerned with __.

a) episodic, our past, personal experiences
b) semantic, our general, factual knowledge about the world
c) procedural, our ability to use and understand language
d) a and b

13 According to the levels of processing approach, __.

a) it is not rehearsal as such which affects long-term storage but the attentional and perceptual processes involved when learning takes place
b) memory is the by-product of the processing of information
c) the durability of memory is a direct function of how deeply the incoming information is processed
d) all of these

14 Asking __ involves a __ level of processing.

a) if a word is written in capital letters, semantic
b) if a word rhymes with some other word, structural
c) if a word means the same as some other word, phonetic/phonemic
d) none of these

15 Baddeley's model of working memory __.

a) rejects the multi-store's view of short-term memory as being unitary
b) adopts a functional approach, concerned with what memory is for
c) sees short-term memory as an active store, the focus of consciousness
d) all of these

16 As far as the multi-store model is concerned, forgetting can be explained in terms of __.

a) what prevents information staying in short-term memory long enough to be transferred to long-term memory (availability)
b) what prevents us from locating the information that has been transferred to

long-term memory (accessibility)
c) lack of availability and failure to retrieve
d) all of these

17 The central idea in __ is that __.

a) trace decay, forgetting in short-term memory increases with the passage of time
b) interference, a stimulus decays from short-term memory as its neural after-effects decay
c) trace decay, learning leaves a trace in the brain and spontaneous fading of this memory trace over time is forgetting
d) a and c

18 Forgetting from short-term memory may occur because __.

a) new information displaces information from one of the limited number of slots
b) new information has higher trace strength than older information
c) extraneous material interferes with the transfer of new information from short-term to long-term memory
d) all of these

19 __ inhibition involves the __ and works in a __ direction.

a) retroactive, learning of a second, later, list which interferes with the recall of the first, earlier, list, backwards
b) proactive, learning of an earlier list which interferes with the recall of a second, later, list, forwards
c) retroactive, learning of an earlier list which interferes with the recall of a second, later, list, backwards
d) a and b

20 According to __ forgetting, subjects who learn in one room and recall in another, should __ compared with subjects who both learn and recall in the same room.

a) cue-dependent, show poorer recall
b) context-dependent, show better recall
c) context-dependent, show poorer recall
d) a and c

21 Scripts are one kind of __. They __.

a) schema, represent commonly experienced social events, such as going to a restaurant
b) packet of information, allow us to fill in details which are not specified in the text
c) schema, contain the sequence of actions and other participants involved in stereotypical social events
d) all of these

22 Imagery represents a form of __ and is used in mnemonics which aid retention by __.

a) organization, reducing the amount of information to be remembered
b) organization, elaborating the information to be remembered
c) semantic memory, finding a path through the network
d) a and b

23 According to Bartlett, __.

a) remembering is a reconstruction of the past
b) remembering involves trying to make past events more logical and coherent by fitting them into our schemata
c) remembering often involves inferring what could or should have happened
d) all of these

24 Loftus has applied the view of memory as __ to the study of __. She argues that our memory of past events can be __ as the result of being asked __.

a) reconstructive, eye-witness testimony, altered, 'leading questions'
b) fallible, identity parades, changed, complex questions
c) reconstruction, eye-witness testimony, improved, 'leading questions'
d) none of these

SELF-ASSESSMENT QUESTIONS

1 Summarize the major differences between short- and long-term memory in terms of a) capacity b) duration and c) coding.

2 Explain how chunking can expand the limited capacity of short-term memory.

3 Describe the major features of the multi-store model of memory.

4 To what extent do the findings from two-component tasks support the multi-store model?

5 To what extent do the findings from studies of coding support the multi-store model?

6 To what extent do the findings from studies of brain-damaged patients support the multi-store model?

7 Explain the difference between a) episodic b) semantic and c) procedural memory.

8 Give some examples from studies of brain-damaged patients which suggest the need to distinguish different kinds of long-term memory.

9 Outline and evaluate the levels of processing approach.

10 Outline and evaluate the working memory model.

11 Compare and contrast any two theories of forgetting.

12 Explain the difference between availability and accessibility. How does this distinction help in the classification of theories of forgetting?

13 Outline and evaluate network models of semantic memory.

14 Discuss the role of a) organization and b) imagers in memory.

15 Explain what is meant by reconstructive memory.

16 Discuss the claim that eye-witness testimony is almost completely unreliable.

KEY TERMS/CONCEPTS

accessibility
acoustic/visual/semantic coding
amnesic syndrome
anterograde amnesia
articulatory loop
articulatory suppression
asymptote
availability
Brown–Peterson technique
capacity
central executive
chunking
coding
consolidation process
control processes
cue-dependent forgetting
decay through disuse
declarative/non-declarative memory
displacement
distinctiveness of processing
duration
echoic store (pre-categorical acoustic store)
efforts after meaning

elaboration of processing
elaborative rehearsal
encoding specificity principle (ESP) (Tulving)
episodic memory
experimenter-imposed organization (EO)
eye-witness testimony
flashbulb memories
free recall
gestalt theory of forgetting
hierarchical network model (of semantic memory)
iconic store
interference
knowing that/knowing how
levels of processing (LOP) (Craik and Lockhart)
long-term memory (LTM)/long-term storage (LTS)/secondary memory
maintenance (rote) rehearsal
mnemonic devices/

mnemonics (memory aids)
motivated forgetting
multi-store model (dual memory theory) (Atkinson and Shiffrin)
organization
paired associate learning
pattern recognition
perceptual defence
primacy effect
primary acoustic store
proactive inhibition (PI)
procedural memory
recency effect
reconstructive/inferential memory (Bartlett)
registration (reception)/storage/retrieval
rehearsal
repeated/serial reproduction
repression (Freud)
retention of learning
retroactive inhibition (RI)
retrograde amnesia
schema theories (of semantic memory)

scripts (Schank and Abelson)
semantic memory
sensory memory
serial position curve
serial probe technique
short-term memory (STM)/short-term storage (STS)/primary memory
spreading activation
state-dependent/context-dependent forgetting
structural components
structural or shallow/phonetic or phonemic/semantic levels (of processing)
subjective organization (SO)
trace decay
transfer-appropriate processing
two-component tasks
visuo-spatial scratch pad
whole/partial reports
working memory (WM) (Baddeley and Hitch)

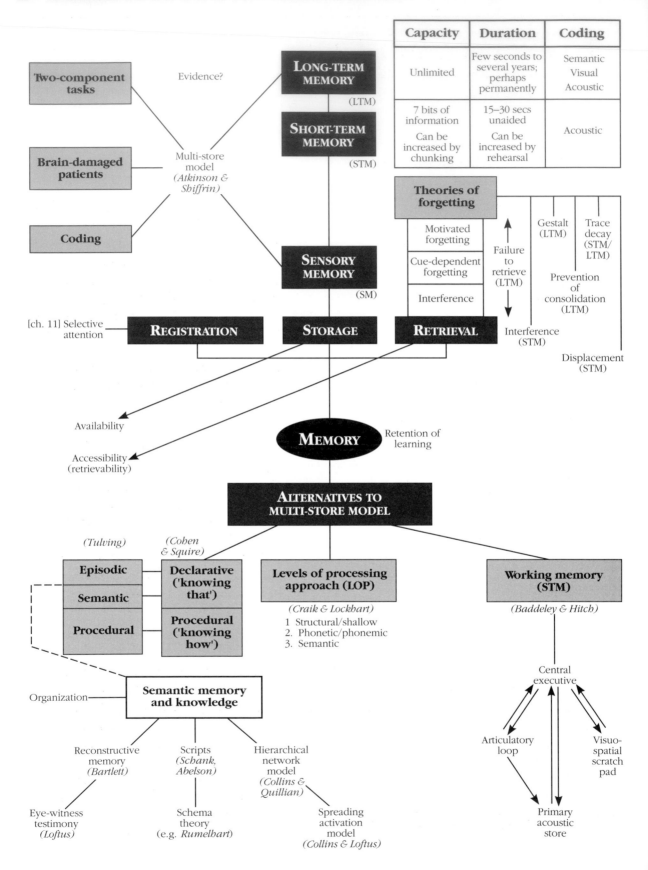

13 LANGUAGE AND THOUGHT

MULTIPLE-CHOICE QUESTIONS

1 According to linguistic determinism, __.

a) language determines our concepts
b) we can only think with the use of concepts
c) language is determined by our concepts
d) a and b

2 The belief that people with different languages will have different world-views is called __.

a) cultural relativism
b) cultural determinism
c) the linguistic relativity hypothesis
d) ethnocentrism

3 An example of linguistic differences which, according to __ cause different perceptions of the world, is __.

a) Whorf, the possession by Eskimos of more than twenty specific words for snow
b) Whorf, the absence of time-related words in the Hopi Indian language
c) Sapir, the Zuni Indians' failure to distinguish verbally between yellow and orange
d) all of these

4 According to the __ version of the linguistic relativity hypothesis, __.

a) weak, language affects perception and memory
b) strong, language determines thought
c) weak, thought is determined by language
d) a and b

5 The Navaho language puts a great deal of stress on the perception of __; according to Sapir and Whorf, children who speak only Navaho __.

a) form, should show superior development of form perception to children who speak only English
b) shape, should be inferior in their shape perception to children who speak only English
c) form, should develop form perception at the same rate as children who speak only English
d) none of these

6 According to the linguistic relativity hypothesis, __.

a) Zuni speakers will not be able to perceive the difference between yellow and orange because Zuni does not have separate labels for these colours
b) Zuni speakers will be 'blind' for yellow and orange because Zuni does not distinguish between them
c) Zuni speakers will easily learn new labels for colours
d) a and b

7 Although different languages denote colour in many different ways, __.

a) all languages seem to select colour terms from eleven basic colour categories
b) the colour spectrum is not divided up in an arbitrary way
c) perception of basic colours seems to correspond across different languages
d) all of these

8 Based on studies of colour perception and the learning of colour labels __.

a) there is very little support for the strong version of the linguistic relativity hypothesis
b) there is quite a lot of support for the claim that language determines how much attention we pay to an object/situation and how easily we recognize it
c) there is quite a lot of evidence that language predisposes people to think or perceive in certain ways or about certain things
d) all of these

9 Evidence that babies can discriminate between different colours long before they ever learn verbal labels for colours indicates that __.

a) language does not dictate the way that colours are perceived
b) colour perception has a biological basis
c) differences between languages in the use of colour labels conceal the basic similarities in colour perception between native speakers of these languages
d) all of these

10 __ claim that all thought processes are in fact the sensations produced by tiny, silent, movements of the speech apparatus, is called __.

a) Whorf's, linguistic determinism
b) Watson's, behaviourism
c) Watson's, peripheralism
d) Wundt's, introspectionism

11 If someone who is completely paralyzed, but kept breathing artificially, can still report his/her thoughts and perceptions, then we may infer that __.

a) thinking cannot be determined by the movements of muscles in the larynx
b) peripheralism cannot be valid
c) movements of the larynx may normally accompany thinking
d) all of these

12 The finding that people born deaf and mute, and who do not learn any sign language, are not intellectually below average as adults suggests that __.

a) cognitive development is not dependent on language
b) it is the development of cognitive structures that is of primary importance
c) both Watson and Piaget are correct
d) a and b

13 When the Russian twins, studied by Luria and Yudovich, were separated, their __ speech began to disappear, suggesting that __.

a) synpraxic, an objective language system is necessary for normal cognitive development
b) synpraxic, backwardness can be caused by language deficiency
c) syncretic, they were emotionally too dependent on one another
d) a and b

14 According to __, working-class children lack a(n) __ code and this __.

a) Bernstein, elaborated, prevents them from developing their intellectual potential
b) Watson, restricted, prevents them from being able to think properly
c) Bernstein, elaborated, puts them at a serious disadvantage in the educational system
d) a and c

15 Lack of an elaborated code is an educational disadvantage because __.

a) schooling is conducted almost exclusively in an elaborated, formal, code
b) the educational system becomes increasingly abstract
c) working-class children are not used to attending to long sequences of speech or asking questions and using reference materials
d) all of these

16 According to Bernstein, black children and adults __.

a) are limited to a restricted code
b) use both a restricted and elaborated code
c) think in a less logical way than white, middle-class children and adults
d) a and c

17 According to Labov, black dialects are called illogical and substandard because __.

a) they are the only known languages which omit the present tense of the verb 'to be'
b) they prevent their users from expressing ideas logically and coherently
c) of white prejudice against blacks
d) none of these

18 The poorer linguistic abilities and intelligence of black and working-class children compared with their white, middle-class, counterparts may reflect _ .

a) the fact that intelligence tests are administered in standard, 'elaborated', English
b) their reluctance to express themselves fully and freely in the presence of a white, middle-class, adult tester
c) biologically determined differences between the two groups
d) a and b

19 According to __, language and thought are initially __.

a) Vygotsky, separate and independent
b) Vygotsky, parts of the same process
c) Bruner, separate and independent
d) Piaget, interdependent

20 Actions, images and perceptions are all examples of __.

a) pre-linguistic thought
b) pre-intellectual language
c) egocentric behaviour
d) none of these

21 After the appearance of verbal thought and rational speech at __ years of age, the child confuses two basic functions of language, namely __.

a) two, monitoring internal thought, communicating one's thoughts to others
b) seven, monitoring internal thought, communicating one's thoughts to others
c) two, internal speech for oneself, external speech for others
d) a and d

22 According to __, the function of egocentric speech is to __.

a) Piaget, act as a running commentary on the child's behaviour
b) Vygotsky, serve mental orientation, help overcome difficulties
c) Vygotsky, act as speech for oneself, eventually becoming inner speech
d) all of these

23 Since thinking develops earlier than language, it seems plausible that __.

a) language builds on the cognitive structures and abilities which have emerged during the pre-linguistic sensorimotor stage
b) language determines thought
c) language is the servant of thought
d) a and c

24 Fodor's 'modularity of mind' sees different cognitive abilities or __ as operating __. It follows that __.

a) modules, independently of each other, language is not influenced by thought
b) nodules, as part of a wider system, language and thought influence each other
c) modules, as part of a wider system, language and thought influence each other
d) cognitive processors, independently of each other, language determines thought

SELF-ASSESSMENT QUESTIONS

1 Briefly outline the three major views as to the relationship between language and thought.

2 Briefly explain what is meant by linguistic determinism and how this is related to the linguistic relativity hypothesis.

3 Give some examples of the characteristics of languages which led Whorf and Sapir to propose the linguistic relativity hypothesis.

4 Explain what is meant by 'the limits of my language mean the limits of my world' (Wittgenstein).

5 What is the difference between the strong and the weak versions of the linguistic relativity hypothesis?

6 Describe two studies which relate to either the strong or the weak versions of the linguistic relativity hypothesis. What conclusions may be drawn from these studies?

7 Outline and evaluate Watson's theory of peripheralism.

8 Discuss the Luria and Yudovich study of the Russian twins in relation to the influence of language on cognitive development.

9 Describe the main differences between restricted and elaborated codes.

10 What are the educational implications of only possessing a restricted code?

11 Discuss the claim that Black English is a substandard form of English.

12 According to Vygotsky, what is the relationship between language and thought?

13 How do Vygotsky and Piaget differ in their explanation of the function and fate of egocentric speech?

KEY TERMS/CONCEPTS

autistic speech
Bassa (Liberia)
BITCH test (Black Intelligence Test of Cultural Homogeneity)
Black English (Labov)
Dani (Indonesian New Guinea)
egocentric speech
elaborated code
Eskimos
external function of

speech
Hopi Indians
Ibibio (Nigeria)
internal function of speech
Jalé (New Guinea)
linguistic determinism
linguistic relativity hypothesis (Sapir, Whorf): strong/weak versions
modes of representation (Bruner): enactive/

iconic/symbolic
modules of the mind (cognitive processors) (Fodor)
Navaho Indians
non-standard English
peripheralism (Watson)
pre-intellectual language (Vygotsky)
pre-linguistic thought
rational speech
restricted code

sensorimotor stage (of cognitive development) (Piaget)
Shone (Zimbabwe)
socialized speech (communicative speech)
substandard English
synpraxic speech
universal linguistic structures
verbal thought
Zuni Indians

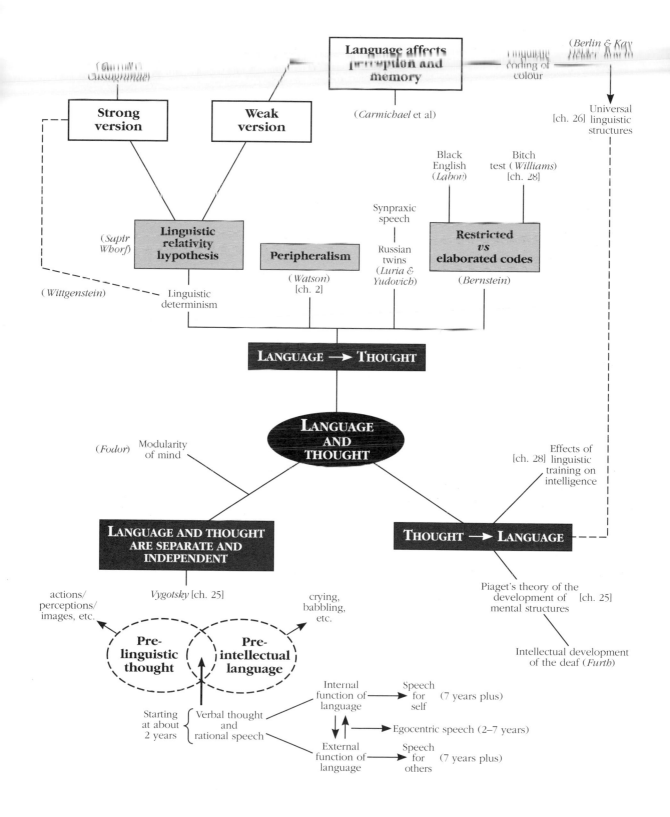

14 THINKING, PROBLEM-SOLVING AND ARTIFICIAL INTELLIGENCE

MULTIPLE-CHOICE QUESTIONS

1 Attempts to produce computer programs capable of solving human problems __.

a) aim to increase our understanding of how people solve them
b) assume that both computers and humans are information-processing machines
c) form a major part of the activity of computer simulation and artificial intelligence
d) all of these

2 The 'General Problem Solver' (GPS) was a computer program, originally based on people's verbal reports of how they are trying to solve a problem as they attempt it, called __.

a) problem-solving analysis
b) introspection
c) protocol analysis
d) behavioural analysis

3 A problem with protocol analysis as a research methodology is that __.

a) people are not always honest about what they are thinking
b) it is unclear how people's reports of their problem-solving relates to the mental operations actually helping them to solve the problem
c) with certain kinds of problem, such as object recognition and language understanding, none of the mental operations underlying these abilities is available to consciousness at all
d) b and c

4 __ refer to strategies for solving problems which help to select actions most likely to lead to a solution but which cannot actually guarantee one.

a) algorithms
b) heuristics
c) expert systems
d) habits

5 Means End Analysis (MEA) is a general __ strategy which __.

a) heuristic, consists of progress tests which inform the solver how close he/she is to the goal
b) heuristic, involves choosing operations which will reduce the distance between the current situation and the current goal
c) algorithmic, consists of progress tests which inform the solver how close he/she is to the goal
d) a and b

6 Many real life situations involve problems __.

a) which are insoluble because they cannot be broken down into sub-goals
b) whose main goal cannot be achieved all in one step
c) whose main goal needs to be broken down into a number of sub-goals
d) b and c

7 Sub-goal MEA __.

a) is an algorithmic strategy
b) is a heuristic strategy

c) involves the creation of sub-goals, each of which must be achieved before the final (main) goal can be reached
d) b and c

8 The kind of knowledge relevant to puzzle problems, such as the Missionaries and Cannibals, is called __. Because this is generally applicable but not always very efficient, it is called __.

a) general purpose, universal and weak
b) domain specific, general purpose and unreliable
c) domain independent, universal and weak
d) a and c

9 What distinguishes experts from non-experts is __.

a) differences in their working memory (WM) capacity
b) differences in their ability to apply MEA
c) differences in their appreciation of the overall structure of the problem
d) differences in IQ

10 Chess experts are superior mainly in terms of .

a) their long-term storage of different board positions
b) their ability to take in more information from briefly presented, meaningful, board positions
c) their ability to make use of stored information in order to cope with the current problem
d) all of these

11 The process of encoding the knowledge of human experts into the expert system is called __. The construction of an expert system is made difficult by the fact that __.

a) transfer of training, not many experts exist
b) transfer of expertise, experts cannot

always express explicitly the knowledge they use
c) transfer of expertise, experts often cannot say how they combine different items of information to make a judgement about a particular case
d) b and c

12 According to Boden, expert systems __.

a) are much less flexible than human experts
b) lack higher-level representations of the knowledge domain
c) cannot integrate knowledge from distinct domains in order to reason by analogy, as can human experts
d) all of these

13 Artificial intelligence (AI) is __.

a) the science of thinking machines
b) a part of computer science which tries to understand intelligence by reproducing it in the form of computer simulation
c) the science of making machines do the sorts of things that are done by human minds
d) all of these

14 A(n) __ is an abstract computing device which reads and writes symbols on a tape. A __ can mimic the operation of any other __.

a) abacus, universal abacus, abacus
b) Turing machine, universal Turing machine, Turing machine
c) Tulving machine, general Tulving machine, Tulving machine
d) program, universal Turing machine, program

15 An important distinction is between the computer as __ and as __.
a) a physical machine, the carrying out of operations as required by the program
b) a metallic object, an information-processing device
c) hardware, software
d) all of these

16 According to __.

a) strong AI, the computer is more than merely a very powerful research tool
b) strong AI, computers given the right program literally understand and have other cognitive states
c) weak AI, the computer is a very powerful tool for formulating and testing hypotheses
d) all of these

17 Underlying __ is the __, according to which intelligence is __.

a) strong AI, Computational Theory of Mind (CTM), the ability to manipulate symbols
b) weak AI, Computational Theory of Mind (CTM), the ability to process information
c) strong AI, Calculational Theory of Mind (CTM), the ability to link symbols to the objects and events they represent
d) none of these

18 The Chinese Room is a __ which is intended to __.

a) Gedanken experiment, demonstrate that there is more to intelligence and understanding than just manipulating symbols
b) thought experiment, show that strong AI is false
c) hypothetical situation, show how easy it is to learn Chinese
d) a and b

19 The __ is meant to be an objective way of trying to answer the question __. It represents the major __ presupposition of strong AI.

a) imitation game, can machines think? methodological
b) Turing test, can machines think? theoretical
c) Chinese room, can people think? methodological
d) all of these

20 According to Searle, mental states and processes are __.

a) real biological phenomena
b) caused by processes going on in the brain
c) not possible in robots because they are not made of flesh and blood
d) all of these

21 According to the Computational Theory of Mind (CTM), __.

a) cognitive processes are defined as the processing of information
b) it is unimportant in what form information is stored and manipulated
c) computers do not need to physically resemble the brain in order to display cognitive abilities
d) all of these

22 Parallel distributed processing (PDP) or __ models have their origins in early computers which tried to develop __.

a) connectionist, abstract models of brain cells
b) neural network, understanding of how large networks of cells work together
c) 'neurally inspired', abstract models of cognitive processes
d) all of these

23 What distinguishes connectionist machines from digital, von Neuman computers is that __.

a) they use parallel as opposed to serial processing
b) they use serial as opposed to parallel processing
c) they are capable of learning to perform tasks as opposed to being programmed to perform them
d) a and c

Self-Assessment Questions

1 Give some examples of the ways in which psychologists have used the term 'problem'.

2 Give two examples of problems used by the Gestalt psychologists.

3 Explain the difference between a) adversary and b) non-adversary problems.

4 Explain the difference between a) a heuristic and b) an algorithm.

5 Outline and evaluate Means End Analysis (MEA) as a strategy for solving problems.

6 Explain what is meant by a 'well-defined' problem. How does this relate to the difference between puzzle-type and everyday problems?

7 Describe the key differences between expert and non-expert chess players.

8 What are expert systems? How well do they perform compared with their human counterparts?

9 What is a computer?

10 Explain the difference between a) hardware and b) software.

11 Define the term 'artificial intelligence' (AI).

12 Explain the difference between strong and weak AI.

13 Describe and discuss the Computational Theory of Mind (CTM).

14 Discuss the Chinese Room thought experiment as an attempt to refute the Computational Theory of Mind.

15 Explain what is meant by a connectionist machine and how it differs from traditional, serial digital, computers.

Key Terms/Concepts

adversary/non-adversary problems
algorithms
analogue computer
artificial intelligence (AI) weak versus strong AI
associationist approach
Backwards Error Propagation Using The Generalized Delta Rule (GDR) ('back propagation')
binary (arithmetic)
carbon/protoplasm chauvinism
cell assemblies
Chinese Room (Searle)
cognitive science
computational theory of mind (CTM)

computer simulation
control strategies (rules)
digital computer
domain-specific knowledge
dualism
engram
expert systems (intelligent knowledge-based systems)
experts versus novices
functional fixedness
functionalism
Gedanken experiment
general problem solver (GPS) (Simon and Newell)
general-purpose/domain-independent knowledge
Gestalt problems

hardware versus software
heuristics
information-processing machine/device
input/output/hidden interconnected units
intentionality
lateral thinking
logical theory machine (or logic theorist) (Newell and Simon)
machinomorphism
Means End Analysis (MEA)
minimax procedure
pandemonium
parallel distributed processing (PDP) (or connectionist models)
perception

physical realization
problem restructuring
problem-solving
problem-reduction representation
problem-solving set
protocol analysis
serial versus parallel processing
state-space representations
state-space theory
supervised learning
transfer of expertise
Turing machine
Turing test (or the Imitation Game)
universal Turing machine
well-defined problems

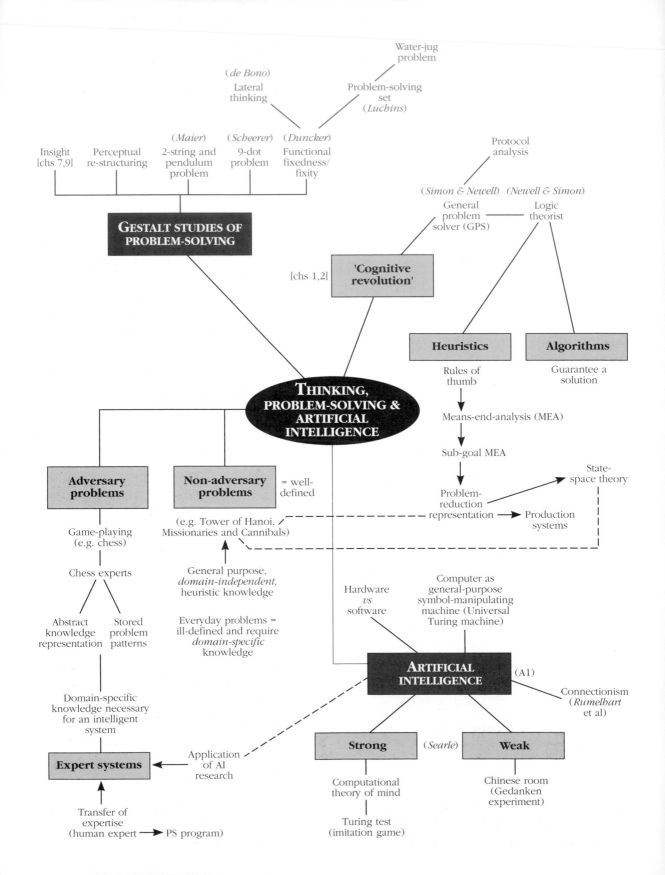

15 THE ETHOLOGICAL AND SOCIOBIOLOGICAL APPROACH TO THE STUDY OF BEHAVIOUR

MULTIPLE-CHOICE QUESTIONS

1 Immediate cause, function, ontogeny and phylogeny correspond to __.

   a) Tinbergen's 'four whys'
   b) Lorenz's 'four whys'
   c) Darwin's 'four whys'
   d) Tinbergen's 'four hows'

2 Ethologists are __ who believe that __.

   a) zoologists, the evolution of behaviour can be studied by comparing species which are related morphologically
   b) biologists, if species with similar skeletons also display similar behaviour, then behaviour is very probably inherited
   c) biologists, learning plays no part in the explanation of behaviour
   d) a and b

3 A basic idea from classical ethology is that __.

   a) a wide range of behaviours should be described in basic terms (the ethogram)
   b) sensible experiments, designed to be as natural as possible, should be encouraged
   c) animals are best studied under highly controlled, laboratory conditions
   d) a and b

4 __ is a process of adaptation through __.

   a) evolution, natural selection
   b) natural selection, evolution
   c) learning, evolution
   d) evolution, learning

5 __ are particular manifestations of an instinct and represent a more __ way of studying instincts. An example is __.

   a) fixed action patterns (FAPs), objective; the egg rolling of the greylag goose
   b) sign stimuli, reliable, the begging response of the herring-gull chick
   c) fixed action patterns (FAPs), objective, the zigzag dance of the male stickleback
   d) a and c

6 A fixed action pattern (FAP) is triggered by a specific stimulus called __.

   a) a releaser
   b) a trigger
   c) a sign stimulus
   d) a and c

7 The red spot on the herring-gull's beak has evolved solely to produce the __ and so is called a __.

   a) begging response in the herring-gull chick, releaser
   b) begging response in the herring-gull chick, sign stimulus
   c) egg-rolling response, releaser
   d) a and b

8 Examples such as the pecking behaviour of laughing-gull chicks and the song of the chaffinch and American white-crowned sparrow demonstrate the __.

   a) the importance of inherited, instinctive, factors
   b) the importance of environmental factors
   c) the interaction between inherited and environmental factors
   d) none of these

9 The hypothetical mechanism within the animal's nervous system which mediates between __ and __ is called the __.

a) the actual, overt behaviour, the sign stimulus, innate releasing mechanism (IRM)
b) the FAP, the releaser, action-specific energy (ASE)
c) the FAP, the releaser, innate-releasing mechanism (IRM)
d) a and c

10 According to the psychohydraulic model, __.

a) a particular FAP may not occur in the presence of a releaser because of insufficient action-specific energy (ASE)
b) a whole sequence of behaviour may occur in the absence of a releaser if sufficient action-specific energy (ASE) has built up
c) whether or not a releaser will be either necessary or sufficient to produce a particular FAP depends on the amount of action-specific energy (ASE)
d) all of these

11 Vacuum activity occurs __.

a) in response to a releaser
b) in the absence of a releaser, spontaneously
c) when the innate-releasing mechanism (IRM) is activated due to the build-up of action-specific energy (ASE)
d) b and c

12 Many FAPs function as __, concerned with __ between members of the same species and triggered by __.

a) sign stimuli, communication, releasing mechanisms
b) signals, communication, social releasers
c) signals, sexual attraction, hormonal levels
d) none of these

13 An animal finding a source of food and potential threat in the same place at the same time __.

a) faces an approach-avoidance conflict
b) faces an approach-approach conflict
c) is likely to engage in some displacement activity, such as preening, washing, feeding or even sleeping
d) a and c

14 The exaggerated, displaced, form of an originally functional response is called __; the process by which it becomes detached from the original sign stimulus and motivation is called __.

a) ritualization, detachment
b) exaggeration, emancipation
c) emancipation, ritualization
d) ritualization, emancipation

15 Much courtship ritual involves the __ necessary for mating to take place and some __ displays involve adopting postures associated with __.

a) reduction in aggression, appeasement, mating
b) increase in aggression, courtship, aggression
c) reduction in aggression, courtship, feeding
d) action-specific energy (ASE), aggressive, mating

16 The difference in the size and nature of the male and female __ is called __ and to a large extent determines the different __ of males and females.

a) sex cells, anisogamy, parental role
b) gametes, polygyny, sexual behaviour
c) gametes, anisogamy, parental role
d) a and c

17 In __, one male has exclusive access to a group of females or __.

a) anisogamy, one male has exclusive access to several females
b) polygyny, a small group of males has access to a larger group of females
c) a pair-bond, two males have access to the same female
d) anisogamy, a small group of females has access to a larger group of males

18 An advantage of living in groups is that
___.

a) a mate is more readily available
b) finding food is easier
c) it is more visible to predators
d) a and b

19 Where some group members have
precedence over others for access to mates
and food, there exists a(n) ___.

a) social class system
b) hierarchy of needs
c) dominance hierarchy
d) inequality of opportunity

20 A territory is basically ___.

a) an area of space which is held and
defended by a solitary animal
b) an area of space which is held and
defended by a family group
c) an area of space in which food is found
and offspring reared
d) all of these

21 Lorenz defined ___ as the learning which
occurs in a young bird when following a
moving object.

a) conditioning
b) imprinting
c) bonding
d) attachment

22 Instinct provides the young bird with ___.

a) the ability to recognize its mother
b) a 'concept' of the mother, without the
details
c) a template of the mother, without the
details
d) b and c

23 According to Lorenz, imprinting is a
unique form of learning because ___.

a) it only occurs during a genetically
determined critical period
b) once it has occurred, it is irreversible
c) it has no effect on behaviours which
haven't yet developed, such as choice of
sexual partner
d) a and b

24 The critical period for imprinting (or the
period of ___) can be extended by ___.

a) imprintability, keeping the young bird
in isolation
b) imprintability, keeping the young bird
in a visually unstimulating environment
c) susceptibility, putting the young bird
with several others
d) a and b

25 The finding that ducklings imprinted on
a pair of yellow rubber gloves showed
normal sexual preferences on reaching
maturity, demonstrates the ___ of
imprinting.

a) irreversibility
b) reversibility
c) flexibility
d) inflexibility

26 Robins, thrushes and titmice warning
others of an approaching hawk, and ants
bees and wasps dying in order to save the
nest against attack, are all examples of ___.

a) psychological altruism
b) biological altruism
c) inclusive fitness
d) kin selection

27 According to ___, the paradox of altruism
can be explained by seeing altruism as ___.

a) sociobiology, only apparent
b) sociobiology, selfish behaviour in
disguise
c) Hamilton, reflecting kin selection and
individual animals being distributed
across kin
d) all of these

28 According to ___, all apparently altruistic
behaviour is a means of maximizing ___.
Altruism has evolved by natural selection
through ___, the sharing of common genes
by related individuals.

a) Wilson, inclusive fitness, kinship
b) Wilson, individual fitness, kinship
c) Darwin, inclusive fitness, inbreeding
d) Lorenz, attachment, imprinting

SELF-ASSESSMENT QUESTIONS

1 Briefly explain the difference between the experimental and the ethological approaches to the study of animal behaviour.

2 What are Tinbergen's 'four whys'?

3 What is the relationship between a) classical and modern ethology and b) sociobiology?

4 Briefly explain the relevance of ethology to psychology.

5 Define the following terms: evolution, sexual (diploid) reproduction, natural selection, fitness adaptedness, selective pressure, species.

6 Define the term instinct and explain how it is related to the concept of a fixed action pattern (FAP).

7 Describe two examples of fixed action patterns (FAPs) and show how they illustrate the major characteristics of FAPs in general.

8 Discuss the role of environmental and hormonal factors on the production of FAPs.

9 Outline and evaluate Lorenz's psycho-hydraulic model of motivation.

10 Explain the relationship between FAPs, displacement activity and evolution.

11 Describe some of the arrangements for courtship and mating within animal species.

12 Describe different kinds of social structure that are found within different animal species.

13 Define the terms 'territory' and 'home range'.

14 What evidence exists that there is a critical period for imprinting and that the effects of imprinting are irreversible?

15 What is the 'paradox of altruism'?

16 Discuss the sociobiological solution to the 'paradox of altruism'.

KEY TERMS/CONCEPTS

action-specific energy (ASE)
adaptedness
agonistic behaviour
anisogamy
approach-avoidance conflict
asexual cell division
behavioural ecology
biological/psychological altruism
classical/modern ethology
consummatory behaviour
critical/sensitive period
delayed reciprocal altruism
displacement activity
distributed across kin
dominance hierarchy
ecological niche

emancipation
ethogram
eusocial insects
evolution
exposure learning
fitness
fixed action patterns (FAPs)
gene exchange
home range
imprintability
imprinting
inclusive fitness
innate releasing mechanism (IRM)
instinct
intention movements
irreversibility
kin selection

matriline
mobility
natural selection
nidifugous birds
ontogeny
pair-bond
paradox of altruism
perceptual learning
pheromones
phylogeny
polygyny
precocial/altricial species
promiscuity
psycho-hydraulic model (of motivation)
reductionism
reification
releaser
ritualization

selective pressure
selfish gene
sexual (diploid) reproduction
sibling groups
sign stimulus
social ethology
social releaser
sociobiology
species
species-specific behaviour
supernormal stimulus (super releaser)
supra-individual
territoriality
Tinbergen's 'four whys'
Umwelt (surroundings)
vacuum activity

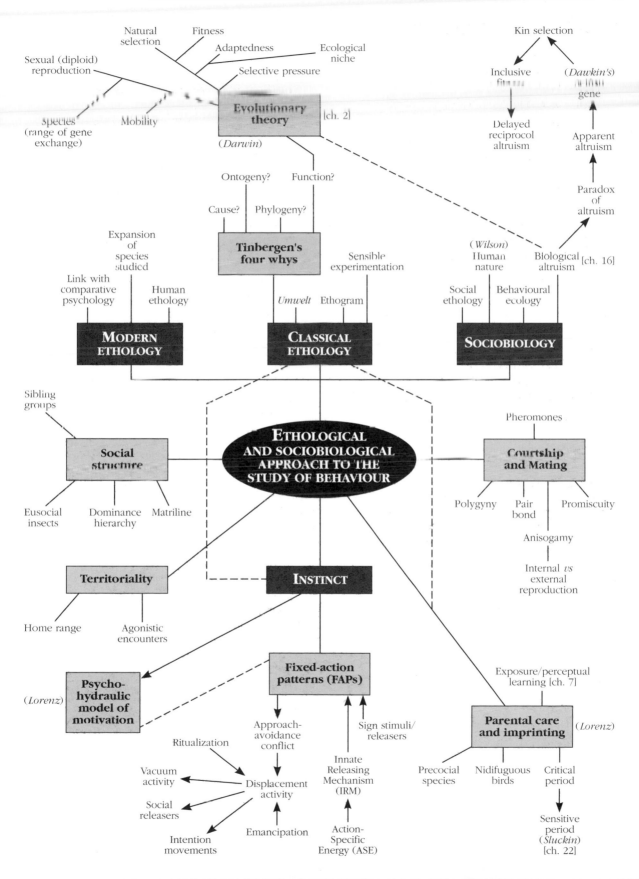

16 PRO- AND ANTI-SOCIAL BEHAVIOUR

MULTIPLE-CHOICE QUESTIONS

1 A strict definition of altruism is an act performed __.

a) in order to receive some extrinsic reward

b) in order to benefit another person without any personal gain or self-interest

c) in order to receive some intrinsic reward

d) in order to benefit another person and to receive some intrinsic or extrinsic reward

2 The Kitty Genovese murder __.

a) stimulated scientific investigation of bystander intervention

b) gave rise to the concept of the unresponsive bystander

c) was remarkable because all 38 witnesses to the crime attempted to contact the police

d) a and b

3 When people in an emergency situation all try to look calm so as not to betray their anxiety and, as a result, each defines the situation as 'safe', __ is being demonstrated.

a) bystander intervention

b) diffusion of responsibility

c) pluralistic ignorance

d) bystander apathy

4 Laboratory experiments have shown that the __ subjects there are (or thought to be) in an emergency situation, the __ likely any one of them is intervene. This is usually explained in terms of __.

a) fewer, more, bystander apathy

b) fewer, less, diffusion of responsibility

c) more, more, pluralistic ignorance

d) more, less, diffusion of responsibility

5 Diffusion of responsibility is __ likely to occur if __.

a) more, the victim can only be heard and not seen

b) more, other witnesses are perceived as more competent to provide the required help

c) less, the emergency occurs in an enclosed space

d) all of these

6 The New York subway experiment found __.

a) no evidence of diffusion of responsibility

b) that an ill victim is very much more likely to be helped than a drunk victim

c) that a black drunk victim is as likely to be helped by a white as a black bystander

d) a and b

7 A motive for not helping is __.

a) loss of time

b) if the victim's plight is seen as self-inflicted

c) if the victim is disfigured in some way

d) all of these

8 If the costs of helping are low and the costs of not helping are high, __.

a) the likelihood of intervention will be very high and direct

b) the likelihood of intervention will be fairly high but indirect

c) the likelihood of intervention will be very low
d) the likelihood of intervention will be fairly high but people will vary considerably

9 Cognitive reinterpretation involves __ and represents a way of resolving the __ dilemma.

a) redefining the situation as one not requiring help, high cost for helping/high cost for not helping
b) diffusing responsibility, high cost for helping/low cost for not helping
c) denigrating/blaming the victim, high cost for helping/high cost for not helping
d) a and c

10 __ may be __ but __ must involve __.

a) aggression, verbal, violence, physical injury
b) aggression, symbolic, violence, the use of great force
c) violence, verbal, aggression, physical injury
d) a and b

11 According to __, aggression __.

a) Lorenz, is the fighting instinct directed against members of the same species
b) Lorenz, is basically constructive in animals but has become distorted in humans
c) Lorenz, in humans is no longer under the control of rituals
d) all of these

12 __ refers to a way of discharging aggression in a __ pattern which ensures that __.

a) rationalization, fixed, fights between animals of the same species do not end in bloodshed
b) ritualization, stereotyped, fights between animals of different species do not end in bloodshed
c) ritualization, stereotyped, fights between animals of the same species do not end in bloodshed

d) repression, fixed, fights between people do not end in bloodshed

13 Infanticide is found among __ and demonstrates that __.

a) lions, animal aggression does not always stop before animals are killed
b) Hanuman langurs, killing members of their own species is not confined to human beings
c) all species, all species are equally aggressive
d) a and b

14 The __ refers to a set of interconnected pathways and centres in the __ which play a vital role in aggressive behaviour.

a) Klüver–Bucy circuit, limbic system
b) Papez circuit, limbic system
c) Papez circuit, cortex
d) reticular activating system, brain stem

15 Even if brain centres exist for different kinds of aggression, __.

a) the elicitation of aggressive behaviour depends on aspects of the experimental situation
b) the limbic system of primates is massively interconnected with the brain's thinking centres in the cortex
c) a monkey's position in the hierarchy has a strong influence on how it behaves when its 'aggression area' is stimulated
d) all of these

16 In humans, __.

a) there is no reliable evidence that stimulation of the amygdala produces aggressive outbursts or violent attacks of rage
b) there is some evidence that tumours of the limbic system are associated with abnormally aggressive behaviour
c) there is no reliable evidence that aggressive emotion or violent behaviour is caused by neurotransmitters, hormones or genetic factors
d) all of these

17 According to Freud, aggression is the major component of __ and represents a(n) __.

a) Thanatos, inborn self-destructiveness
b) Thanatos, an inborn aggression directed primarily against other people
c) the death instinct, an innate tendency to self-destruction
d) a and c

18 Cases of __ individuals who commit brutal crimes but who are typically very unaggressive, lend some support to __ view that aggression is __.

a) overcontrolled, Freud's, spontaneous
b) undercontrolled, Lorenz's, reactive
c) overcontrolled, Lorenz's, spontaneous
d) a and c

19 According to __.

a) social learning theory, aggression is always caused by frustration
b) the frustration-aggression hypothesis, frustration always results in aggression
c) the frustration-aggression hypothesis, aggression is only caused by frustration
d) b and c

20 According to Berkowitz, __.

a) for anger to be converted into actual aggression, certain cues are needed
b) the name of a character in a violent film can act as an environmental cue to aggression
c) the mere physical presence of weapons can increase the likelihood of aggressive behaviour
d) all of these

21 Investigation of viewers' perceptions of television violence suggests that __.

a) realistic portrayals of violence are judged to be more serious than cartoon portrayals
b) real-life incidents in news/documentaries are rated as more violent than fictional violence
c) children discriminate between cartoon and realistic portrayals of violence
d) all of these

22 A reduction in emotional response to TV violence as a result of repeated viewing is called __.

a) arousal
b) disinhibition
c) desensitization
d) imitation

23 A(n) __ of field experiments of the effects of TV violence compared with laboratory experiments is that __.

a) advantage, they are more ecologically valid
b) disadvantage, they often involve pre-selected groups of subjects, such that individuals are not randomly allocated to control and experimental groups
c) advantage, they allow far more control over situational variables
d) a and b

24 If watching TV violence helps the viewer to discharge his/her own aggression, then __ is taking place.

a) modelling
b) vicarious catharsis
c) sublimation
d) repression

25 The concept of __ has been used to explain why people in groups behave in an uncharacteristically __ way relative to their __ behaviour.

a) anonymity, passive, solitary
b) displacement, aggressive, individual
c) dehumanization, demoralized, normal
d) de-individuation, aggressive, individual

26 According to __.

a) Festinger, being able to submerge oneself in a group is one of the attractions of group membership
b) Zimbardo, anonymity is a major source of de-individuation
c) Zimbardo, anonymity can be operationalized by having subjects wear hoods and masks
d) all of these

SELF-ASSESSMENT QUESTIONS

1 How useful is the concept of biological altruism in explaining altruistic behaviour in human beings?

2 Define the following terms: a) definition of the situation b) diffusion of responsibility c) pluralistic ignorance

3 How can we explain the failure to intervene by the 38 witnesses of the murder of Kitty Genovese?

4 Describe one study which demonstrates a) diffusion of responsibility and b) defining the situation as an emergency.

5 Discuss the costs of helping and not helping as factors influencing the likelihood of bystander intervention.

6 Discuss the Arousal:Cost-Reward Model of bystander intervention.

7 Explain the difference between a) universal egoism and b) the empathy-altruism hypothesis.

8 Is there such a thing as a truly altruistic act?

9 Define the term aggression.

10 Outline and evaluate Lorenz's theory of human aggression.

11 Outline and evaluate Freud's theory of aggression.

12 Evaluate the evidence for the claim that aggression and violence, in animals and humans, is controlled by specific centres in the brain.

13 What is the frustration-aggression hypothesis? How has it been subsequently modified?

14 Under what conditions is frustration likely to lead to aggression?

15 Explain what is meant by the 'weapons effect'.

16 In what ways is viewing TV violence thought to affect attitudes and behaviour?

17 Evaluate the evidence for the claim that watching TV violence increases aggressive behaviour in the viewer.

18 Define the term vicarious catharsis. Is there any evidence to show that watching TV violence reduces levels of aggression in the viewer?

19 Explain what is meant by de-individuation. How useful is the concept of de-individuation in accounting for human aggression?

KEY TERMS/CONCEPTS

aggression: hostile/
  instrumental/natural/
  pathological
aggression/source of
  arousal/anger
aggression versus violence
aggressive-cue theory
anonymity
appeasement rituals
  (gestures)
arousal
Arousal:Cost-Reward
  Model
biological altruism
bystander intervention
catharsis
cause and effect
cognitive reinterpretation
communal versus agentic
  helping
competence
correlational surveys

death instinct (Thanatos)
  versus life instinct (Eros)
definition of the situation
de-individuation
delayed reciprocal altruism
depersonalization/
  dehumanization
desensitization
diffusion of responsibility
direct/indirect helping
disinhibition
displacement
dissolution of
  responsibility
ecologically valid
empathy-altruism
  hypothesis
ethological approach
exchange theory
frustration as: instigator of
  aggression/source of
  arousal/anger

frustration-aggression
  hypothesis (Dollard et al)
imitation
infanticide
intrinsic/extrinsic rewards
kin selection
Klüver–Bucy syndrome
laboratory/field
  experiments
learning theory approach
limbic system:
  hypothalamus/amygdala/
  septum
longitudinal panel studies
low cost altruism
neurophysiological
  approach
observational learning
  (modelling)
other-oriented versus self-
  oriented
over- versus under-

controlled individuals
Papez circuit
personal/empathy costs
pluralistic ignorance
psychological altruism
psychoanalytic approach
rationalization
ritualization
sham rage
social learning theory
  approach
sublimation
technology
territoriality
the costs of helping/not
  helping
TV content analysis
universal egoism
vicarious catharsis
warrior versus hunter-
  gatherer
weapons effect (Berkowitz)

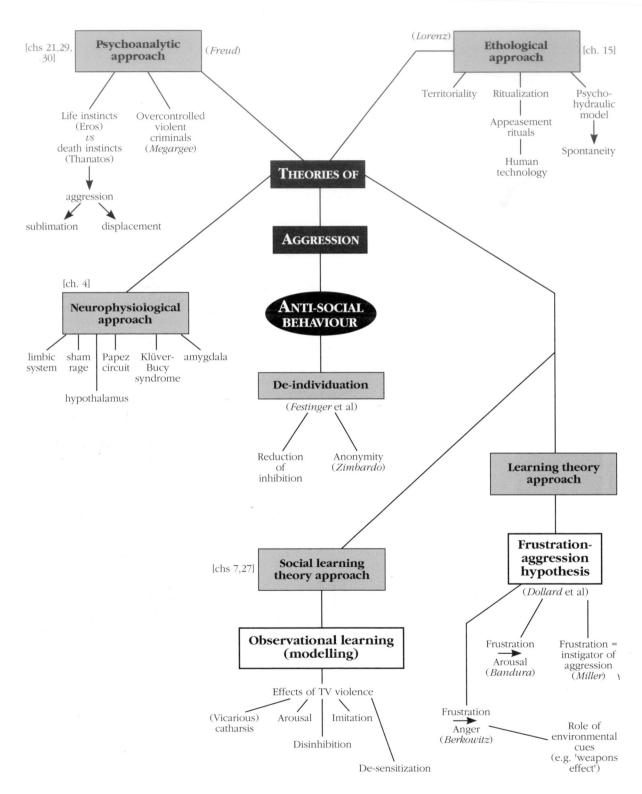

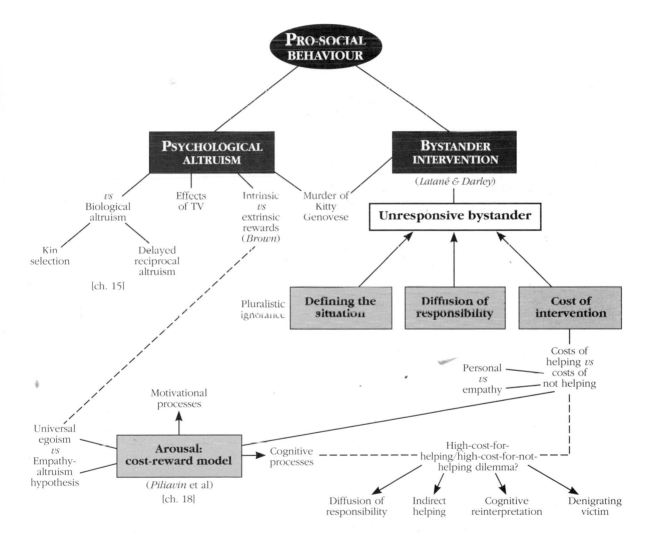

17 INTERPERSONAL PERCEPTION

MULTIPLE-CHOICE QUESTIONS

1 Compared with the professional psychologist, the ___.

a) layperson uses his/her theories for practical purposes
b) amateur psychologist is usually emotionally involved in others' behaviour to some degree
c) lay psychologist uses theories which are implicit or intuitive
d) all of these

2 ___ refers to the study of the role of ___ in forming impressions of people.

a) social cognition, cognitive processes
b) social perception, cognitive processes
c) social influence, power and authority
d) the intuition model, gut reactions

3 ___ traits are those which ___.

a) central, exert a major influence over our global perception of others
b) peripheral, have very little influence on the overall impressions we form of others
c) central, appear in the middle of a list of adjectives describing a hypothetical person
d) a and b

4 As a ___ psychologist, Asch believed that ___.

a) Gestalt, a set of traits produces an integrated impression
b) behaviourist, impressions are formed by summing all the individual traits
c) Gestalt, central traits exert a major organizing influence on the impression formed compared with peripheral traits
d) a and c

5 When subjects are asked to infer traits from the central traits 'warm' and 'cold', ___.

a) the inferred traits are almost identical to those inferred when 'warm' and 'cold' are presented in a list of traits
b) the inferred traits are very different from those inferred when 'warm' and 'cold' are presented in a list of traits
c) their answers indicate that they already possess implicit personality theories in which traits are associated with 'warm' and 'cold'
d) a and c

6 If we are told that a person has a particularly ___ characteristic, we tend to attribute them with ___. This is called a ___.

a) favourable, other favourable characteristics, positive halo effect
b) unfavourable, other unfavourable characteristics, negative halo effect
c) favourable, unfavourable characteristics, broken halo effect
d) a and b

7 According to the ___ effect, if the first words in a list of words describing a person are positive and those at the end are negative, we will form a ___ impression of the person.

a) primacy, negative
b) recency, positive
c) primacy, positive
d) none of these

8 The __ effect is more likely to occur if __.

a) primacy, the impression formed is of someone we are meeting for the first time
b) recency, we are warned against making snap judgements
c) primacy, we already know the person very well
d) a and b

9 The __ refers to our attempts to explain why people behave as they do by identifying the __ of their behaviour.

a) primacy-recency effect, causes
b) attribution process, consequences
c) attribution process, causes
d) inference model, meaning

10 According to Jones and Davis's __, the goal of the attribution process is to __.

a) co-variation model, make correspondent inferences
b) correspondent inference theory, infer that some behaviour and the intention behind it both correspond to an underlying, stable, feature of the person
c) correspondent inference theory, make inferences about people's dispositions
d) b and c

11 An indicator of personal dispositions is __.

a) the analysis of uncommon effects
b) the display of socially undesirable or unconventional behaviour
c) the display of out-of-role behaviour
d) all of these

12 If John is late on this occasion for psychology but is usually punctual for all his classes as are the other psychology students, then __.

a) there is low consistency, high distinctiveness, low consensus
b) we can make an external attribution
c) we can 'blame' John's lateness on circumstances
d) all of these

13 General ideas about how certain kinds of causes interact to produce a specific kind of effect are called __.

a) mental maps
b) multiple necessary causes
c) causal schemata
d) multiple sufficient causes

14 The correspondent inference theory and co-variation model are __, which means that they describe how people __. A more accurate account of how people actually make causal attributions comes from study of __.

a) normative, should ideally make causal attributions, errors and biases in the attribution process
b) normative, make causal attributions in experimental situations, real-life attributions
c) idealistic, would make attributions in an ideal world, errors and biases in the attribution process
d) all of these

15 The __ refers to the tendency to overestimate the importance of __ factors relative to __ factors as causes of behaviour.

a) fundamental attribution error, dispositional, environmental,
b) actor-observer effect, personal, environmental
c) fundamental attribution error, environmental, dispositional
d) self-protecting bias, internal, external

16 The __ refers to the tendency for __.

a) actor-observer effect, actors to attribute their own behaviour to situational factors
b) actor-observer effect, observers to attribute other people's behaviour to dispositional factors
c) fundamental attribution error, dispositional factors to be overestimated relative to situational factors
d) all of these

17 When judging negative behaviours, __.

a) the actor-observer effect is most pronounced
b) we are more likely to make a situational attribution, regardless of whose behaviour is being judged
c) the self-protecting bias is likely to be used, especially if it is our own behaviour or that of someone close to us
d) all of these

18 Generally, the more serious the consequences of someone else's behaviour, __, and this is made even more likely by __.

a) the more likely the fundamental attribution error is to be made, hedonic relevance
b) the more likely we are to hold the actor as responsible, regardless of his/her perceived intentions, personalism
c) the less likely a situational attribution is to be made, personal relevance
d) all of these

19 A schema which associates a set of personality traits with members of a particular age, sex, ethnic, national or occupational group is called a __.

a) prejudice
b) group attitude
c) stereotype
d) monotype

20 Individual stereotypes or __ can be related to __.

a) 'person type' implicit personality theories, people's names
b) person schemas, people's physical attractiveness
c) 'person type' implicit personality theories, any characteristic possessed by individuals as individuals
d) all of these

21 Stereotypes, as schemas about people, __.

a) are inherently different from other kinds of schema
b) illustrate the general cognitive

tendency to store knowledge as simplified, generalized, representations
c) are universal and inevitable
d) b and c

22 Stereotypes can influence behaviour by their effect on other cognitive processes, such as __.

a) selective remembering and negative memory bias
b) the illusion of outgroup homogeneity
c) the ingroup differentiation hypothesis
d) all of these

23 Trying to influence the way others perceive us is called __.

a) interpersonal perception
b) self-disclosure
c) impression management
d) manipulation

24 Impression management is closely related to the concept of __ and is often likened to the process of __. This comparison is central to the __ analysis of social interaction.

a) self-presentation, acting, dramaturgical
b) self-actualization, growth, humanistic
c) self-presentation, disguise, 'detective'
d) all of these

25 How accurately others perceive us is partly determined by __.

a) our ability and willingness to reveal ourselves to others
b) the extent of our self-disclosure
c) what we fail to say or do
d) all of these

26 Compared with __ self-monitors, __ self-monitors __.

a) low, high, monitor the situation, looking for cues as to what is appropriate behaviour
b) high, low, have poor social skills
c) low, high, show greater cross-situational consistency in their behaviour
d) a and b

SELF-ASSESSMENT QUESTIONS

1 Discuss the basic similarities and differences between the perception of objects and the perception of people.

2 In what ways can we all be described as psychologists?

3 Define the term interpersonal perception.

4 Explain briefly the relationship between the intuition and inference models of interpersonal perception.

5 Discuss either central versus peripheral traits or the primacy-recency effect as an explanation of global perception.

6 How have Gestalt psychologists contributed to our understanding of the process of impression formation?

7 Give a definition of the attribution process.

8 Outline and evaluate one major theory of attribution.

9 Explain what is meant by the fundamental attribution error. How is it related to the actor-observer effect and under what conditions is it most likely to occur?

10 Describe the other major sources of error and bias in the attribution process.

11 What is a stereotype? How is stereotyping related to human cognition in general?

12 Discuss some of the ways in which stereotypes can influence a) cognitive processes and b) behaviour.

13 Define the following terms: a) impression management b) self-disclosure c) self-monitoring.

14 Describe some of the factors which influence either impression management or self-disclosure.

15 What is the difference between high and low self-monitors?

KEY TERMS/CONCEPTS

actor-observer effect
analysis of uncommon
  effects
attribution process
authenticity
causal information
causal schemata: multiple
  necessary/multiple
  sufficient causes
central versus peripheral
  traits
choice/social desirability/
  roles/prior expectations
complementary roles
consistency/consensus/
  distinctiveness
correspondent inference
  theory (Jones and Davis)
co-variation model
  (Kelley)
discounting principle
disposition

dramaturgical analysis of
  social interaction
exceptionless
  generalizations
fallacy of representative
  behaviour
fundamental attribution
  error
general (object) perception
Gestalt psychology
global perception
high versus low self-
  monitors
illusion of outgroup
  homogeneity
illusory causation effect
implicit personality
  (intuitive) theories
impression management
inference
inference model (Cook)
ingroup differentiation

hypothesis
internal (personal/
  dispositional) versus
  external (situational)
  causes
interpersonal perception
  (perception of others/
  person perception)
inter-role conflict
intra-role conflict
intuition model
negative halo effect
norms
organization
person schema
personal (hedonic)
  relevance
personalism
phenomenological
  psychologists
polarized judgements
positive halo effect

primacy-recency effect
principle of co variation
role sets
role strain
selection
self-disclosure
self-fulfilling prophecy
self-monitoring
self-perception (perception
  of self/self-concept)
self-presentation
self-serving attributional
  bias: self-enhancing/self-
  protecting bias
seriousness of the
  consequences
social cognition
social (people) perception
social phenomenology
social roles
stereotypes: individual/
  group

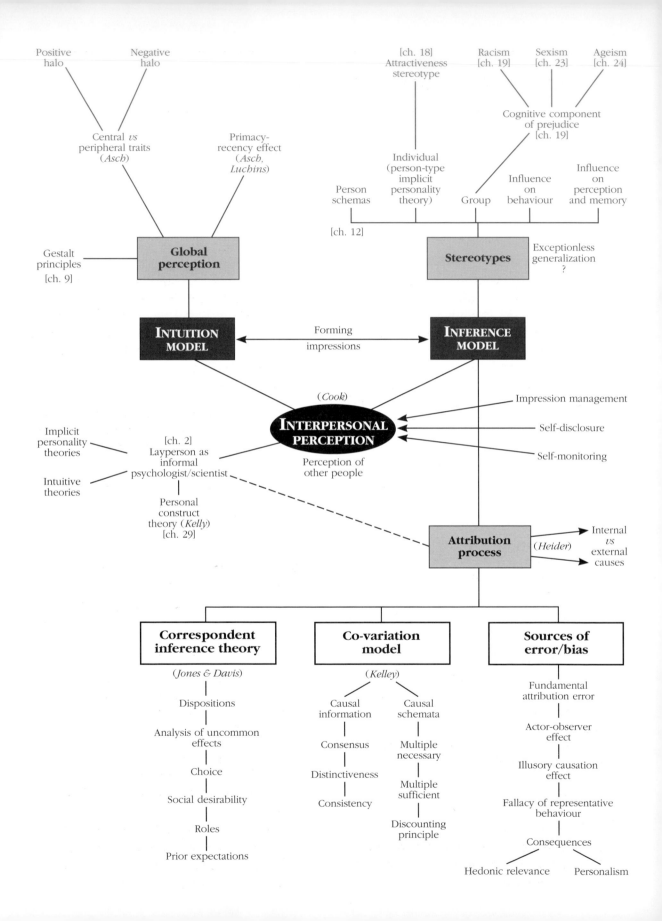

18 INTERPERSONAL ATTRACTION

MULTIPLE-CHOICE QUESTIONS

1 According to __ version of Exchange
Theory, __.

a) Homans', we view our feelings for
others in terms of profits
b) Blau's, relationships are expensive and
so what we put into them must exceed
what we get in return
c) Berscheid and Walster's, relationships
involve the exchange of rewards and
attraction reflects an evaluation of rewards
received relative to rewards given
d) a and c

2 __ couples are those in which __.

a) communal, each partner gives out of
concern for the other
b) exchange, each partner is preoccupied
with getting their fair share
c) exchange, the partners tend to be
suspicious and insecure
d) all of these

3 Exchange theory is really a special case of
__ theory, according to which __.

a) equality, everyone should receive
exactly the same rewards
b) equity, the principle of fairness is
defined as a constant ratio of rewards to
costs
c) equity, people accept the fairness of the
unequal distribution of rewards among
individuals
d) b and c

4 According to __.

a) Thibaut and Kelley, comparison level
(CL) is the reward:cost ratio we are used
to in relationships

b) Thibaut and Kelley, comparison level
for alternatives (CL alt) is the reward:cost
ratio we believe could be obtained from
alternative relationships
c) Duck, staying in a relationship could
be determined by the negative features of
perceived alternatives or the perceived
costs of leaving
d) all of these

5 According to the __, individuals who are
willing to become romantically involved
will be closely matched in their ability to
reward each other.

a) frustration-aggression hypothesis
b) matching hypothesis
c) gain-loss theory
d) a and b

6 Since we can only dream about finding
our perfect partner, __.

a) we compromise in the form of a value
match
b) most of us will avoid romantic
relationships altogether
c) we settle for a partner whom we believe
is the most rewarding we could
realistically hope to find
d) a and c

7 Early computer dance studies __ the
matching hypothesis by finding that the
probability of a woman being asked out
again __.

a) supported, depended on her level of
attractiveness, regardless of the man's
b) contradicted, depended on her level of
attractiveness, regardless of the man's

c) supported, depended on the man's level of attractiveness, regardless of her's
d) none of these

8 A major limitation of computer dance studies is that __.

a) they involve artificially created couples
b) they only use photographs and not videotapes of faces
c) they involve deceiving subjects about the use of a computer to match them with a partner
d) all of these

9 The matching phenonemon is __ and is a major ingredient of __.

a) confined to physical attractiveness, compatibility
b) not confined to physical attractiveness, compatibility
c) relevant to any characteristic which can be considered socially rewarding, compatibility
d) b and c

10 Evidence shows that, compared with people who feel they are not benefiting enough from their relationship, those who feel they are benefiting too much __.

a) feel the most guilty
b) are the most unhappy
c) have more extramarital affairs
d) have extramarital affairs early into their marriage

11 The 'field of availables' refers to __.

a) the range of people that are actually available for us to meet
b) the range of people that are theoretically available for us to meet
c) people from our own racial, religious, social class and educational groups
d) a and c

12 The importance of proximity for attraction is that __.

a) it increases the opportunity for interaction

b) it increases exposure
c) increased exposure results in more polarized attitudes towards others
d) all of these

13 Greater exposure __ attraction because __.

a) increases, it increases familiarity
b) increases, it increases similarity
c) decreases, familiarity breeds contempt
d) increases, birds of a feather flock together

14 If a stranger comes and sits right next to you, moving away or erecting some kind of barrier are both ways of __.

a) playing hard to get
b) trying to assert your independence
c) trying to preserve your personal space
d) trying to make yourself less conspicuous

15 The distance commonly found between __ is __.

a) close friends, social-consultative distance
b) work colleagues, casual-personal distance
c) public speakers and their audience, intimate distance
d) none of these

16 The (largely) unwritten rules regarding the appropriate distance that should be kept between people in different social situations are called __.

a) the level of intimacy
b) proxemic rules
c) the rules of prosperity
d) status rules

17 Violent compared with non-violent criminals, and schizophrenics compared with other kinds of psychiatric patients, __.

a) have a smaller body buffer zone
b) have a larger body buffer zone
c) begin to feel uneasy more quickly when

approached by another person
d) b and c

18 According to Kerckhoff and Davis, __.

a) relationships pass through a series of filters
b) similarity of sociological or demographic variables determines the field of availables
c) similarity of basic values is necessary for the relationship to become relatively stable and permanent
d) all of these

19 While __ may be relatively more important early on in a relationship, __ becomes more important as it progresses.

a) physical attractiveness, familiarity
b) similarity, complementarity of needs
c) complementarity of needs, similarity
d) reciprocal liking, similarity

20 According to the gain-loss theory, we are most attracted to those who __.

a) give us consistently positive feedback
b) begin by disliking us, then adopt a positive attitude towards us
c) give us consistently negative feedback
d) begin by liking us, then adopt a negative attitude towards us

21 Although we generally admire people who are capable and competent, __.

a) we prefer competent people who are also fallible
b) we prefer competent but fallible people if we ourselves are of average self-esteem
c) we prefer competent but fallible people if we are ourselves of very high or very low self-esteem
d) we prefer people who never make mistakes

22 Marriages are more likely to be unhappy and/or end in divorce if they are between __.

a) teenage partners, especially those from lower socio-economic and educational backgrounds
b) partners from different ethnic, religious and other demographic backgrounds
c) partners who experienced divorce as children
d) all of these

23 Relationship rules refer to the __ partners have of each other regarding __.

a) expectations, personal space, especially the intimate zone
b) hopes, marriage and having children
c) expectations, loyalty, fidelity, honesty and trustworthiness
d) all of these

24 The breaking of __ represents a major cause of relationship breakdown. Another cause of breakdown is __.

a) proxemic rules, incompatibility
b) relationship rules, lack of stimulation
c) relationship rules, the moving away of one partner in order to start college or university
d) b and c

25 The break-up of a relationship is a(n) __ which goes through a number of __. According to Duck, these are __.

a) event, changes, the intra-psychic, dyadic, social and grave-dressing phases
b) process, stages, dissatisfaction, exposure, negotiation, resolution and termination
c) process, stages, the intra-psychic, dyadic, social and grave-dressing phases
d) none of these

SELF-ASSESSMENT QUESTIONS

1 How valid is Exchange Theory as an explanation of human relationships?

2 Explain how the concept of equity differs from that of equality.

3 How is the matching hypothesis related to Exchange Theory?

4 Evaluate the evidence for the matching hypothesis.

5 Explain the difference between a) communal and b) exchange couples. How useful is this distinction in accounting for the likelihood of a relationship breaking up?

6 How are proximity, exposure and familiarity related as influences on interpersonal attraction?

7 What is meant by personal space? In what ways can spatial behaviour affect interactions between people?

8 'Birds of a feather flock together'. Discuss this statement by reference to the psychological evidence.

9 What is meant by complementary needs?

10 Explain the following: a) reciprocal liking b) the reward:cost principle c) gain-loss theory.

11 How important an influence on attraction is physical attractiveness and how is perception of physical attractiveness influenced by culture, gender and context?

12 Explain the difference between liking and loving?

13 Analyze some of the major factors which cause relationships to break up.

14 Discuss the claim that the break-up of relationships is best thought of as a process.

KEY TERMS/CONCEPTS

attachment/caring/
 intimacy
body buffer zone
communal versus
 exchange couples
companionate versus
 passionate (romantic)
 love
comparison level (CL)
comparison level for
 alternatives (CL alt)
compatibility
competence
complementarity needs
computer dance method

contact versus non-contact
 cultures
dissatisfaction
 (D)/exposure (E)/
 negotiation
 (N)/resolution
 (R)/termination (T)
 (Lee)
equilibrium model (of
 intimacy) (Argyle and
 Dean)
equity theory
Exchange Theory
exposure
'fait accompli' matching

familiarity
field of availables
 (Kerckhoff)
gain-loss theory (Aronson
 and Linder)
intimate distance/casual-
 personal distance/social-
 consultative distance/
 public distance
intra-psychic/dyadic/
 social/grave-dressing
 phases (Duck)
investment
liking versus loving
 matching hypothesis

(similarity hypothesis)
personal space
physical attractiveness
polarized attitudes
proxemic rules (Hall)
proximity
reciprocal liking
relationship breakdown as
 a process
relationship rules
reward:cost principle
reward:cost ratio
similarity
social skills
value match

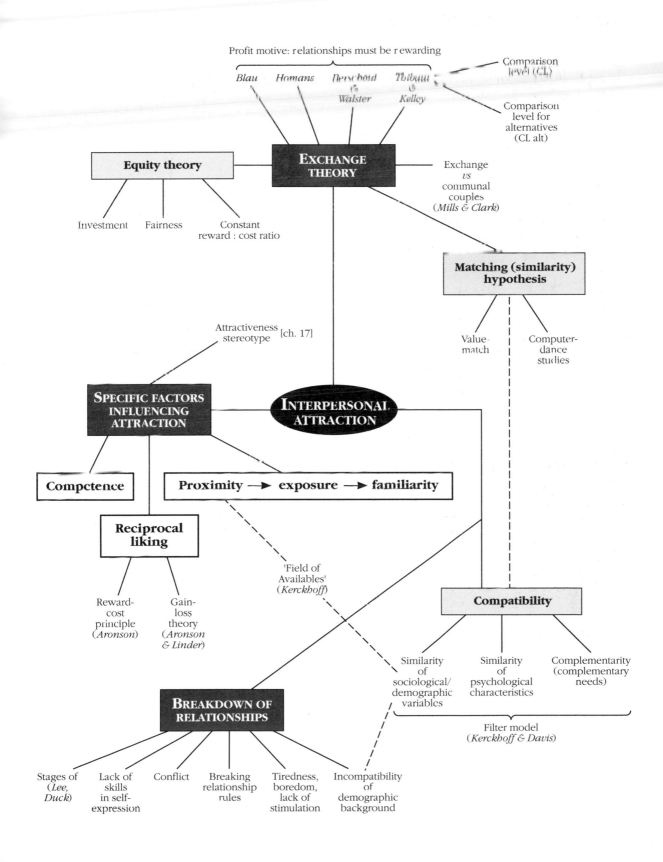

Profit motive: relationships must be rewarding

Blau   Homans   Berscheid   Thibaut
                  &   &
                  Walster   Kelley

Comparison level (CL)

Comparison level for alternatives (CL alt)

EXCHANGE THEORY

Equity theory

Investment   Fairness   Constant reward : cost ratio

Exchange *vs* communal couples (*Mills & Clark*)

Matching (similarity) hypothesis

Value-match   Computer-dance studies

Attractiveness stereotype [ch. 17]

SPECIFIC FACTORS INFLUENCING ATTRACTION

INTERPERSONAL ATTRACTION

Competence

Proximity → exposure → familiarity

Reciprocal liking

Reward-cost principle (*Aronson*)   Gain-loss theory (*Aronson & Linder*)

'Field of Availables' (*Kerckhoff*)

Compatibility

Similarity of sociological/ demographic variables   Similarity of psychological characteristics   Complementarity (complementary needs)

Filter model (*Kerckhoff & Davis*)

BREAKDOWN OF RELATIONSHIPS

Stages of (*Lee, Duck*)   Lack of skills in self-expression   Conflict   Breaking relationship rules   Tiredness, boredom, lack of stimulation   Incompatibility of demographic background

19 ATTITUDES, ATTITUDE CHANGE AND PREJUDICE

MULTIPLE-CHOICE QUESTIONS

1 The cognitive, affective and behavioural are the components shared by all __.

a) attitudes
b) values
c) beliefs
d) all of these

2 An individual's sense of what is desirable, good, important, worthwhile etc. defines his/her __.

a) attitudes
b) values
c) beliefs
d) prejudices

3 The La Piere study demonstrates that __.

a) behaviour is determined solely by our attitudes
b) attitudes represent predispositions to behave
c) behaviour is affected by situational factors
d) b and c

4 Giving answers on attitude scales which the subject believes are expected or 'proper' is called __. This source of bias can be detected by the inclusion of a __.

a) response set, response set scale
b) demand characteristics, lie scale
c) social desirability, lie scale
d) social desirability, number of irrelevant items

5 The __ comprises a number of statements, for each of which subjects must indicate the extent to which they agree or disagree.

a) Bogardus Social Distance Scale
b) Likert Scale
c) Thurstone Scale
d) Semantic Differential

6 In experimental studies of persuasive communication, __.

a) measuring subject's attitude towards the attitude object before any attempt to change it is called the post-test
b) manipulating some characteristic of the source or message is the independent variable
c) measuring subject's attitude following the attempt to change it is called the pre-test
d) the attitude object is always of great personal significance to the subjects

7 The effectiveness of a high-fear message depends upon __.

a) the high availability factor
b) the precise level of fear arousal
c) the subject's initial level of concern
d) all of these

8 Attitudes which serve a(n) __ function are likely to be the __ to change.

a) externalization, most difficult
b) knowledge, most difficult
c) ego-defensive, most difficult
d) a and c

9 Resistance to persuasion can be increased by __.

a) inoculating people against attempts to persuade them
b) warning people that an attempt will be made to persuade them
c) reducing the credibility and trustworthiness of the source
d) all of these

10 The greater the discrepancy between the attitude a person already holds and the one the communicator wants him/her to hold, the more likely it is that the message __.

a) will fall inside the person's latitude of acceptance
b) will fall inside the person's latitude of rejection
c) will produce attitude change
d) will be assimilated

11 According to Chaiken's heuristic model of persuasion, when personal involvement in an issue is __, then __.

a) low, we tend to rely on heuristics or mental short cuts to determine our attitudes
b) high, we cognitively analyze the message
c) high, the degree of attitude change is largely determined by the quality of the arguments put forward
d) all of these

12 In the one-dollar/twenty-dollar experiment, the finding that the __ group showed the most liking for the boring tasks indicates that __.

a) one-dollar, these subjects experienced the most dissonance
b) twenty-dollar, these subjects experience the most dissonance
c) one-dollar, these subjects were unable to justify their counter-attitudinal behaviour in terms of their financial reward
d) a and c

13 If counter-attitudinal behaviour is __, then attitude change will be greatest under conditions of __ reward.

a) voluntary, little or no
b) involuntary, large
c) voluntary, large
d) a and b

14 According to Bem's self-perception theory, __.

a) the concept of dissonance is not needed in order to explain the finding of studies such as the one-dollar/twenty-dollar experiment
b) the twenty-dollar subjects could easily make a situational attribution to explain why they lied about the task
c) the one-dollar subjects had to make a dispositional attribution to explain why they lied about the task
d) all of these

15 According to __ theory, the results of dissonance experiments can be explained in terms of __.

a) self-perception, inferences subjects draw about their attitudes from their own behaviour
b) impression management, the need to appear consistent
c) impression management, the need to avoid social anxiety and embarrassment
d) all of these

16 Stereotypes constitute the __ component of prejudice, while __ is one form in which the __ component may be expressed.

a) cognitive, discrimination, behavioural
b) affective, anti-locution, cognitive
c) cognitive, avoidance, behavioural
d) a and c

17 According to Adorno et al, the authoritarian personality is __.

a) prejudiced against particular minority groups
b) hostile to people of higher status and

servile to those of lower status
c) highly conventional in their beliefs and values
d) flexible and introspective

18 According to Rokeach, a person who obtains a high score on the __ scale __.

a) dogmatism, has a closed mind
b) F-scale, believes in extreme left-wing political views
c) dogmatism, may have extreme right or left wing political views
d) a and c

19 While personality is an important factor involved in prejudice, __.

a) it is society which defines the legitimate targets for prejudice and discrimination
b) conformity to social norms can prove more powerful as an influence on behaviour
c) we acquire prejudice against particular out-groups, rather than out-groups in general
d) all of these

20 Prejudice and hostility often arise __.

a) as a result of the need to find a scapegoat at times of recession and economic hardship
b) from competition for scarce resources
c) whenever there is a conflict of interests between two or more groups
d) all of these

21 The results of __ experiments are explained by __ theory, according to which __.

a) maximal group, cognitive dissonance, individuals strive to achieve/maintain a positive self-image
b) minimal group, social identity, a person's social identity reflects the various social groups with which he/she identifies
c) minimal group, social identity, emphasising the desirability of the in-group and the undesirability of the out-group helps to enhance an individual's

social identity and self-image
d) b and c

22 If prejudice and discrimination are to be reduced, contact between members of different racial groups must be __ and they must pursue __ goals.

a) non-competitive, common
b) equal status, subordinate
c) equal status, superordinate
d) a and c

23 Studies of equal-status contact, such as those of racially integrated housing and schooling, typically find that __.

a) positive feelings towards members of other groups are generalized to those groups as a whole
b) positive feelings towards members of other groups do not generalize to those groups as a whole
c) inter-group relationships are fundamentally changed
d) interpersonal relationships are not affected

24 The jigsaw classroom technique __.

a) is aimed at making children from different racial groups dependent on one another
b) tends to enhance self-esteem, increase academic performance and increase liking for classmates
c) changes attitudes towards the racial groups to which classmates belong
d) a and b

25 A way of trying to reduce prejudice is to __.

a) discourage people from using category-driven processing
b) encourage people to use attribute-driven processing
c) shift people's perceived boundaries between 'us' and 'them'
d) all of these

SELF-ASSESSMENT QUESTIONS

1 What is an attitude?

2 What is the difference between attitudes, beliefs and values and how are they related?

3 How well do attitudes predict behaviour?

4 Describe some of the ways in which psychologists have attempted to measure attitudes. What are some of the problems involved in attitude measurement?

5 Discuss experimental studies of persuasive communication.

6 To what extent does the function served by an attitude affect the ease with which it can be changed?

7 Describe two studies of cognitive dissonance showing how they support the predictions of dissonance theory.

8 Evaluate dissonance theory in the light of alternative explanations of the results of dissonance experiments.

9 Explain the difference between prejudice and discrimination.

10 Describe and discuss the authoritarian personality theory of prejudice.

11 How adequate is personality as an explanation of the causes of prejudice?

12 Give some examples of prejudice and/or discrimination as conformity to social norms.

13 Discuss either inter-group conflict or minimal groups as explanations of prejudice and/or discrimination.

14 Evaluate the success of attempts to reduce prejudice, based on the principles of equal status contact and the pursuit of common goals.

KEY TERMS/CONCEPTS

anti-locution/avoidance/ discrimination/physical attack/extermination

attitudes

attitudes as predispositions to behave

attractiveness (of source)

authoritarian personality (Adorno et al)

autistic hostility

balance theory (Heider)

beliefs

Bogardus social distance scale

category-driven versus attribute-driven processing (Fiske and Neuberg)

cognitive consistency

cognitive dissonance theory (Festinger)

cognitive/affective/ behavioural components

commitment

congruity theory (Osgood and Tannenbaum)

correspondence (between attitudes and behaviour)

dissonance following a decision

dissonance resulting from counter-attitudinal

behaviour

dissonance resulting from effort

dogmatism scale (Rokeach)

equal status, non-competitive, contact

explicit or implicit message

F (Fascism) scale

function of attitudes (Katz/Smith et al)

heuristic model of persuasion (Chaiken)

high availability factor

Ideological dogmatism

impression management theory

initial level of concern

inter-group conflict

inter-group versus interpersonal relationships

interpersonal simulation

jigsaw classroom technique (Aronson et al)

latitude of acceptance and rejection

less-leads-to-more effect

level of emotional appeal (in the message)

lie scale

Likert scale

minimal groups (Tajfel et al)

mirror image phenomenon (Bronfenbrenner)

negative attitude change

one- versus two-sided arguments

open-ended versus structured interviews

opinion leaders

out-group homogeneity

people as rationalizing creatures

persuasive communication

prejudice

prejudice as conformity to social norms

primacy-recency

radicalism-conservatism (R factor)

reactance

reinforcement or incentive theory (Janis et al)

response set

scapegoating

selective exposure/ attention/interpretation

self-inoculation

self-perception theory (Bem)

semantic differential (Osgood et al)

sleeper effect

social desirability

social identity theory (SIT) (Tajfel and Turner)

sociogram

sociometry (Moreno)

specificity (of attitude and behaviour measurement)

status/credibility (of source)

suffering-leads-to-liking effect

superordinate goals

terminal versus instrumental values (Rokeach)

Thurstone scale

toughmindedness-tendermindedness (T factor) (Eysenck)

trustworthiness (of source)

two-step flow hypothesis (Lazarsfeld et al)

values

volitional (voluntary) behaviour

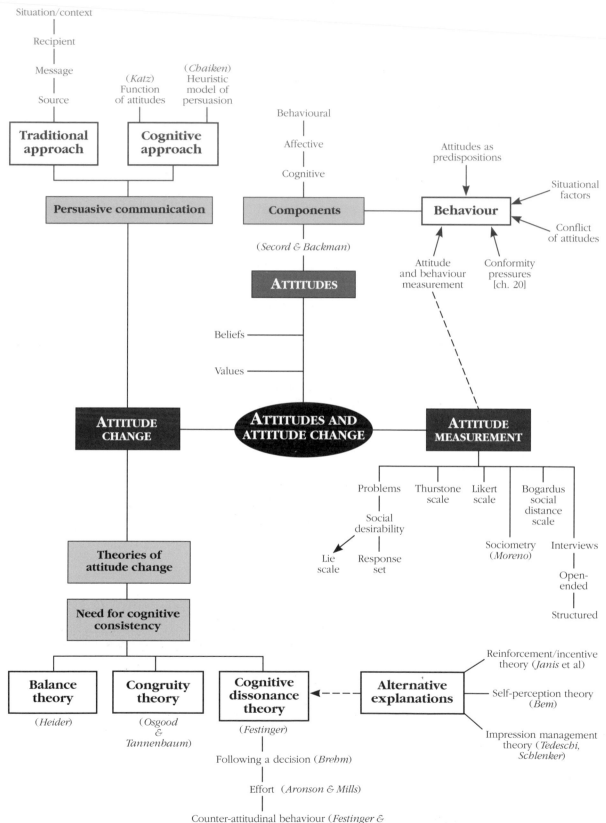

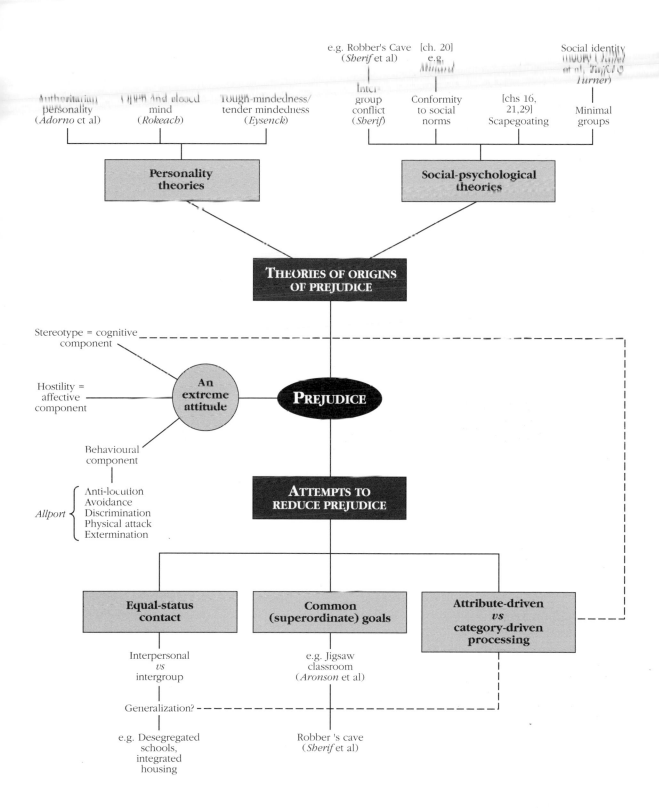

20 SOCIAL INFLUENCE

MULTIPLE-CHOICE QUESTIONS

1 __ has been defined as responding to the actual or implied presence of one or more others.

a) social influence
b) social psychology
c) normative influence
d) social norm

2 Social norms refer to how people are __ to behave in particular situations.

a) found
b) believed
c) expected
d) all of the above

3 The co-action effect refers to increases in performance as a result of __.

a) seeing others working on the same task
b) believing that others are working on the same task
c) performing in front of an audience
d) a and b

4 Performing better on a task in front of others (than when alone) is called the __

a) co-action effect
b) audience effect
c) actor-observer effect
d) narcissism effect

5 Trying to identify the kind of person a leader is describes the __ approach to leadership.

a) attributional
b) situational
c) trait
d) behaviourist

6 An alternative to the search for specific personality characteristics is the attempt to identify different kinds of __.

a) personality style
b) leadership style
c) attributional style
d) leader

7 The situational approach to the study of leadership focuses on __.

a) the process of the leadership (as opposed to the leader's personality)
b) the leader's leadership style
c) the interaction between leader, group members, the groups task etc.
d) a and c

8 In a(n) __ group, the leader is __ by a(n) external authority, while in a(n) __ group, the leader __ his/her authority from the members.

a) formal, assigned, informal, achieves
b) informal, assigned, formal, achieves
c) formal, appointed, informal, derives
d) a and c

9 Central to Fiedler's model is the LPC score, which stands for __.

a) lowest perceived cost
b) least preferred co-worker
c) least preferred co-leader
d) lowest price contingency

10 A high LPC score indicates a leader who is __, and a low LPC score indicates a leader who is __.

a) relationship oriented, task oriented
b) task oriented, relationship oriented

c) democratic, autocratic
d) autocratic, democratic

11 People put into the central position in a five-person wheel, 'Y' or chain communication network tend to __ .

a) accept the challenge and behave like leaders
b) be recognized as leaders by the rest of the group
c) send more messages, solve problems more quickly, make fewer errors
d) all the above

12 The five kinds of power identified by French and Raven are __ .

a) expert, referent, legitimate, reward, autocratic
b) coercive, expert, referent, legitimate, dictator
c) reward, coercive, expert, referent, democratic
d) legitimate, reward, coercive, expert, referent

13 Yielding to group pressure is a way of defining __ .
a) social influence
b) obedience
c) conformity
d) leadership

14 In Sherif's conformity experiment, when subjects heard others' estimates of how far the light moved, convergence took place. This means that __ .

a) individual estimates became different
b) individual estimates became more similar
c) individual subjects became confused about their answers
d) none of these

15 Because of the ambiguous nature of the task, Sherif's subjects engaged in a process of __ in order to help them define the situation.

a) social exchange
b) social comparison
c) social disengagement
d) social reinforcement

16 In Asch's experiment, conformity was measured in terms of the __ .

a) number of incorrect answers given on the critical trials
b) number of correct answers given on the critical trials
c) number of incorrect answers given on the neutral trials
d) number of correct answers given on the neutral trials

17 The overall conformity rate in the Asch experiment was __ .
a) 64%
b) 23%
c) 32%
d) 5%

18 The effect of having someone agree with the subject, or disagree with the subject and the majority, is to __ .

a) greatly reduce conformity to 5.5%
b) greatly increase conformity to 65%
c) destroy the unanimity of the majority
d) a and c

19 Studies of personality factors associated with conformity suggest that uniformity may reflect our underlying need for __ .
a) power
b) acceptance
c) security
d) b and c

20 According to Deutsch and Gerard, the two major kinds of influence involved in conformity are __ .
a) social and informational
b) informational and normative
c) social and normative
d) internalization and compliance

21 In situations which are ambiguous, we come under __ influence, while in situations where we don't want to be rejected by others, __ influence is brought to bear.

a) normative, informational
b) informational, normative
c) informational, social
d) normative, social

22 Subjects in Asch's and Crutchfield's experiments were (mainly) under __ and the kind of conformity involved was __.

a) informational, internalization
b) informational, compliance
c) normative, internalization
d) normative, compliance

23 Complying with the demands of an authority figure is a definition of __.

a) conformity
b) leadership
c) social influence
d) obedience

24 Being in the same room as the learner caused obedience to __ to __ and having to keep his hand on the shock plate caused a further __ to __.

a) rise, 70%, rise, 95%
b) fall, 40%, fall, 30%
c) fall, 20%, fall, 10%
d) rise, 40%, rise, 30%

25 Having two other 'teacher subjects' refuse to carry on giving shocks caused the obedience rate to __, apparently through a process of __.

a) rise, modelling
b) fall, modelling
c) fall, obedience
d) fall, leadership

26 When the experimenter left the room and gave subsequent orders by telephone, obedience __ to __.

a) rose, 75%
b) fell, 40%
c) fell, 20.5%
d) fell, 5%

27 The highest obedience rate (__), was obtained when __.

a) 100%, the experimenter prompted the subject by telling him the shocks were not harmful
b) 95%, the subject could both see and hear the learner
c) 92.5%, another 'subject' actually threw the switch
d) 92.5%, another 'subject' read out the questions and the real subject threw the switch

28 A way of accounting for Milgram's results is in terms of __.

a) denial of personal responsibility
b) the 'agentic state'
c) coming to see ourselves as the instrument of someone else's will
d) all of these

29 A __ experiment by Hofling et al of psychiatric nurses provides evidence for the __ of Milgram's experiments.

a) naturalistic/field, experimental realism
b) naturalistic/field, mundane realism
c) naturalistic/field, everyday relevance
d) b and c

30 The prison simulation experiment demonstrates the powerful role of __ in determining human social behaviour.

a) personality variables
b) male hormones
c) social, institutional forces
d) sex-role stereotypes

SELF-ASSESSMENT QUESTIONS

1 What is meant by the term social influence?

2 Explain the difference between the audience effect and the co-action effect.

3 What variables affect performance on a task in the presence of an audience?

4 Outline the trait and the situational approaches to the study of leadership.

5 Give some examples of leadership style. How does leadership style differ from a leader's traits?

6 What is the difference between an appointed and an emergent leader?

7 Outline Fiedler's Contingency Model. How does it link the concepts of leadership style and situational variables to predict the effectiveness of a leader?

8 Give some examples of communication networks. How can they help to explain the process of leadership?

9 Explain the difference between conformity and obedience.

10 What is the difference between informational and normative influence?

11 What is the difference between internalization and compliance?

12 Outline one study of conformity and analyze the kind of influence and the kind of conformity involved.

13 To what extent do Milgram's obedience experiments display experimental and mundane realism?

14 Outline two of Milgram's later experiments and analyze the factors influencing obedience (in relation to the voice feedback condition).

15 Outline Zimbardo et al's prison simulation experiment. What social psychological factors help to explain the behaviour of the participants, both prisoners and prison guards?

KEY TERMS/CONCEPTS

agentic state
anti-conformity
appointed/emergent leaders
audience effect
authoritarian personality
authority figure
autocratic/democratic/ laissez-faire
autokinetic effect
banality of evil
co-action effect
communication networks
compliance
conformity

convergence
experimental realism
Fiedler's contingency model
formal/informal groups
independence
informational influence
internalization
leadership style
least preferred co-worker score (LPC)
legitimate/reward/ coercive/expert/referent power
mundane realism

non-conformity
normative influence
obedience (Milgram)
position power
power of social, institutional, forces
prison simulation experiment (Zimbardo et al)
quality of leader-member relationship
relationship-oriented leader
responsibility
role playing

self-categorization
situational approach
social comparison
social facilitation
social influence
social norm
socio-emotional specialist
task specialist
task structure
task-oriented leader
trait approach
true conformity
unanimity
validation

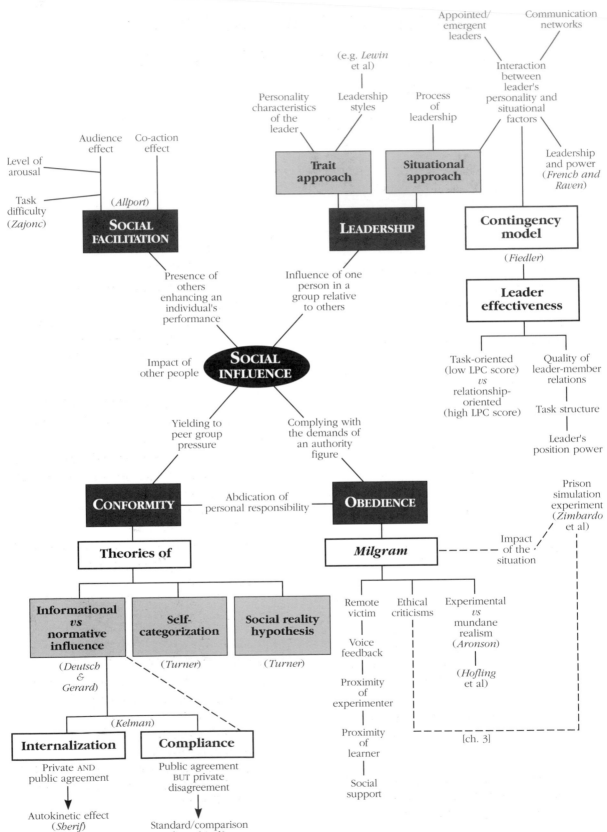

21 CHILDHOOD AND ADOLESCENCE — DEVELOPMENT OF PERSONALITY AND THE SELF-CONCEPT

MULTIPLE-CHOICE QUESTIONS

1 According to Freud, the id __.

a) represents the biological, pre-socialized part of the personality
b) is governed by the reality principle
c) engages in secondary process thinking
d) is the rational, decision-making part of the personality

2 The __ is the part of the personality _ .

a) ego, which takes external reality into account
b) id, which engages in primary process thinking
c) superego, which represents the continuing influence of parents within the individual's personality
d) all of these

3 According to the notion of infantile sexuality, __.

a) babies and young children have genital sexual needs
b) babies and young children have sexual needs and are capable of sexual pleasure
c) the sexual needs of babies and young children are much weaker than those of adults
d) the sexual needs of babies and young children are much more powerful than those of adults

4 Personality develops through a series of __ stages, the order of which is determined by __. Both excessive gratification and frustration can result in __ at that particular stage.

a) psychosexual, learning, neurotic conflict
b) psychosocial, maturation, fixation
c) psychosexual, maturation, fixation
d) biosocial, environmental influence, psychological arrest

5 The boy's Oedipus Complex is resolved through __, while the girl's is (probably) resolved through __.

a) repressing his desire for the mother and jealousy of his father, identification with the aggressor
b) identification with the aggressor, anaclitic identification
c) repressing his desire for the father and jealousy of his mother, anaclitic identification
d) anaclitic identification, identification with the aggressor

6 The case of Little Hans can be criticized on the grounds that __.

a) Freud had already made up his mind that Hans was 'a little Oedipus' and so interpreted all the data accordingly
b) Hans' psychoanalysis was conducted primarily by his father
c) there are alternative interpretations to Freud's which are at least as plausible
d) all of these

7 Orderliness, parsimony and obstinacy are characteristics of the __ personality.

a) anal
b) oral
c) phallic
d) neurotic

8 The state of being subject and object simultaneously is called __.

a) consciousness
b) self-consciousness
c) introspectiveness
d) the subjective-objective state

9 The set of attitudes a person holds towards him/herself refers to the __. This consists of __.

a) self-concept, self-image or ego identity
b) self, self-esteem or self-regard
c) self-concept, ideal self or ego ideal
d) all of these

10 According to __ theory of the 'looking-glass self', __.

a) Mead's, the self is reflected in the reactions of other people
b) Cooley's, in order to understand what we are like, we need to know how others see us
c) Cooley's, children gradually build up an impression of what they are like from others' reactions to them
d) b and c

11 According to Mead, __.

a) knowledge of self and others develops separately and independently
b) the self is a structure rather than a process
c) the central process by which we come to represent ourselves to ourselves is role-taking
d) pretend play comes later in children's development than games

12 The Coopersmith study suggests that high self-esteem in the child is most likely to develop when __.

a) parents firmly enforce limits on the child's behaviour
b) the child is given a good deal of freedom and independence
c) the child is allowed to do whatever it wants to regardless of how it affects others
d) a and b

13 Part of the reaction of others involves __ and we often do the same thing when trying to evaluate our own abilities. This is related to the view of the self-concept as __.

a) comparing us with others, implying not-self
b) being critical of our behaviour, intrinsically judgmental
c) comparing us with others, intrinsically bipolar
d) a and c

14 Babies' ability to recognize themselves in the mirror __.

a) has been tested by using a version of the 'red dot' technique used by Gallup with young chimps
b) does not usually appear before 15 months and is much more common after 18 months
c) seems to require the development of object permanence
d) all of these

15 Names represent an important aspect of __ and may form the basis for __.

a) self-recognition, self-definition
b) self-definition, the self-fulfilling prophecy
c) self-categorization, comparison with others
d) the psychological self, self-definition

16 The __ is the first aspect of the self-concept to develop in the baby and it undergoes a dramatic change during __ which marks the beginning of __.

a) categorical self, puberty, adolescence
b) bodily self, puberty, adolescence

c) psychological self, late childhood, puberty
d) bodily self, puberty, young adulthood

17 Compared with boys, the effects of early or late maturation on girls are ___ but the greater media pressure to conform to ideal body types may partly account for ___.

a) much less marked, anorexia nervosa
b) much more marked, anorexia nervosa
c) much less marked, slimming-related diseases among 16 to 19-year-old girls
d) a and c

18 Erikson's ___ theory differs from Freud's in that Erikson ___.

a) psychosocial, saw development as continuing throughout the life-cycle
b) psychosexual, saw the id as the most powerful part of the personality
c) psychosocial, believed that conflict can arise within the ego itself
d) a and c

19 The psychosocial crisis facing the ___ is between ___, while the radius of significant relationships is ___.

a) baby, autonomy and shame and doubt, mother/mother figure
b) toddler, basic trust and basic mistrust, neighbourhood and school
c) 7 to 12-year-old, initiative and guilt, parents
d) none of these

20 Erikson sees adolescence as an authorized delay of adulthood or ___, with the major developmental task being to ___.

a) pre-adulthood stage, prepare for adulthood
b) moratorium, achieve a sense of identity
c) moratorium, achieve a sense of intimacy
d) prolonged puberty, achieve sexual maturity

21 The inevitability of some form of stress or emotional turmoil or disturbed identity during adolescence is called the ___.

a) adolescent moratorium
b) identity crisis
c) normative crisis
d) b and c

22 According to psychoanalytic theories, ___.

a) the balance within the child's personality is disturbed with the onset of puberty
b) in adolescence there is a re-emergence of strong Oedipal feelings
c) adolescence is a second individuation process
d) all of these

23 Compared with traditional societies, the transition from childhood dependence to relative independence in Western culture is ___.

a) smooth, gradual and continuous
b) discontinuous and involves the unlearning of much childhood-appropriate behaviour
c) made easier by the use of initiation ceremonies and puberty rites
d) made easier by the existence of a common set of values by which the adolescent can make sense of the world

24 ___ has been studied by measuring the adolescent's ___.

a) storm and stress, display of psychiatric symptoms
b) identity crisis, level of self-esteem
c) generation gap, perception of their relationships with parents and siblings
d) all of these

25 According to Coleman's focal theory, ___.

a) adolescents spread the process of adaptation over a number of years
b) adolescents try to resolve all their problems and relationship issues in the shortest period of time possible
c) it is those adolescents who have to deal with more than one issue at a time who are most likely to face problems
d) a and c

SELF-ASSESSMENT QUESTIONS

1 Outline the part played by the id, ego and superego within the psychic apparatus.

2 Briefly describe the main sources of conflict facing the ego.

3 Define the term 'infantile sexuality' and outline the stages of psychosexual development.

4 Discuss Freud's theory of the Oedipus Complex.

5 Explain Freud's theory of the relationship between stages of psychosexual development and personality types.

6 What is self-consciousness?

7 Define the terms: a) self-concept b) self-image c) self-esteem d) ideal-self.

8 Outline Mead's theory of self.

9 Describe and discuss the major factors affecting the development of the self-concept.

10 Describe the development of one of the following: a) self-recognition b) self-definition c) the psychological self d) the categorical self.

11 Describe some of the major changes that occur to the body image in adolescence.

12 Compare and contrast Freud's and Erikson's developmental theories.

13 Explain what Erikson means by the following terms: a) moratorium b) identity diffusion (or confusion) c) normative crisis (or identity crisis).

14 What evidence is there to suggest that not being in work is psychologically harmful to young people?

15 Compare and contrast any two theories of adolescence.

16 Outline and evaluate the 'classical' view of adolescence.

KEY TERMS/CONCEPTS

adolescence
affect and object hunger
ambivalence
anaclitic identification
anal personality
anorexia nervosa
asceticism
body image/bodily self
bulimia (secondary anorexia)
case of Little Hans
categorical self
comparison with others
conscience
consciousness versus self-consciousness/self-awareness
cultural anthropology
cultural relativism (Benedict)
death instincts (Thanatos)
disengagement

ego ideal
epigenetic principle
external/reality conflict
fear of castration/castration anxiety
fixation
focal theory of adolescence (Coleman)
generalized other (Mead)
generation gap
id/ego/superego
ideal-self/ego ideal/idealized self-image
identification with the aggressor
industry
infantile sexuality
intellectualization
intimacy
libido
life instincts (Eros)
'looking-glass self'

(Cooley)
moral conflict
moratorium
negative identity
neurotic conflict
normative crisis/identity crisis
Oedipus Complex
oral personality
penis envy
pleasure principle
primary process thinking
psychic apparatus
psychic energy
psychoanalysis
psychoanalytic theory (Freud)
psychological self
psychosocial crisis
psychosocial modalities
psychosocial stages of development (Erikson)

radius of significant others
reaction of others
reality principle
role-taking
second individuation process (Blos)
secondary process thinking
seduction theory
self as reflexive process
self-definition
self-esteem/self-regard
self-fulfilling prophecy
self-image/ego identity
self-recognition
self/self-concept
stages of psychosexual development
storm and stress
time perspective

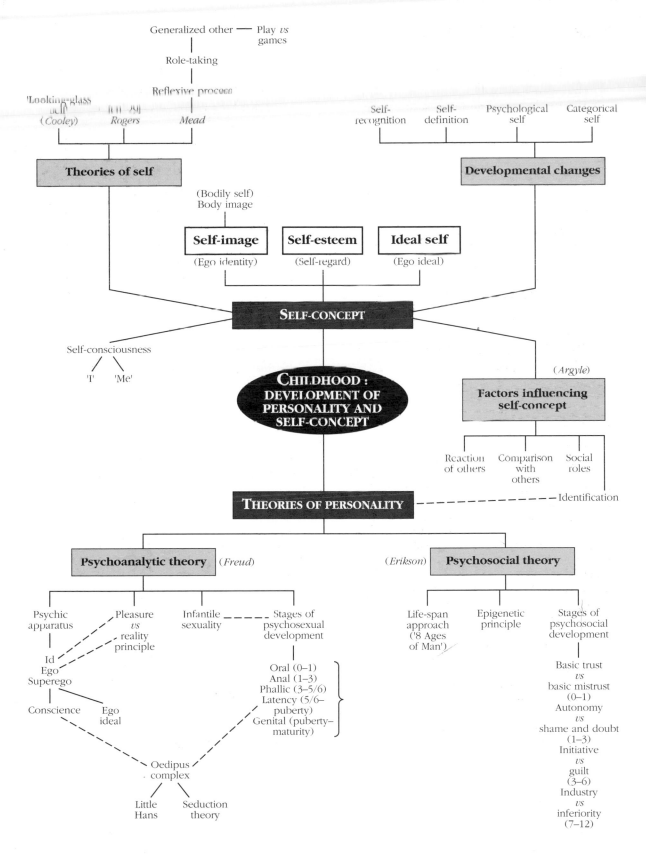

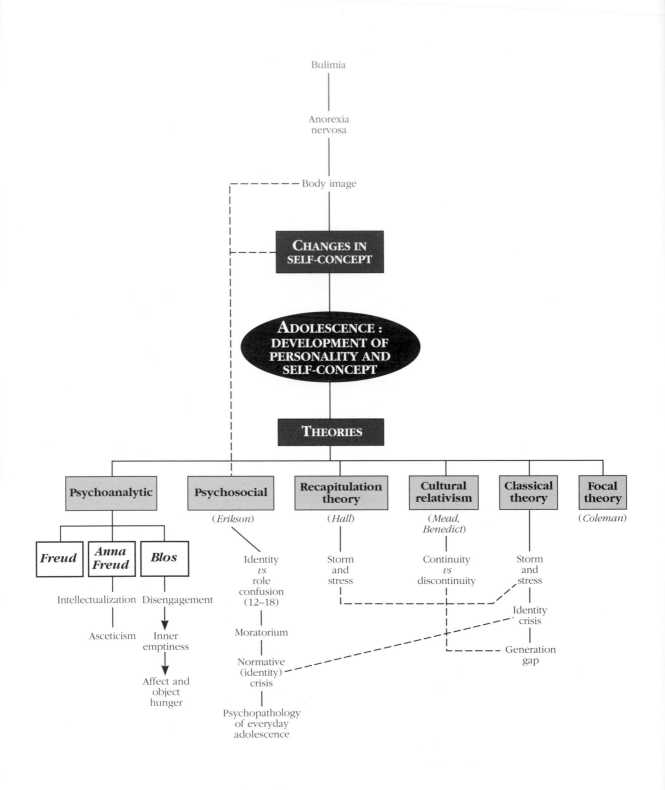

22 ATTACHMENT AND SEPARATION: THE EFFECTS OF EARLY EXPERIENCE

MULTIPLE-CHOICE QUESTIONS

1 Attachments are indicated by __.

a) the baby's ability to miss the mother when she is even briefly out of sight
b) the baby's fear response to strangers
c) the baby's ability to discriminate between familiar people and strangers, as shown by the baby smiling
d) a and b

2 A 'clingy' child whose mother has just had another baby, and a 'blasted' baby rhesus monkey clinging to its surrogate mother are both displaying __ attachments

a) strong, secure
b) strong, insecure
c) weak, secure
d) weak, insecure

3 The whole purpose of bonding is __.

a) to enable the child to feel secure in strange environments
b) to reduce attachment behaviours and to increase exploration and independence
c) detachment
d) all of these

4 As revealed by the 'strange situation', type __ children seem to be displaying __ towards their mother.

a) A, anxious-avoidant, indifference
b) B, securely attached, ambivalence
c) C, anxious resistant, ambivalence
d) a and c

5 According to __ theory, __.

a) 'cupboard love', babies become attached to the mother who feeds them
b) Freud's psychoanalytic, love has its origin in attachment to the satisfied need for nourishment
c) Dollard and Miller's drive-reduction, the baby acquires a secondary drive for the mother based on her satisfaction of the baby's primary hunger drive
d) all of these

6 When baby rhesus monkeys are raised from birth with two surrogate mothers, __.

a) they become attached to the one which provides milk
b) they become attached to the cloth mother who provides contact comfort
c) they use the cloth mother as a safe base and a source of comfort when frightened
d) b and c

7 According to Schaffer and Emerson, the best predictor of a baby's attachment to an attachment figure is __.

a) the responsiveness of the attachment figure to the baby's behaviour
b) the total amount of stimulation provided by the attachment figure
c) how much of the baby's physical needs the attachment figure is responsible for
d) a and b

8 The influence of ethology on Bowlby's theory of attachment can be seen in his emphasis on __.

a) the instinctive nature of attachment behaviour
b) the importance of parental responsiveness to the baby's innate attachment behaviours
c) a critical period for the development of attachments
d) all of these

9 In contradiction of Bowlby's theory of monotropy is the research finding that __.

a) attachment to the mother/mother figure is not qualitatively different from other attachments
b) attachment to the mother/mother figure is not always the first to appear or the most intense
c) fathers are attachment figures in their own right
d) all of these

10 The belief that breaking the maternal bond in early childhood will inevitably result in serious and permanent damage to all aspects of development is called the __.

a) theory of monotropy
b) maternal privation hypothesis
c) maternal deprivation hypothesis
d) cupboard love theory

11 In the institutions studied by Goldfarb and by Spitz and Wolf, __.

a) it was the lack of adequate maternal care which was responsible for the developmental retardation
b) there was a very low level of stimulation which accounts for at least some of the developmental retardation
c) the lack of adequate maternal care was irrelevant to the children's developmental progress
d) children's development did not suffer compared with children living with their families

12 Children raised in institutions suffer from the __ effects of __, which can be summarized as __.

a) short-term, deprivation, distress
b) long-term, deprivation, developmental retardation
c) short-term, privation, distress
d) long-term, privation, developmental retardation

13 The degree of distress experienced by a child undergoing separation from its mother is likely to be increased if __.

a) the child is aged between 12 and 18 months
b) the child is male and has experienced behavioural or emotional problems prior to the separation
c) the child has previously experienced satisfactory separations and has multiple attachments
d) a and b

14 The effects of day care on attachment __.

a) are always harmful
b) depend on the quality of the substitute care and how stable an arrangement it is
c) may be beneficial if the mother enjoys her work and is more fulfilled as a person
d) b and c

15 A major effect of long-term separation is separation anxiety, which may manifest itself as __.

a) school phobia/refusal
b) increased clinginess
c) detachment
d) all of these

16 According to attachment theories such as Bowlby's, __.

a) loss of the father through divorce should not have more serious consequences for the child than his death
b) the mother-child relationship is the crucial one

c) loss of the father through divorce will have very different consequences compared with those resulting from his death
d) a and b

17 The inability to have deep feelings for others and the resulting lack of meaningful interpersonal relationships, together with lack of guilt and the inability to keep rules, is called __.

a) sociopathy
b) affectionless psychopathy
c) the authoritarian personality
d) affective disorder

18 According to Bowlby, __.

a) mothering is almost useless if delayed until after two and a half to three years
b) mothering is almost useless, for most children, if delayed until after twelve months
c) there is no sensitive or critical period for the development of attachments
d) a and b

19 The longitudinal study by Hodges and Tizard of children brought up in institutions shows that __.

a) the critical period is much less critical than Bowlby believed
b) it is possible to develop attachments after age two to three if these are encouraged and wanted by the parents
c) early institutional upbringing can have lasting detrimental effects on peer relationships
d) all of these

20 The Freud and Dann study of concentration camp survivors and the Koluchova study of the Czech twins suggest that __.

a) the mother-child relationship is qualitatively different from all others and there is no substitute for it
b) bond formation is the crucial process for later social and emotional development
c) it is with whom the bond is formed that is crucial for social and emotional development
d) children cannot become attachment figures for each other

21 Harlow's studies of rhesus monkeys show that __.

a) it is more harmful for a baby to be reared with just its mother than with just other babies
b) babies reared with surrogate mothers will reject their own first offspring but will care for their second baby quite normally
c) the effects of early isolation can be reversed by a period of 'therapy' provided by young, female monkeys
d) all of these

22 According to Rutter, __.

a) the term 'maternal deprivation' is no longer of value because it is too general and its effects are too varied
b) development consists of both consistencies and discontinuities of personality and behaviour
c) study of maternal (de-)privation should be seen in the wider context of the effect of early experience on later development
d) all of these

23 The case of Mary shows that __.

a) the effects of early privation are irreversible
b) recovery can occur long after the period of privation has ended
c) most human characteristics are capable of surviving even the most dire early environments
d) b and c

SELF-ASSESSMENT QUESTIONS

1 Define the following terms: a) attachment b) bond c) attachment behaviour.

2 Explain how the strength and security of attachments are related, giving examples.

3 Describe and evaluate the 'strange situation' as a way of investigating attachments.

4 Discuss 'cupboard love' theories of attachment.

5 Discuss Bowlby's theory of monotropy.

6 Describe some of the influences on the development of attachments.

7 Explain the difference between separation and privation. How does this distinction help to understand the effects of early experience?

8 Discuss the long-term effects of separation.

9 Assess the evidence relating to the claim that maternal deprivation causes affectionless psychopathy.

10 Discuss the claim that there is a critical period for the development of attachments.

11 What can studies of children suffering extreme privation tell us about the nature and function of attachments?

KEY TERMS/CONCEPTS

adoption
affectionless psychopathy
anaclitic depression
anxious-avoidant (Type A) attachment
anxious-resistant (Type C) attachment
attachment
attachment behaviours
bonds (selective attachments)
conflict

continuities versus discontinuities (in development)
critical or sensitive periods
'cupboard love theory'
death and divorce as processes
deprivation versus privation
detachment
developmental retardation
distress: protest/despair/

detachment
drive-reduction or secondary drive theory (Dollard and Miller)
fear response to strangers
hospitalism
institutional upbringing
loss versus absence
maternal deprivation hypothesis
monkey 'therapists'
monotropy (Bowlby)

psychoanalytic theory (Freud)
reversibility
rhesus monkey surrogate mothers
school phobia/refusal
securely attached (Type B)
security (of attachments)
separation anxiety
strength/intensity (of attachments)
the 'strange situation'

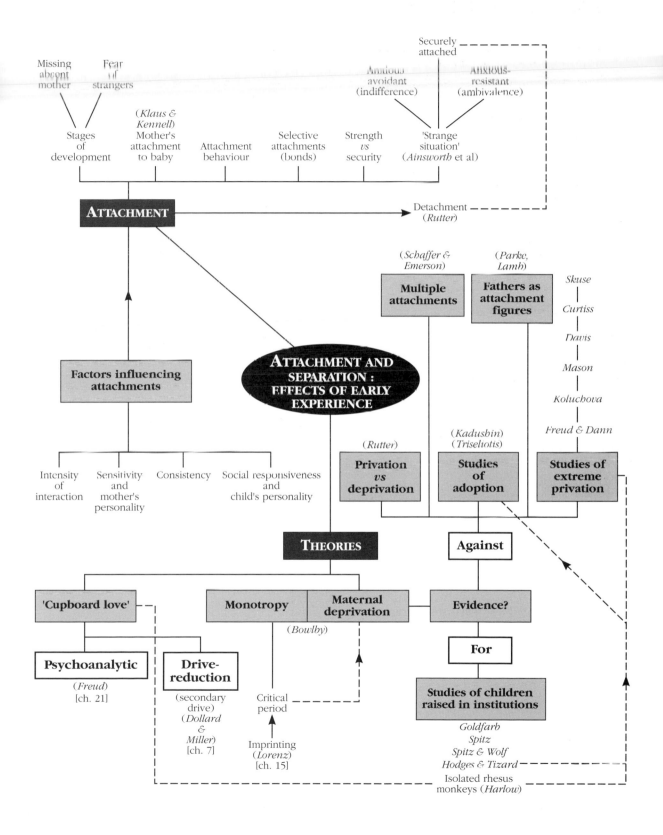

Missing absent mother

Fear of strangers

Securely attached

Anxious avoidant (indifference)

Anxious-resistant (ambivalence)

Stages of development

(*Klaus & Kennell*) Mother's attachment to baby

Attachment behaviour

Selective attachments (bonds)

Strength *vs* security

'Strange situation' (*Ainsworth* et al)

ATTACHMENT

Detachment (*Rutter*)

(*Schaffer & Emerson*)

(*Parke, Lamb*)

Multiple attachments

Fathers as attachment figures

Skuse

Curtiss

Davis

Mason

Koluchova

Freud & Dann

Factors influencing attachments

ATTACHMENT AND SEPARATION : EFFECTS OF EARLY EXPERIENCE

(*Rutter*)

Privation *vs* deprivation

(*Kadushin*) (*Triseliotis*)

Studies of adoption

Studies of extreme privation

Intensity of interaction

Sensitivity and mother's personality

Consistency

Social responsiveness and child's personality

THEORIES

Against

'Cupboard love'

Monotropy

Maternal deprivation

Evidence?

(*Bowlby*)

Psychoanalytic

(*Freud*) [ch. 21]

Drive-reduction

(secondary drive) (*Dollard & Miller*) [ch. 7]

Critical period

Imprinting (*Lorenz*) [ch. 15]

For

Studies of children raised in institutions

Goldfarb
Spitz
Spitz & Wolf
Hodges & Tizard
Isolated rhesus monkeys (*Harlow*)

23 SEX AND GENDER

MULTIPLE-CHOICE QUESTIONS

1 __ refers to __.

a) gender, how we classify ourselves as male or female
b) gender role, how society expects us to behave, think and feel based on our biological sex
c) gender identity, how we classify ourselves as male or female
d) all of these

2 The male hormones are __, the most important being __, secreted by the testes. The ovaries secrete two distinct types of female hormone, namely __.

a) the androgens, testosterone, oestrogen and progesterone
b) the androgens, progesterone, oestrogen and testosterone
c) the oestrogens, testosterone, androgen and progesterone
d) the oestrogens, progesterone, androgen and testosterone

3 The strict definition of a hermaphrodite is __.

a) any discrepancy between any of the components of sexual anatomy and physiology
b) a person who has functioning organs of both sexes
c) an anatomically normal person who believes that he/she is a member of the opposite sex
d) someone who enjoys dressing in the clothes of the opposite sex

4 __ is caused by an excessive amount of androgens or progesterone and refers to __.

a) the adrenogenital syndrome, a chromosomally normal male with female-looking external genitalia
b) the adrenogenital syndrome, a chromosomally normal female with male-looking external genitalia
c) testicular feminizing syndrome, a chromosomally normal male with female-looking external genitalia
d) none of these

5 To ask if boys and girls really do behave in accordance with gender roles is to ask __.

a) are boys more masculine than girls
b) are girls more feminine than boys
c) do psychological sex differences exist
d) all of these

6 While gender differences may be found in a given area of behaviour, __.

a) the behaviour of individual males and females is often very similar
b) the similarities between men and women are greater than the differences
c) the differences within each gender are at least as great as the differences between them
d) all of these

7 That children understand and accept gender role differences from an early age is demonstrated by the finding that __.

a) Two-and-a-half to three-year-olds

categorize certain behaviours as 'boy' or 'girl' behaviours
b) girls are more likely to avoid 'tomboy' behaviours than boys are to avoid 'sissy' behaviours
c) by age three, children play more with same-gender playmates
d) a and c

8 Male development can be regarded as __.

a) the natural form of human beings
b) the result of interference with the female route
c) the lack of interference by factors causing female development
d) what happens when female development goes wrong in some way

9 The case of the Batista boys who were reared as girls until they were ten when they grew full-size penises, suggests that __.

a) their brains had been masculinized by the testosterone present before birth
b) there is no critical period for the learning of gender identity and gender role
c) there may be differences between male and female brains which affect gender identity and gender role
d) all of these

10 A suggested difference between male and female brains is in the size of the __, with females' being __ and as different as male and female __.

a) cerebral hemispheres, larger, arms
b) corpus callosum, larger, arms
c) cerebral hemispheres, smaller, legs
d) corpus callosum, smaller, legs

11 Emphasising the interaction between biological and social factors is what distinguishes __ theory from other attempts to account for gender differences.

a) psychoanalytic
b) social learning
c) biosocial
d) cognitive-developmental

12 According to Money and Ehrhardt __.

a) it is the very fact of a child's sexual identity which is crucial for understanding how it is socialized
b) anatomy is destiny
c) how the child is raised will determine its gender identity, giving rise to its gender role identity and sexual preference
d) all of these

13 Money and Ehrhardt believe that __.

a) a child's sex of rearing can be changed at any age up to ten without causing any psychological harm
b) psychological sexuality is differentiated at birth and this is reinforced during the course of growing up
c) the first two and a half to three years represents a critical or sensitive period for the development of gender identity
d) biological sex is more important than sex of rearing

14 Based on Freud's psychoanalytic theory, __.

a) being brought up in a single-parent family should not affect the child's psychosexual development
b) being brought up in a conventional, heterosexual family will prevent the child from becoming homosexual
c) being brought up in a homosexual household will seriously increase the probability that the child will become homosexual
d) none of these

15 Social learning theorists see gender differences as being acquired through __.

a) the imitation of same-sex model's behaviour, based on observational learning
b) the reinforcement of imitation of same-sex model's behaviour
c) sex typing
d) all of these

16 When adults are asked to rate the emotional behaviour of infants whom they believe are girls, ___.

a) they are more likely to be seen as displaying fear than anger
b) they are more likely to be seen as displaying anger than fear
c) they are just as likely to be seen as displaying anger as fear
d) they are likely to be seen as displaying little or no emotion

17 Cultural relativism ___.

a) represents the most direct challenge to the biological approach to gender differences
b) maintains that the same gender differences will occur in different cultures
c) maintains that any gender differences which occur between cultures must be culturally determined
d) a and c

18 The existence of societies in which more than two gender role categories are used ___.

a) supports the biological explanation of gender differences
b) supports the cultural-relativism approach
c) shows that there is more to gender roles than biological sex
d) b and c

19 According to Kohlberg's ___ theory, ___.

a) cognitive-developmental, the child labels itself before it selectively attends to same-sex models
b) cognitive-developmental, the child first develops a gender identity which determines who it will imitate

c) social learning, the child first imitates same-sex models and then acquires a gender identity
d) a and b

20 A two or three-year-old girl who can tell you that she is a girl but also believes that she could become a boy or a daddy if she wanted to, is displaying ___.

a) basic gender identity
b) gender stability
c) gender constancy
d) gender consistency

21 A person who possesses characteristics, behaviours, attitudes etc. which are both 'masculine' and 'feminine', regardless of biological sex, is called ___.

a) bisexual
b) androgynous
c) hermaphrodites
d) transsexual

22 A major scale for measuring androgyny is the ___.

a) Bem sex role index
b) Bem sex role inventory
c) both sexes represented inventory
d) Bem sexual response index

23 As measured by the BSRI, androgynous subjects ___.

a) show sex-role flexibility across situations
b) behave in sex-inappropriate ways if the situation requires
c) may not always show higher levels of self-esteem than sex-typed subjects, especially sex-typed men
d) all of these

SELF-ASSESSMENT QUESTIONS

1 Define the following terms: a) sexual identity b) gender identity c) gender role d) sexual orientation e) transsexual.

2 Describe the five major categories of biological sex.

3 Explain the difference between true and other kinds of hermaphrodites.

4 Describe what is involved in either the testicular feminizing syndrome or the adrenogenital syndrome.

5 Summarize the evidence relating to psychological sex differences.

6 Compare and contrast any two theories of gender differences.

7 Define the term androgyny.

8 Outline and evaluate attempts to measure androgyny.

9 Is it possible and/or desirable for everyone to be androgynous?

KEY TERMS/CONCEPTS

adrenogenital syndrome
androgens
androgyny
basic gender identity
Bem sex role inventory (BSRI)
biological approach
biosocial theory (Money and Ehrhardt)
chromosomal sex
cognitive-developmental theory (Kohlberg)
cultural relativism (Mead)

external genitalia
gender (gender identity)
gender (sex) differences
gender constancy (consistency)
gender role
gender role behaviour
gender role identity
gender role stereotype
gender schema theory (Bem)
gender stability
gonadal sex

hermaphroditism/ hermaphrodite
heterosexual
homosexual
hormonal sex
internal accessory organs
masculine/feminine
oestrogen
personal attributes questionnaire (PAQ) (Spence et al.)
progesterone
psychoanalytic theory

(Freud)
sex (sexual identity)
sex-typing
sexual orientation (preference)
social learning theory
testosterone
testosterone insensitivity (testicular feminizing syndrome)
transsexual

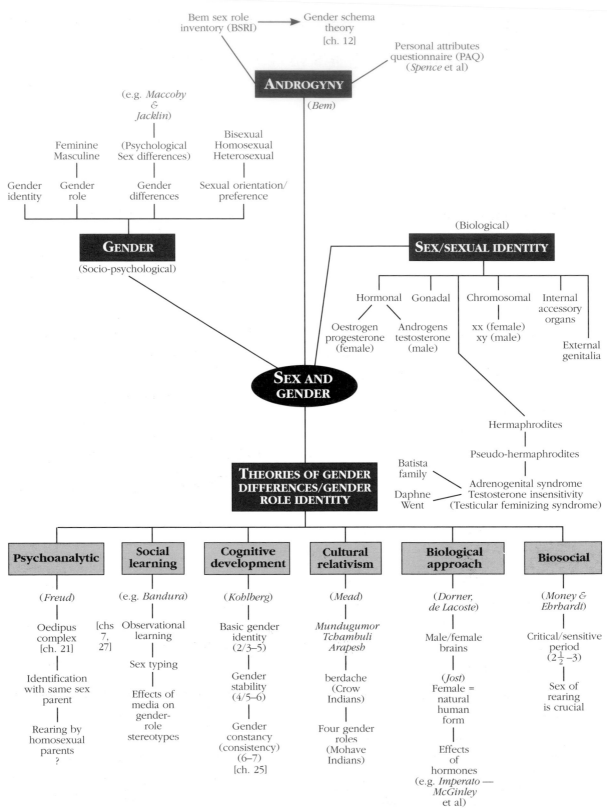

24 ADULTHOOD AND OLD AGE – DEVELOPMENT OF PERSONALITY AND THE SELF-CONCEPT

MULTIPLE-CHOICE QUESTIONS

1 Psychological adulthood has been defined in terms of   .

a) chronological age
b) mental age
c) maturity
d) all of these

2 Maturity is often taken to imply __.

a) possession of an accurate self-concept
b) emotional stability and satisfying social relationships
c) accepting responsibility for one's choices and decisions
d) all of these

3 For Erikson, young adulthood is achieved when we __, before which we must have __.

a) have developed intimacy in one special relationship, achieved a sense of identity
b) are able to share ourselves with another person and to care for them, achieved a sense of basic trust
c) display generativity, produced children of our own
d) have developed a sense of identity, achieved intimacy

4 Both Levinson et al's and Gould's theories are attempts to __.

a) describe how adulthood is experienced
b) extend some of Freud's ideas to adulthood
c) test out hypotheses about adulthood derived from work with psychiatric patients on a sample of non-patients

d) describe adulthood by comparing it with childhood

5 According to Levinson et al, the underlying pattern or design of a person's life at a given time is called their __.

a) adult consciousness
b) psychosocial stage of development
c) life structure
d) self-concept

6 A major theme of the __ is __.

a) early adult transition, separation from the family of origin
b) settling down phase, becoming one's own man (BOOM)
c) mid-life transition, soul-searching and assessing the meaning of the achievements of the life structure
d) all of these

7 According to Gould, in order to achieve psychological growth and maturity we must __.

a) come to terms with separation anxiety stemming from childhood
b) free ourselves of the illusion of absolute safety
c) replace our childhood consciousness with adult consciousness
d) all of these

8 The 'mid-life crisis' has been defined as

a) a time of soul-searching, questioning and assessing the real meaning of the achievements of the life structure

b) the pain and distress produced by the passing, in opposite directions, of men and women in their forties
c) a time when a large number of stressful life changes are likely to occur together
d) all of these

9 __ represents an __ loss of work. Reactions to loss of work are in many ways similar to other kinds of loss, such as __.

a) unemployment, unanticipated, bereavement
b) retirement, unanticipated, bereavement
c) unemployment, anticipated, the death of a loved one
d) retirement, unanticipated, the death of a loved one

10 Unemployed people are __.

a) likely to experience mental ill health and distress as a result of losing their jobs
b) likely to have lost their jobs because of physical ill health
c) likely to experience poorer physical health as a result of losing their jobs
d) a and c

11 The distress caused by unemployment is likely to be increased __.

a) the more committed people are to their jobs
b) for middle-aged women and younger men
c) the more structured the time is which was previously spent at work
d) when the local level of unemployment is high

12 Retirement, although anticipated, may produce distress because of __.

a) the loss of income, personal identity, meaning to life and the company of workmates
b) the assumption of an ambiguous, economically non-productive role
c) a failure to plan or prepare for retirement, both financially and

psychologically
d) all of these

13 According to the __ model, ageing is a time __.

a) decrement, when our intellectual abilities and social relationships decay or decline
b) personal growth, when we can give priority to the things that really matter in life
c) decrement, when our sense of responsibility declines and we behave in a much more irresponsible way
d) a and b

14 If we infer someone's abilities, lifestyle and self-concept from their chronological age, __.

a) we will obtain a very accurate profile of the person
b) we will obtain a very inaccurate picture of the whole person
c) we are failing to acknowledge the biological, subjective, functional and social definitions of age
d) b and c

15 A factor which might contribute to increasing life expectancy is __.

a) being allowed to contribute to the economy of the community by not having to retire at a particular age
b) enjoying a high social status within an extended family context
c) having a spouse and remaining sexually active
d) all of these

16 Fluid intelligence __.

a) involves memory span and mental agility
b) is thought to be more sensitive to changes in the central nervous system
c) goes on improving in the second half of our lives
d) a and b

17 The popular and traditional view of intelligence as declining quite rapidly in old age is based on __.

a) the definition of intelligence as an overall ability rather than composed of a number of separate abilities
b) the tendency to emphasize overall IQ as opposed to verbal or performance IQ
c) the use of cross-sectional as opposed to longitudinal studies
d) all of these

18 A major problem with __ studies of intelligence is __. This can be partly overcome by the use of the __ method.

a) cross-sectional, the cohort effect, longitudinal
b) cross-sectional, the cohort effect, cross-longitudinal
c) longitudinal, the practice effect, cross-sectional
d) cross-longitudinal, the practice effect, cross-sectional

19 In contrast with Piaget's claim that formal operational thought is the final kind of thought to develop, others have proposed that __.

a) there is a fifth stage of development, corresponding to the ability to think divergently
b) mature thought involves accepting that something can be true and not true at the same time
c) formal operations is just the beginning of the development of adult thought
d) a and b

20 According to Social Disengagement Theory, __.

a) ageing involves a mutual withdrawal of society from the individual and the individual from society
b) mutual withdrawal is the most

appropriate and successful way to age
c) those who remain active in their old age will be the most content
d) a and b

21 Critics of Social Disengagement Theory argue that __.

a) engagement and activity are at least as likely to be sought by the elderly
b) disengagement is neither natural nor an inherent aspect of ageing
c) the tendency to disengage is a personality dimension and so will not apply equally to all elderly people
d) all of these

22 According to Erikson, the task of old age is to resolve the conflict between __.

a) basic trust versus basic mistrust
b) identity versus role confusion
c) ego integrity versus despair
d) intimacy versus isolation

23 The process of grieving through which a bereaved person adjusts to their loss is called __. The three stages or phases involved are __.

a) grief work, disbelief and shock, developing awareness, resolution
b) grief work, protest, despair, detachment
c) mourning, disbelief and shock, developing awareness, resolution
d) bereavement, protest, despair, detachment

24 __ represents a way of preparing for one's own death and a common feature of this in the elderly is __.

a) anticipatory grief, ambivalence
b) grief work, reminiscing
c) anticipatory grief, reminiscing
d) a and c

SELF-ASSESSMENT QUESTIONS

1 What criteria have been proposed for psychological adulthood?

2 Discuss Erikson's theory of psychosocial development as it relates to adulthood.

3 Outline either Levinson et al's or Gould's theory of adulthood.

4 How useful are stage theories of adulthood?

5 What is the 'mid-life crisis'?

6 Compare and contrast the effects of unemployment and retirement.

7 Define the term 'ageism', giving some examples.

8 Distinguish between a) lifespan and b) life expectancy.

9 Describe the major physical changes involved in ageing.

10 'Ageing is a period of intellectual decline'. Discuss.

11 Describe and assess Social Disengagement Theory.

12 Define the following terms: a) bereavement b) grief c) mourning d) grief work.

13 How easy is it to draw the line between normal and abnormal grieving?

14 Define the following terms: a) anticipatory grief b) reminiscing c) life review

KEY TERMS/CONCEPTS

activity (re-engagement) theory (Havighurst, Maddox)
ageing
ageism
ambivalence
anticipated versus unanticipated loss of work
anticipatory grief
bereavement
chronological/biological/ subjective/functional/ social age
cohort effect
conservation tasks
convergent versus divergent thinking
cross-longitudinal method
cross-sectional versus

longitudinal studies
decrement model
ego integrity versus despair (Erikson)
ego transcendence versus ego preoccupation (Peck)
evolution of adult consciousness (Gould)
fluid versus crystallized intelligence
formal operational thinking (Piaget)
generativity versus stagnation (Erikson)
geriatrics
gerontology
grief
grief work (Engel)
'growing up' versus 'growing old'

illusion of absolute safety
intimacy versus isolation
life expectancy
life review
life structure
lifespan
lifespan approach
marker events
mature thought
maturity
menopause (climacteric)
'mid-life crisis'
mourning
normal versus abnormal grieving
personal growth model
problem-finding
psychological adulthood
reminiscing (Butler)
retirement

'seasons of a man's life' (Levinson et al)
separation anxiety
social disengagement theory (Cumming and Henry)
social exchange theory (Dyson, Dowd)
stable (structure building)/ transitional (structure changing) phases
STM versus LTM
test of primary mental abilities (PMA)
unemployment
verbal/performance/total IQ
Wechsler adult intelligence scale (WAIS)

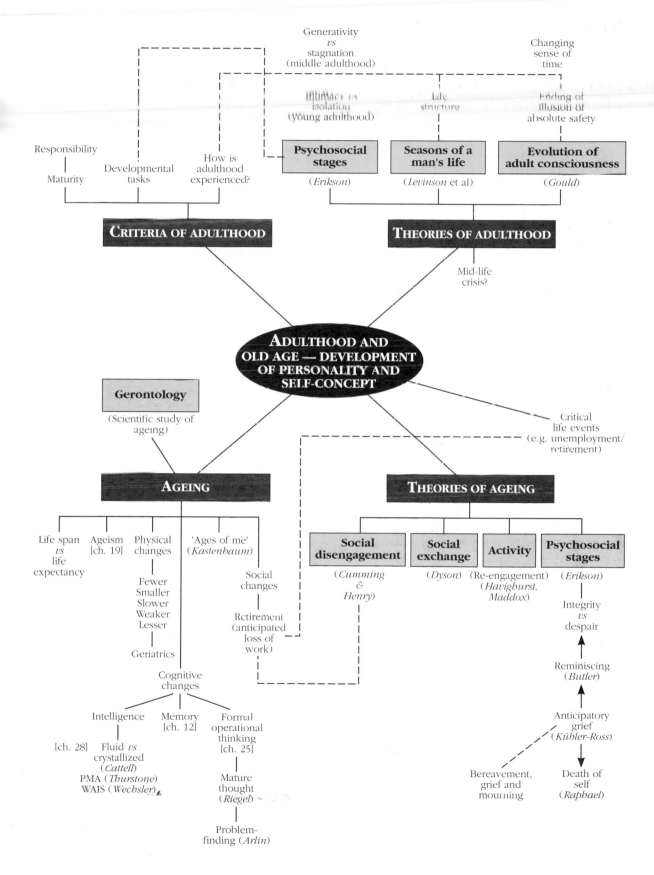

25 COGNITIVE DEVELOPMENT

MULTIPLE-CHOICE QUESTIONS

1 The study of how knowledge develops in human beings is called __.

a) sociobiology
b) epistemological genetics
c) genetic epistemology
d) cognitive genetics

2 Piaget believed that __.

a) children's mistakes on IQ tests are much more revealing about how they think than correct answers
b) children's errors are not random but systematic
c) how children think is much more important than what they think
d) all of these

3 According to Piaget, intelligence is __.

a) a process of adaptation to the environment
b) essentially the individual's construction of an understanding of reality through interaction with it
c) something which can be validly measured by the right kind of IQ test
d) a and b

4 When we apply the schemas we currently have to new situations, we are showing __.

a) assimilation
b) accommodation
c) equilibration
d) adaptation

5 The stages of cognitive development __.

a) occur in a fixed, invariant sequence
b) occur in a different order for different children

c) are the oral, anal, phallic, latency and genital
d) occur at exactly the same age in all children

6 During most of the __ stage, objects only exist for the child __.

a) sensorimotor, if they are being perceived
b) pre-operational, if they are being acted upon
c) sensorimotor, if they are being acted upon
d) a and c

7 Centration is manifested in __.

a) the child's inability to sort objects on the basis of more than one attribute at a time
b) the child's egocentrism
c) the child's inability to conserve
d) all of these

8 The word 'intuitive' in the second sub-stage of the __ stage is meant to imply that the child's thinking is dominated by __.

a) pre-operational, the appearance of objects
b) sensorimotor, how things look
c) pre-operational, the belief that things are how they seem
d) a and c

9 The Swiss mountain scene __.

a) is used to study conservation
b) involves two three-dimensional models, one of which is on a turntable which the

child is able to move
c) reveals that children as young as four are able to see things from someone else's perspective
d) none of these

10 According to Donaldson, compared with the Swiss mountain scene the policeman-doll experiment __.

a) provides a meaningful context for the child
b) makes 'human sense'
c) allows children as young as three and a half years old to display their ability to take the perspective of another person
d) all of these

11 Understanding that things remain constant despite changes in their appearance __.

a) is called conservation
b) involves being able to mentally reverse the operation by which something is originally made to look different
c) first develops in the pre-operational stage
d) a and b

12 When conservation first develops, __.

a) it can only be applied to actual objects and situations
b) the child is only capable of number and liquid quantity conservation
c) all different types of conservation appear together
d) a and b

13 Formal operational thinking involves the ability to __.

a) follow the form of an argument regardless of the particular content
b) think hypothetically
c) consider possible and not just actual states of affairs
d) all of these

14 Play is an adaptive activity which involves __. It differs from intellectual activity in that __.

a) assimilation, play is engaged in for its own sake
b) accommodation, intellectual activity involves an external aim or purpose
c) mainly assimilation, intellectual activity is concerned with solving problems posed by the environment
d) all of these

15 If a child can conserve number but not volume it is displaying __. Being able to perform all kinds of classification task but not all types of conservation is called __.

a) horizontal décalage, vertical décalage
b) vertical décalage, horizontal décalage
c) a horizontal slip in level of performance, a vertical slip in level of performance
d) a and c

16 According to Piaget, the crucial form of learning involved in the educational process is __.

a) programmed learning
b) tutorial training
c) active self-discovery
d) observational learning

17 Based on Piaget's theory, the role of the teacher is to __.

a) impart information to the child
b) assess the child's current stage of cognitive development
c) encourage the child to ask questions, experiment and explore
d) b and c

18 Cross-cultural studies __.

a) strongly support the sequence of stages in Piaget's theory
b) provide strong evidence that the stages are invariant and universal, at least up to and including concrete operations
c) suggest that Piaget's theory applies only to Western culture
d) suggest that Piaget's theory applies only to non-Western culture

19 Bruner and Piaget agree that __.

a) the child's underlying cognitive structure matures over time
b) all children pass through the same sequence of stages of cognitive development
c) interaction with the environment is vital for cognitive growth
d) a and c

20 Bruner's developmental theory comprises __.

a) three fundamental ways in which we represent knowledge
b) three stages of cognitive development
c) the enactive, iconic and symbolic modes
d) a and c

21 Initially our knowledge and understanding are expressed through __ and this refers to the __ mode. This corresponds to Piaget's __ stage.

a) mental images, symbolic, pre-operational
b) actions, enactive, sensorimotor
c) symbols, symbolic, concrete operational
d) actions, iconic, sensorimotor

22 According to __.

a) Bruner, language and logical thinking are inseparable
b) Piaget, language is merely a tool used for operational thinking
c) Bruner, language training will have no effect on cognitive development
d) a and b

23 If, in a conservation experiment, children are allowed to reshape a ball of plasticine themselves and have to describe the new shape, __.

a) they are using their enactive, iconic and symbolic modes
b) they are less likely to be dominated by the appearance of the plasticine
c) they are more likely to demonstrate conservation

d) all of these

24 Even though Piaget saw operational thought developing independently of language, __.

a) he believed that linguistic interaction between children can help their cognitive development
b) he believed that verbal training can speed up intellectual growth
c) he acknowledged that language may be necessary for formal operations
d) a and c

25 According to Vygotsky, __.

a) all speech is social in nature
b) speech is essentially concerned with communication and human interaction
c) babies are social beings who gradually become self-sufficient and independent
d) all of these

26 At about two years of age, __.

a) pre-intellectual language and pre-linguistic thought converge to produce verbal thought
b) the child's intelligence is no longer similar to that of apes
c) speech becomes social
d) a and b

27 What the child can do with help today __.

a) is called its zone of proximal development
b) it will be able to do without help tomorrow
c) is called its zone of actual development
d) a and b

28 According to Vygotsky, __.

a) two children with the same mental age may still be of different intelligence
b) when we try to understand and assess intelligence we should ask what the child could do if given help
c) IQ tests are appropriate ways of assessing intelligence
d) a and b

SELF-ASSESSMENT QUESTIONS

1 Define the term genetic epistemology.

2 Explain how Piaget used the term intelligence.

3 Define the following terms: a) adaptation b) assimilation c) accommodation d) equilibration e) schema.

4 Outline the stages of development of object permanence.

5 What is egocentrism? To what extent has recent research cast doubt on this part of Piaget's theory?

6 Describe and evaluate the evidence relating to the ability to conserve.

7 What are the implications of Piaget's theory for the education of young children?

8 Outline Bruner's modes of representation. How are they different from stages of development?

9 Compare and contrast the views of Piaget and Bruner regarding the role of language in cognitive development.

10 Explain what Vygotsky means by internalization and convergence.

11 How useful is Vygotsky's concept of the zone of proximal development in understanding and assessing intelligence?

KEY TERMS/CONCEPTS

accidental versus incidental transformations
accommodation
active self-discovery (discovery learning)
adaptation
animistic thinking (animism)
assimilation
centration
class-inclusion tasks
clinical method
compensation
conservation
constructivism (convergence)

deferred imitation
egocentrism
equilibration
functional invariants
general symbolic function
genetic epistemology
horizontal versus vertical décalage
identity
infer invisible displacements
intelligence
interiorized schemas
internalization
mastery (practice) play
mental operation
modes of representation

(Bruner): enactive/ iconic/symbolic
object permanence
play with rules
pre-intellectual language
pre-linguistic thought
primary circular reactions
profound egocentrism
readiness
reversibility
schema
secondary circular reactions
seriation
stages of cognitive development: sensorimotor/pre-

operational (pre-conceptual/intuitive)/ concrete operational/ formal operational
superordinate versus subordinate classes
symbolic (make-believe or representational) play
symbols versus signs
syncretic thought
tertiary circular reactions
transductive reasoning
tutorial training
zone of proximal (or potential) development (Vygotsky)

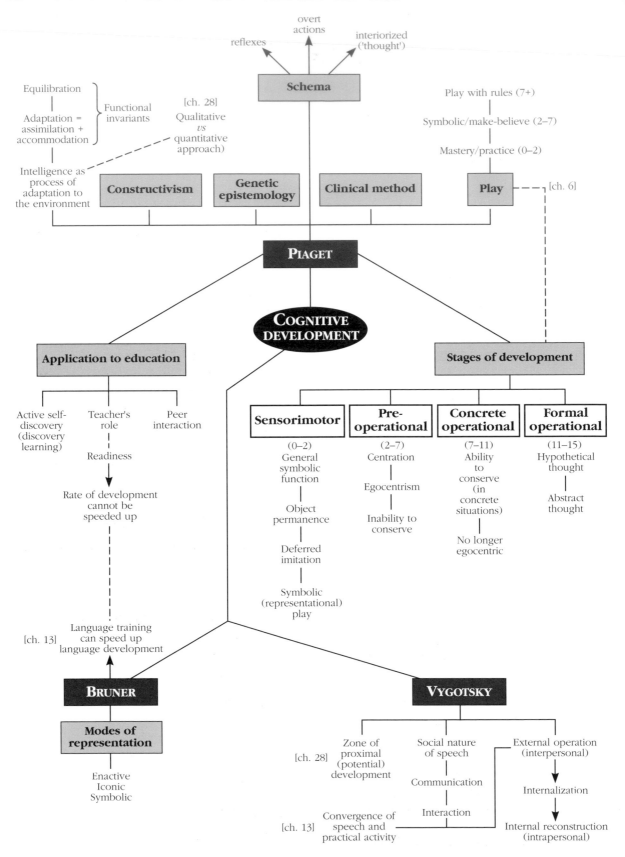

26 LANGUAGE DEVELOPMENT

MULTIPLE-CHOICE QUESTIONS

1 Psychologists who study language __.

a) are interested in language for its own sake
b) are interested in how language is acquired, perceived, understood and produced
c) are called psycholinguists
d) b and c

2 Language has been defined as __.

a) an arbitrary system of symbols
b) a system of rules which allows an infinite variety of messages to be produced
c) any form of communication between members of a species
d) a and b

3 The rule system of a language is called __ and comprises __.

a) semantics, phonology, syntax and grammar
b) grammar, phonology, semantics and syntax
c) syntax, phonology, semantics and grammar
d) phonology, syntax, semantics and grammar

4 Phonological rules determine the permitted sequence of __ which are __.

a) phonemes, the basic units of meaning in a language
b) phonemes, those sounds which are functionally important in a language
c) morphemes, the basic units of meaning in a language
d) morphemes, those sounds which are

functionally important in a language

5 A characteristic of the pre-linguistic stage is __.

a) babbling
b) phonemic contraction
c) imitation with reduction
d) a and b

6 During the pre-linguistic stage, __.

a) no communication is possible between the baby and the mother
b) interactions with the mother help the baby to prepare for language
c) communicative intentionality emerges in the form of pointing gestures and glances
d) b and c

7 Children begin to speak when they __.

a) use their vocal apparatus in any way in order to communicate
b) consistently use the same sound to label the same thing
c) are able to imitate particular words used by other people
d) stop babbling

8 The child's first words __.

a) are often quite different from adult words
b) are often context bound
c) are often used to convey a much more complex message
d) all of these

9 The child's speech during stage 1 grammar typically __.

a) pays no attention to word order
b) uses more functors than contentives
c) involves imitation with expansion
d) none of these

10 During stage 2 grammar, sentences are becoming __, due to __.

a) longer, the gradual inclusion of function words
b) longer, the inclusion of longer words
c) more complex, gradual inclusion of words which correspond to syntactic rules
d) a and c

11 Children demonstrate their understanding of syntactic rules by __.

a) making certain kinds of grammatical mistakes
b) over-generalizing or over-regularizing the rules
c) being able to state the rule
d) a and b

12 According to Skinner, __.

a) speech is learned according to the principles of operant conditioning
b) correct grammar is selectively reinforced
c) the stages of language development reflect the biological process of maturation
d) a and b

13 The evidence suggests that __.

a) parents tend to respond to the truth value of their child's speech rather than its grammatical correctness
b) trying to correct poor grammar may actually hinder the child's development
c) when children imitate adult speech, they convert it to the grammar they themselves are currently using
d) all of these

14 According to Chomsky, Skinner's theory __.

a) fails to capture the complexity and structured nature of language
b) fails to explain the creativity of language

c) cannot account for the spontaneous use of grammatical rules
d) all of these

15 The actual words or phrases used in a sentence are called its __ structure; the meaning of the sentence is its __ and through __ we are able to understand the relationship between them.

a) surface, deep, phrase structure and transformational rules
b) deep, surface, transformational rules
c) surface, deep, transformational grammar
d) a and c

16 Language acquisition device (LAD) __.

a) is an innate, biologically-programmed capacity for learning language
b) basically consists of transformational grammar
c) is a hypothetical model which Chomsky believes is necessary to account for the child's acquisition of grammatical rules
d) all of these

17 Supporting Chomsky's LAD is the finding that __.

a) all known human languages share certain basic features
b) with few exceptions, all human beings acquire language regardless of IQ
c) in the absence of speech, gestures will spontaneously go through the same early stages of development as speech
d) all of these

18 According to Aitchison, it is possible to explain children's language development __.

a) only if it is assumed that their brains naturally contain large amounts of specific information about language
b) by seeing children as being natural puzzle-solvers which enables them to process linguistic data
c) only if it is assumed that an innate language ability exists independently of other innate abilities
d) none of these

19 Both Chomsky and Lenneberg believe that __.

a) language is a human species-specific behaviour
b) chimps and other non-human primates have the capacity for language even though it does not appear spontaneously
c) language is acquired through the principle of selective reinforcement
d) language is simply a manifestation of the child's high level of general intelligence

20 According to Aitchison, what makes human language unique is __.

a) semanticity
b) displacement
c) structure dependence
d) all of these

21 Early attempts to teach chimps to speak failed because __.

a) they have no capacity for language
b) they are very poor imitators
c) their vocal apparatus is unsuited to making English speech sounds
d) they were too old by the time the attempts were started

22 Instead of trying to teach chimps and other non-human primates to speak, attempts have been made to teach language by using __.

a) American sign language (ASL)
b) small plastic symbols on a magnetized board
c) a special typewriter controlled by a computer
d) all of these

23 Critics of attempts to teach language to chimps claim that __.

a) they have been operantly conditioned to use a fixed order of signs and so are not displaying true structure dependence
b) they are often inadvertently cued by their trainers to produce signs in a correct order
c) they are not aware of what the signs mean and so do not display true semanticity
d) all of these

24 Compared with children, most of the non-human primates in language studies __.

a) are much more likely to sign in order to inform their trainers that they have noticed something
b) are much less likely to sign in order to inform their trainers that they have noticed something
c) are much more likely to try to acquire the object rather than simply name it
d) b and c

25 Most chimp studies have involved __ training, which involves __.

a) production-based, putting them through rote learning of symbols
b) comprehension-based, an immersion in a large vocabulary of symbols from the start
c) production-based, gradually building up a vocabulary of symbols one at a time
d) a and c

26 Savage-Rumbaugh has found that __.

a) making the chimp's environment more like a child's enables it to learn symbols without being trained
b) observational exposure is sufficient for the learning of both lexical and vocal symbols
c) the learning of symbols begins with the learning of routines
d) all of these

27 According to Savage-Rumbaugh, __.

a) language is first acquired through comprehension
b) language production stems from language comprehension
c) the difference between the language of chimps and people is merely one of degree
d) all of these

SELF-ASSESSMENT QUESTIONS

1 What is psycholinguistics?

2 Briefly describe what is involved in phonology, semantics and syntax. How are they related?

3 Explain why pre-linguistic communication between the baby and its mother is important for later language development.

4 What is a word? What is known about the child's first words?

5 Summarize the main features of the child's speech during stage 1 grammar

6 Explain how the child's grammatical mistakes are related to its acquisition of grammatical rules.

7 Discuss Skinner's theory of language development.

8 Explain what Chomsky's LAD consists of. How valid is it as an explanation of what is known about language development?

9 Define the following terms: a) semanticity b) displacement c) structure dependence d) creativity (or productivity).

10 Describe some of the methods used to try to teach language to non-human primates.

11 Explain the difference between a) production-based training and b) observational exposure, in relation to studies of language acquisition in chimps. How useful is this distinction for evaluating the findings of these studies?

12 Is language a human species-specific behaviour?

KEY TERMS/CONCEPTS

American sign language (ASL or Ameslan)
babbling
cause-effect analytic device
cognition hypothesis
competence versus performance
comprehension versus production
contentives versus functors
context-bound words
criteria of language: semanticity/ displacement/structure-dependence/creativity (productivity)
critical period
deep versus surface structure
echolalia
emergence of communicative

intentionality
first and second order causality
formats
grammar
holophrase
imitation
imitation with expansion
imitation with reduction
jargon
language
language acquisition device (LAD) (Chomsky)
language acquisition support system (LASS) (Bruner)
language as a communicative tool
lexical rewrite rules
linguistic universals
linguists

maturation
mean length of utterance (MLU)
morphemes
morphology
motherese (baby talk)
observational exposure versus production-based training
one-word stage
over-generalizing/over-regularizing (of rules)
phonemes
phonemic contraction
phonemic expansion
phones
phonological rules
phonology
phrase structure rules
pivotal and categorical (combinatorial) rules
pragmatic rules

pre-linguistic communication
pre-linguistic stage
proto-conversation
psycholinguistics
reduplicated monosyllables
referential words
selective reinforcement (Skinner)
semantics
slot-filling operations
stage 1 grammar
stage 2 grammar
structure-dependent operations
syntactic rule
syntax
telegraphic speech
transformational grammar (Chomsky)
word order

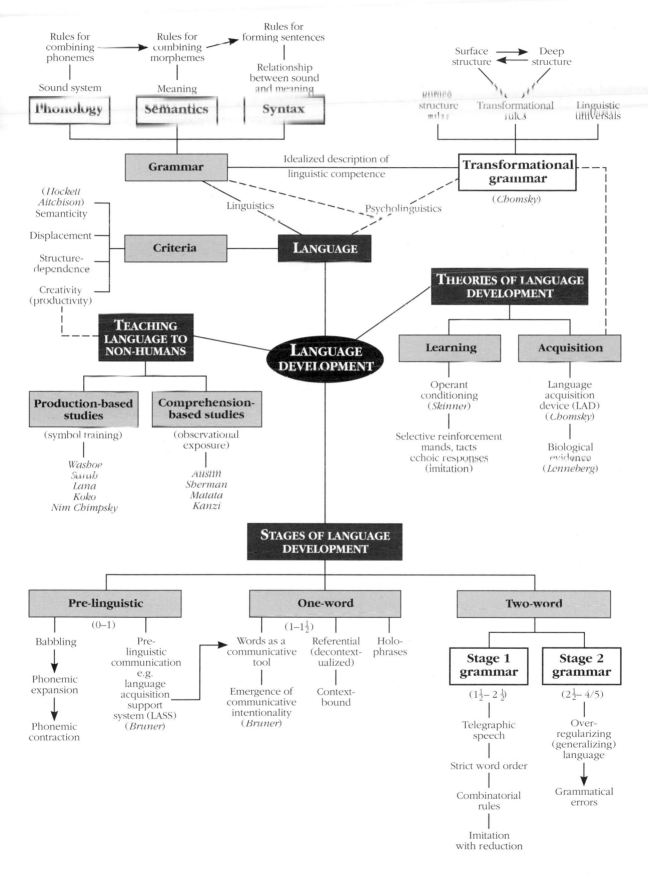

27 MORAL DEVELOPMENT

MULTIPLE-CHOICE QUESTIONS

1 Moral development involves __.

a) knowing what is right and wrong
b) behaving in accordance with moral rules
c) feelings of guilt or pride
d) all of these ✓

2 __ theory focuses on the __ component of morality.

a) psychoanalytic, cognitive
b) social learning, affective
c) cognitive developmental, behavioural
d) none of these

3 The __ stage of psychosexual development is the most important as far as moral development is concerned because of the occurrence in this stage of __.

a) anal, potty training
b) genital, puberty and heterosexual needs
c) phallic, the Oedipus Complex
d) oral, masturbation

4 According to Freud, girls, compared with boys __.

a) have a much weaker motive for identifying with the same-sex parent
b) do not have to repress their attachment to the opposite-sex parent as completely
c) have a weaker superego
d) all of these ✓

5 In the Mackinnon study of cheating, cheats were more likely to __.

a) say they felt guilty than non-cheats were to say they would have felt guilty if they had cheated
b) say they felt guilty about things they did or didn't do in everyday life compared with non-cheats
c) swear and express their frustration more openly than non-cheats ✓
d) say that their parents had used psychological methods of punishment than the non-cheats

6 Children with a strong conscience are likely to have experienced __ methods of punishment, but __.

a) physical, the distinction between physical and psychological punishment is rather artificial
b) psychological, we cannot be certain that the strong conscience was caused by how they were disciplined
c) psychological, these children may have been easier to discipline this way
d) b and c

7 A criticism of Freud's concept of conscience is that __.

a) moral development is a much more gradual process than he claims
b) people's moral behaviour may not be as consistent across different situations as is implied by the concept
c) it was based solely on his self-analysis
d) a and b

8 In classical conditioning terms, conscience is a collection of __.

a) unconditioned emotional responses
b) conditioned emotional responses
c) operant responses brought under stimulus control

d) voluntary behaviours of a moral kind

9 According to Eysenck, conscience refers to __.

a) conditioned anxiety responses which allow us to resist temptation
b) feelings of guilt after doing something wrong
c) an internalized punishing parent
d) a and b

10 If puppies are swatted with a newspaper just before they begin to eat forbidden food, __ than puppies swatted just after eating the food.

a) they will resist the temptation to eat for longer
b) they will show more anxiety once they have started to eat
c) they will show less anxiety once they have started to eat
d) a and c

11 If children are given reasons for not touching a particular toy, __.

a) the timing of punishment becomes irrelevant
b) resistance to temptation persists for longer periods of time
c) the children's age and the kind of reason given will affect their ability to resist temptation
d) all of these

12 An argument against the use of punishment is that __.

a) it can, at best, merely inhibit unacceptable behaviour
b) it can only inform the child how not to behave, rather than how it should behave
c) especially if it takes a physical form, it may demonstrate the very behaviour it is meant to remove
d) all of these

13 If __ rewards are offered for activities which are already intrinsically rewarding, interest in the activity will tend to __. This is called the __.

a) extrinsic, increase, extra reinforcement effect
b) external, decrease, paradox of reward
c) extrinsic, decrease, paradox of reward
d) b and c

14 If reward and punishment are used together, __.

a) it is important that the rewarded behaviour and the punished behaviour are incompatible
b) the combination is likely to be more effective than either used on its own
c) the more intense the punishment and the more sparing the reward the better
d) a and b

15 Models are more likely to be imitated if __.

a) they display sex-appropriate behaviour
b) they are of the same gender as the child
c) they behave in a consistent way
d) all of these

16 If children see an adult model being either rewarded or punished for aggressive behaviour, __.

a) they are less likely to imitate the punished than the rewarded model
b) they will learn equally about how to be aggressive from both models
c) reinforcing the child for imitating the model will produce similarly high levels of imitative aggression in both groups
d) all of these

17 While children are selective in their spontaneous imitation of models, __.

a) mere exposure to a model may be sufficient for learning to occur
b) they may have learnt something from observing a model but not demonstrate this learning in their actual behaviour
c) the consequences of the model's behaviour determine whether or not the child learns anything from observing the model
d) a and b

18 A __ model is imitated because of __.

a) positional, the social role that he/she represents
b) personal, his/her personal qualities or characteristics
c) positional, his/her position in the family
d) a and b

19 Identification involves __.

a) personal modelling
b) generalized imitation
c) a strong emotional relationship between the child and the model
d) all of these

20 In contrast with Skinner, social learning theorists __.

a) believe that cognitive variables intervene between stimulus and response
b) distinguish between internal and external reinforcements and punishments
c) distinguish between learning and performance
d) all of these

21 The only theory which is concerned with the development of morality as such is __.

a) Social Learning Theory
b) operant conditioning
c) cognitive developmental theory
d) classical conditioning

22 Piaget studied children's understanding of the rules of marbles because __.

a) playing marbles forces children to think about moral issues
b) the game involves an extremely complex system of rules or code of laws
c) he believed that the essence of morality is the respect individuals show for rules
d) b and c

23 Children in the heteronomous stage display __.

a) internal responsibility
b) moral relativism

c) a belief in expiatory punishment
d) the principle of reciprocity

24 Children in the autonomous stage __.

a) can now distinguish between deliberate and accidental naughtiness
b) are more skilled at weighing up the relative importance of intentions and the damage done when making moral judgements
c) believe in immanent justice
d) believe that a lie is any departure from the truth

25 The change from heteronomous to autonomous morality takes place __.

a) due to the decline of egocentrism
b) due to the change in the child's social relationships
c) as a result of adult teaching
d) a and b

26 Compared with Piaget, Kohlberg's theory __.

a) sees moral development taking place over a much longer time period
b) places much more emphasis on the role of general cognitive development
c) is based on much more extensive evidence, including longitudinal studies
d) a and c

27 Kohlberg's use of moral dilemmas __.

a) is designed to tap people's level of moral reasoning
b) is an attempt to assess what people think rather than how they think
c) has been criticized on the grounds that they do not represent realistic, complex moral situations
d) a and c

28 Piaget's __ stage corresponds to Kohlberg's __ level.

a) heteronomous, post-conventional
b) heteronomous, pre-conventional
c) autonomous, pre-conventional
d) none of these

SELF-ASSESSMENT QUESTIONS

1 Define the term morality.

2 What similarities are there between language and morality?

3 Briefly show how different theoretical approaches focus on different aspects of morality.

4 Discuss Freud's psychoanalytic theory of moral development.

5 Is moral behaviour determined by moral traits or by moral situations?

6 Is conscience simply a collection of classically conditioned emotional responses?

7 Compare and contrast reward and punishment as influences on the child's moral behaviour.

8 Briefly explain how Social Learning Theory differs from conditioning theory (or learning theory).

9 Describe an experiment which demonstrates the difference between learning and performance.

10 How are imitation and identification related?

11 Compare and contrast Piaget's and Kohlberg's cognitive-developmental theories.

KEY TERMS/CONCEPTS

affective/cognitive/ behavioural aspects of morality
classical conditioning
cognitive developmental theory (Piaget, Kohlberg)
cognitive variables
conditioned emotional responses (CERs)
conscious realization
doctrine of specificity
expiatory punishment
external versus internal reinforcements and punishments
generalized imitation
guilt
heteronomous versus autonomous morality
identification
imitative self-approval

imitative self-disapproval
immanent justice
intervening variables
intrinsic versus extrinsic rewards
justice
learning (acquisition) versus performance (imitation)
love-oriented versus object-oriented child rearing
models
moral dilemmas
moral judgement
moral realism versus moral relativism
negative reinforcement
object-oriented versus person-oriented rationale
objective (external) versus

internal responsibility
observational learning
Oedipus Complex
operant (instrumental) conditioning
paradox of reward
person variables (Mischel): competencies/cognitive strategies/expectancies/ subjective outcome variables/self-regulatory systems and plans
positional versus personal models
positive reinforcement (reward)
practical versus theoretical morality
pre-conventional/ conventional/post-

conventional levels of moral reasoning
psychoanalytic theory (Freud)
psychosexual stages
punishment
reciprocity
resistance to temptation
rules
S-O-R approach
social learning theory
social rules (or conventions) versus moral rules
superego (conscience and ego-ideal)
symbolic renunciation
unilateral versus mutual respect

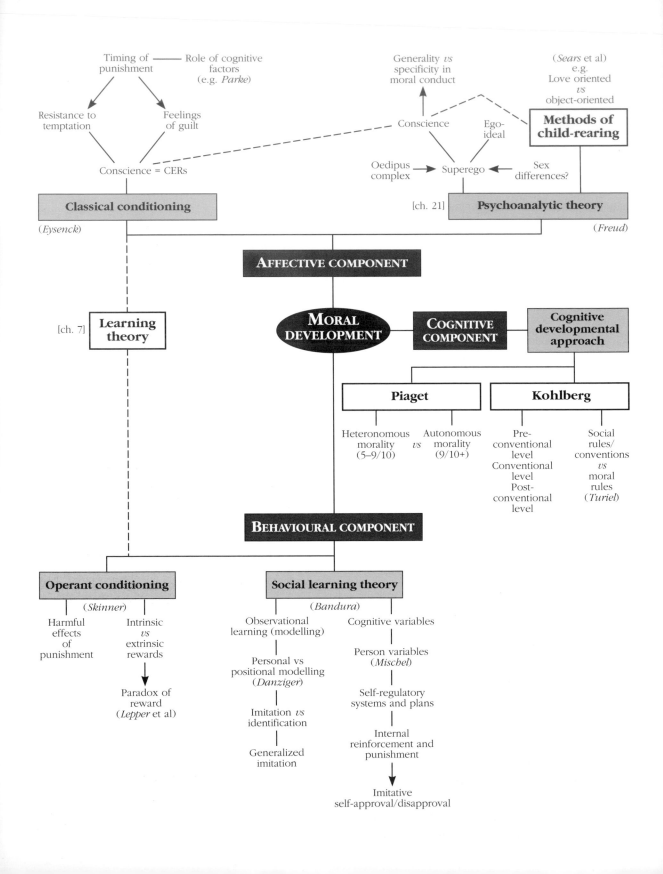

28 INTELLIGENCE

MULTIPLE-CHOICE QUESTIONS

1 Most definitions of intelligence fall into the __ category which is related to the __ approach.

a) biological, qualitative
b) psychological, psychometric
c) operational, qualitative
d) biological, quantitative

2 Factor analysis (FA) __.

a) is a statistical technique used as part of psychometrics
b) involves correlating the scores of large numbers of subjects on a variety of tests
c) assumes that correlations between scores on different tests indicate that those tests measure the same basic ability (or factor)
d) all of these

3 A major difference between theories of the structure of intelligence is that __.

a) American psychologists have stressed the correlations between scores on different tests
b) British psychologists have stressed the lack of correlation between scores on different tests
c) British theories emphasize what different tests have in common
d) American theories emphasize what different tests have in common

4 According to Spearman's __.

a) hierarchical model, every intellectual activity involves both a general and a specific factor
b) two-factor theory, every intellectual activity involves both a general and a

specific factor
c) structure of intellect model, intelligence consists of 120 separate mental abilities
d) primary mental abilities, intelligence consists of seven distinct factors

5 The hierarchical model __.

a) presents a more complex view of intelligence than the two-factor theory
b) sees 'g' as being what all tests are measuring
c) puts major group factors at the top of the hierarchy
d) a and b

6 According to Thurstone, 'g' __.

a) is the innate essence of intelligence
b) is what all tests are measuring
c) is a mental faculty or 'vector of the mind'
d) the grand average of positive correlations for a particular battery of tests

7 According to Guilford, __ is one kind of __ in terms of which a cognitive task can be classified.

a) divergent production, operation
b) convergent production, product
c) transformation, content
d) memory, product

8 Factor analysis (FA) can be criticized on the grounds that __.

a) there are different ways of performing FA which will produce different patterns of factors
b) the factors which emerge will depend on the type of tests and subjects used

c) factors do not exist objectively but are labels applied to patterns of inter-correlations and may/not reflect psychological reality
d) all of these

9 The information processing approach __.

a) denies that individual differences in intelligence exist
b) sees intelligence as the steps or processes people go through in solving problems
c) sees individual differences in intelligence as reflecting differences in speed or efficiency of problem-solving
d) b and c

10 According to Sternberg, although the components involved in solving a particular problem may be common to different cultures, __.

a) cultures will differ widely in the kinds of problem that need solving
b) cultures will differ regarding their definition of intelligence
c) how these components are combined to solve a particular problem will differ between cultures
d) a and b

11 According to Gardner, the existence of distinct, independent, systems of intelligence is suggested by __.

a) the study of brain-damaged patients
b) the identification of a core operation or set of operations
c) the existence of idiots savants, prodigies and other exceptional individuals
d) all of these

12 The first test of intelligence was aimed at identifying children of __ intelligence.

a) superior
b) inferior
c) average
d) genius level

13 The __ test is a(n) __ test of intelligence.

a) WAIS-R, group
b) Stanford-Binet, individual
c) BAS, group
d) 'army alpha', individual

14 __ tests are used __.

a) individual, primarily as diagnostic tools in a clinical setting
b) group, when large numbers of subjects need to be tested at the same time
c) individual, when a timed, pencil and paper test is needed which can be administered and marked by an untrained person
d) a and b

15 The concept of mental age __.

a) is a measure of an individual's intelligence
b) is an absolute assessment of the individual's level of intellectual development
c) only tells us about an individual's intelligence when chronological age is taken into account
d) b and c

16 Most intelligence tests today use a __ IQ, which __.

a) ratio, expresses mental age as a ratio of chronological age
b) deviation, expresses the test score as a standard score
c) deviation, indicates how many standard deviations above or below the mean of the testee's age group the score lies
d) b and c

17 The fact that someone could obtain the same score on two different tests but two different deviation IQs, shows that __.

a) IQ and intelligence are identical concepts
b) IQ is a purely statistical concept
c) measuring someone's intelligence is just as straightforward and uncontroversial as measuring their height
d) all tests are exactly equivalent

18 A good test of intelligence is one which
—.

a) produces a wide distribution of scores
b) has been tested on a large,
representative sample of the population
for whom the test is designed
c) produces consistent scores and actually
measures intelligence
d) all of these

19 Correlating the scores from an IQ test
with future academic performance is a
way of trying to establish the test's __.

a) concurrent validity
b) predictive validity
c) test-retest reliability
d) face validity

20 Critics of IQ tests argue that __.

a) the claim that they are tests of aptitude
rather than attainment is invalid
b) there is no such thing as a culture-free
test
c) intelligence cannot be defined
independently of the culture in which it is
being measured
d) all of these

21 According to the genetic theory, __.

a) differences in intelligence between
individuals and groups are largely
determined by genetic factors
b) the closer the genetic relationship
between any two individuals, the greater
the similarity of their intelligence
c) an individual's IQ should be stable
throughout his/her lifespan
d) all of these

22 Studies of separated monozygotic twins
(MZs) __.

a) consistently show that environmental
factors are more important than genetic
factors
b) represent natural experiments in which
the relative influence of genetic and
environmental factors can be separated
c) sometimes fail to use adequate criteria
for defining separation
d) b and c

23 The proportion of the variance between
the IQ scores of individuals which is
attributable to genetic differences is called
—.

a) a heritability estimate
b) the reaction range
c) standard deviation
d) the hereditarian fallacy

24 Transracial adoption studies __.

a) usually involve a black child being
adopted by a white family with a
biological child of their own
b) show that the child's race has no effect
on the degree of mother-child similarity
in IQ
c) show that the child's adoptive status
has no effect on the degree of mother-
child similarity in IQ
d) all of these

25 Compensatory preschool programmes
such as Headstart __.

a) are bound to fail because of the genetic
inferiority of the children for whom they
are designed
b) can produce significant benefits which
may only show much later on in the
child's school career
c) are most likely to produce benefits for
the child if the parents are actively
involved and help to provide a
stimulating home environment
d) b and c

26 Racial differences in IQ __.

a) can be adequately accounted for in
terms of a heritability estimate based on
twin studies
b) cannot easily be explained in terms of
genetic differences because the genetic
similarities between racial groups are
greater than the differences
c) are very difficult to establish while IQ
tests continue to be culturally biased
d) b and c

SELF-ASSESSMENT QUESTIONS

1 Explain the difference between the qualitative and the quantitative (or psychometric) approaches to the study of intelligence.

2 What is an operational definition of intelligence?

3 Briefly explain what is involved in factor analysis (FA).

4 Compare and contrast two of the following: a) Spearman's two-factor theory b) the hierarchical model (Burt and Vernon) c) Thurstone's primary mental abilities (PMAs) d) Guilford's structure of intellect model.

5 Discuss the use of FA in attempting to understand the nature of intelligence.

6 Explain how the information processing approach differs from both the qualitative and the quantitative (psychometric) approaches to the study of intelligence.

7 Analyze the kind of measurement involved in the use of tests of intelligence.

8 Explain how the concepts of intelligence and IQ are related.

9 How does a ratio IQ differ from a deviation IQ?

10 Discuss the criteria by which an intelligence test should be judged a good test.

11 Can an intelligence test be culture free?

12 Outline the genetic theory of intelligence. What does the theory predict?

13 Discuss the use of either twin studies or fostering and adoption studies in relation to the genetic theory of intelligence.

14 Define the following terms: a) heritability estimate b) reaction range c) natural experiment d) genotype and phenotype e) the hereditarian fallacy.

15 Discuss the claim that intellectual differences between racial groups are due to genetic differences.

KEY TERMS/CONCEPTS

aptitude versus attainment tests
army alpha and beta tests
basal age
Bayley scales of infant development
biological/psychological/ operational definitions
British ability scales (BAS)
compensatory preschool programmes
consistency over time: test-retest method
content/operations/ products
culture-fair/culture-free tests
developmental quotient (DQ)
discriminatory power
divergent versus convergent production
factor analysis (FA)
fluid versus crystallized intelligence (Cattell)

fostering and adoption studies
genetic theory (of intellectual differences)
genotype versus phenotype
hereditarian fallacy (Gould)
heritability estimate
hierarchical model (Burt, Vernon)
idiots savants
individual versus group tests
information processing approach
intelligence
intelligence A and B (Hebb), and C (Vernon)
mental age (MA) versus chronological age (CA)
monozygotic twins (MZs) versus dizygotic twins (DZs)
normal distribution
ordinal versus interval

scale of measurement
performance scale
primary mental abilities (PMAs) (Thurstone)
prototypes
qualitative versus quantitative (psychometric) approach
ratio versus deviation IQ
reaction range
reification
reliability: internal consistency/split-half method/alternate (parallel) forms/Kuder–Richardson method
standard deviations from the mean
standard score
standardization
Stanford–Binet test
structure of intellect model (Guilford)
theory of multiple intelligences (Gardner)

transracial adoption studies
triarchic theory of human intelligence (Sternberg) – componential/ contextual/experiential sub-theories
twin studies
two-factor theory (Spearman)
validity: face (content)/ concurrent/predictive/ construct
verbal scale
Wechsler adult intelligence scale (WAIS-R)
Wechsler intelligence scale for children (WISC-R)
Wechsler preschool primary scale of intelligence (WPPSI)
within-group versus between-group differences

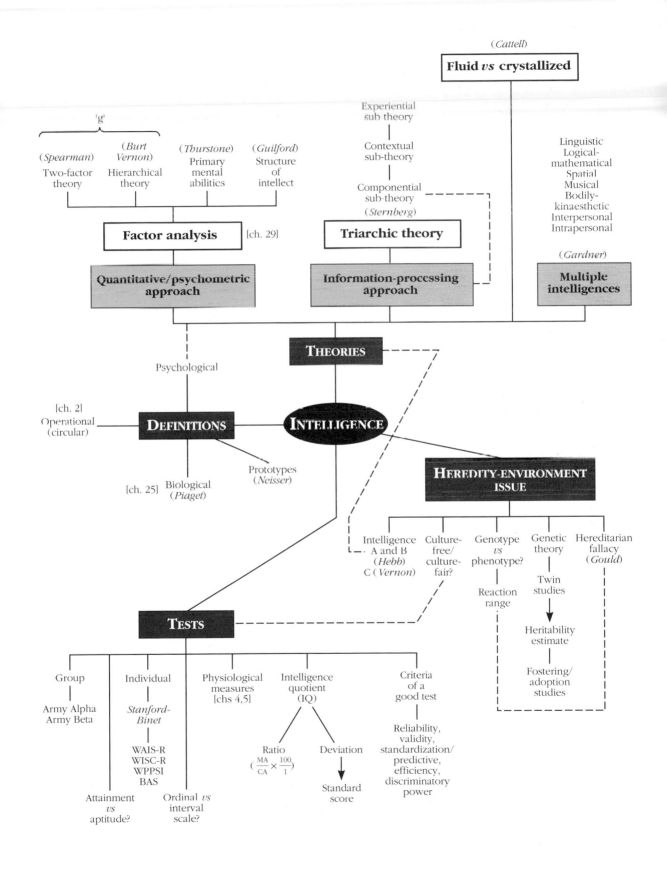

29 PERSONALITY

MULTIPLE-CHOICE QUESTIONS

1 Those relatively stable and permanent aspects of individuals, which make them unique but which also allow people to be compared with each other, define __.

   a) self-concept
   b) personality
   c) psychology
   d) psychometrics

2 Personality theorists who adopt a(n) __ approach, __.

   a) nomothetic, use factor analysis to analyze scores on personality questionnaires
   b) nomothetic, stress the uniqueness of each individual and study the whole person
   c) idiographic, are trying to measure personality in order to make comparisons between people
   d) all of these

3 In Allport's trait theory, __.

   a) common traits apply to all members of a particular culture and so fall within the nomothetic approach
   b) individual traits apply only to unique individuals and so fall within the idiographic approach
   c) a small number of central traits constitute the core of each individual's personality
   d) all of these

4 According to situationalism, behaviour is __.

   a) primarily caused by personality traits
   b) primarily caused by situational factors
   c) the product of an interaction between personality traits and situational factors
   d) none of these

5 When situational factors are very powerful, as in Milgram's obedience experiments, __.

   a) personality factors contribute little to the explanation of people's behaviour
   b) inter-individual consistency is the rule
   c) everyone behaves in an identical fashion
   d) a and b

6 Eysenck prefers an __ method of factor analysis which produces __ factors referred to as __.

   a) orthogonal, second-order, types/surface traits
   b) orthogonal, first-order, types/source traits
   c) oblique, first-order, traits/source traits
   d) oblique, second-order, traits/source traits

7 Introversion-extroversion (E) and neuroticism (N) are __.

   a) both normally distributed
   b) orthogonal, second-order, types/surface traits
   c) dimensions which represent continuums along which everyone can be placed
   d) all of these

8 Introverts __.

   a) have an RAS which is biased towards the build up of excitation

b) are chronically under-aroused
c) have a 'strong' nervous system
d) are much less easily conditioned than extroverts

9 People who score high on neuroticism

a) have an ANS which reacts strongly and quickly to stressful situations
b) have a very labile ANS
c) are also likely to score high on introversion
d) a and b

10 Regardless of an individual's normal position on the scale, __.

a) stimulant drugs should shift behaviour in an introverted direction
b) stimulant drugs should shift behaviour in an extroverted direction
c) depressant drugs should shift behaviour in an extroverted direction
d) a and c

11 Cattell's 16 PF questionnaire is designed to measure __.

a) 16 first-order, oblique, source traits
b) traits which interact to produce surface traits
c) 16 second-order, orthogonal, surface traits
d) a and b

12 Cattell's exvia-invia and anxiety __.

a) are the product of a second-order factor analysis of his 16 source traits
b) correspond to Eysenck's E and N respectively
c) correspond to Eysenck's introversion and extroversion respectively
d) a and b

13 Compared with Eysenck, Cattell __.

a) adopts a much more idiographic approach
b) acknowledges the effect of situational factors on behaviour to a much greater extent
c) acknowledges the effect of mood, state

and motivational factors on behaviour to a much greater extent
d) b and c

14 Kelly's personal construct theory

a) is a nomothetic approach
b) is a phenomenological approach
c) regards people as scientists
d) b and c

15 Personal constructs are __.

a) each individual's unique set of transparent templates or goggles through which he/she perceives the world
b) necessary in order to make sense of the world
c) our interpretations of the world which are constantly being tested and revised in the light of experience
d) all of these

16 The __ is the method used to elicit the individual's personal constructs, which are expressed in a __ way.

a) EPQ, yes/no
b) 16 PF questionnaire, bipolar
c) Repertory Grid Test, bipolar
d) semantic differential, yes/no

17 __ theories represent a 'third force' in psychology, the others being __.

a) humanistic, behaviourism and psychoanalytic theory
b) humanistic, type and trait theories
c) psychoanalytic, humanistic theories and behaviourism
d) behaviouristic, psychoanalytic and humanistic theories

18 According to Maslow, self-actualization __.

a) is unique to human beings
b) is at the top of a hierarchy of needs at the bottom of which are safety needs
c) refers to becoming everything one is capable of becoming
d) a and c

19 According to Rogers, __.

a) most human behaviour can be understood as an attempt to maintain consistency between our self-concept and our actions
b) the self-image of a congruent person is flexible and changes in line with new experiences
c) the greater the gap between self-image and reality, the greater the likelihood of anxiety and emotional disturbance
d) all of these

20 Learning how to act and feel in order to obtain the love and acceptance of significant others is called __.

a) unconditional positive regard
b) conditional positive regard
c) positive self-regard
d) incongruence

21 Psychodynamic theories are concerned with __.

a) those motives which are unique to human beings
b) the active forces within the personality
c) feelings, conflicts, drives and unconscious motivational forces
d) b and c

22 According to Freud, dreams, neurotic symptoms and defence mechanisms are all __.

a) ways of dealing with the inevitable conflict arising within the personality
b) controlled by the unconscious part of the ego
c) forms of everyday psychopathology
d) a and b

23 The view that all behaviour has a cause (often unconscious) is called __.

a) overdeterminism
b) psychic determinism
c) rationalism
d) parapraxis

24 A common criticism of Freud's theories is that __.

a) they overemphasize the biological influences on personality development
b) they are based on a very unrepresentative sample of the human population
c) they are based on the case-study method which is open to many types of distortion and uncontrolled influences
d) all of these

25 According to Jung, __.

a) individuation is the process by which a person becomes a separate, indivisible unity or whole
b) the personal unconscious comprises both Freud's unconscious and pre-conscious
c) the collective unconscious consists of archetypes, including the persona, anima/animus, the shadow and the self
d) all of these

26 According to Adler, __.

a) children come to experience their dependence and powerlessness as a state of inferiority relative to adults
b) a state of inferiority produces an unconscious drive towards superiority, the will to power
c) physical deformity, gender, birth order and the response of parents to the child's successes and failures can all influence an individual's degree of inferiority
d) all of these

27 As a strategy for coping with inferiority, __ refers to attempts to prevent the possibility of failure.

a) escape from combat
b) successful compensation
c) overcompensation
d) giving up the struggle

SELF-ASSESSMENT QUESTIONS

1 Explain the difference between a nomothetic and an idiographic approach to the study of personality.

2 Is it necessary, or valid, to distinguish between a nomothetic and an idiographic approach?

3 Is behaviour the product of personality, the situation or an interaction between the two?

4 Show how the theories of Eysenck and Cattell differ with regard to: a) their preferred method of factor analysis b) the resulting factors.

5 Describe and discuss Eysenck's theory of personality.

6 Summarize the major differences between Eysenck's and Cattell's theories.

7 Outline Kelly's theory of personal constructs.

8 What is meant by a phenomenological approach to the study of personality?

9 Describe the major features of Maslow's hierarchy of needs.

10 Explain the following terms: a) self-concept b) self-actualization c) incongruence d) conditional and unconditional positive regard e) conditions of worth.

11 According to Freud, in what ways does the unconscious mind reveal itself?

12 Discuss the scientific status of Freud's psychoanalytic theory.

13 Compare and contrast the psychodynamic theories of Freud and Jung.

14 Why, according to Adler, do people suffer from feelings of inferiority and how do they try to overcome these feelings?

KEY TERMS/CONCEPTS

Adler's individual psychology
archetypes: persona/anima/animus/shadow/self
Cattell's trait theory
chronic under-/over-arousal
complex
conditionability
conditional/unconditional positive regard
conditions of worth
constructive alternativism
constructs/elements
criterion analysis
day residues
deficiency or D motives versus growth (being) or B motives
depth psychology
descriptive versus generalizing sciences
displacement/condensation/concrete representation
dream work
dysthymics versus hysterics
ego defence mechanisms conscious/pre-conscious/

unconscious
escape from combat
excitation versus inhibition
exvia-invia/anxiety
Eysenck personality inventory (EPI)/questionnaire (EPQ)
Eysenck's type theory
factor analysis (FA): orthogonal versus oblique methods
fictive goals
first-order versus second-order factors
Freud's psychoanalytic theory
group versus idiosyncratic (individual) norms
humanistic theories
idiodynamics (or idiography)
incongruence
individuation
inferiority
interactionism (Bowers)
inter-/intra-individual consistency
introversion-extroversion (E)

Jung's analytical psychology
L data/Q data/T data
lie scale
man the scientist
manifest versus latent content (of dreams)
Maslow's hierarchy of needs
metatrait hypothesis
neurotic symptoms
neuroticism or emotionality/stability (N)
nomothetic versus idiographic approach
overcompensation
overdetermination
parapraxes (Freudian slips)
pathogenic
peak experiences
personal construct theory (PCT) (Kelly)
personal versus collective unconscious
personality
16 PF questionnaire
positive self-regard
psyche
psychic determinism

psychical fatigue
psychodynamic theories
psychoticism (P)
reactivity (or lability) of autonomic nervous system (ANS)
repertory grid test ('rep grid')
reticular activating system (RAS)
Rogers' self theory
rotation to simple structure
self versus organism
self-actualization
situationalism (Mischel)
successful compensation
trait theory (Allport): common versus individual traits (cardinal/central/secondary)
traits (source traits)
type and trait approach
types (surface traits)
will to power
wish fulfilment

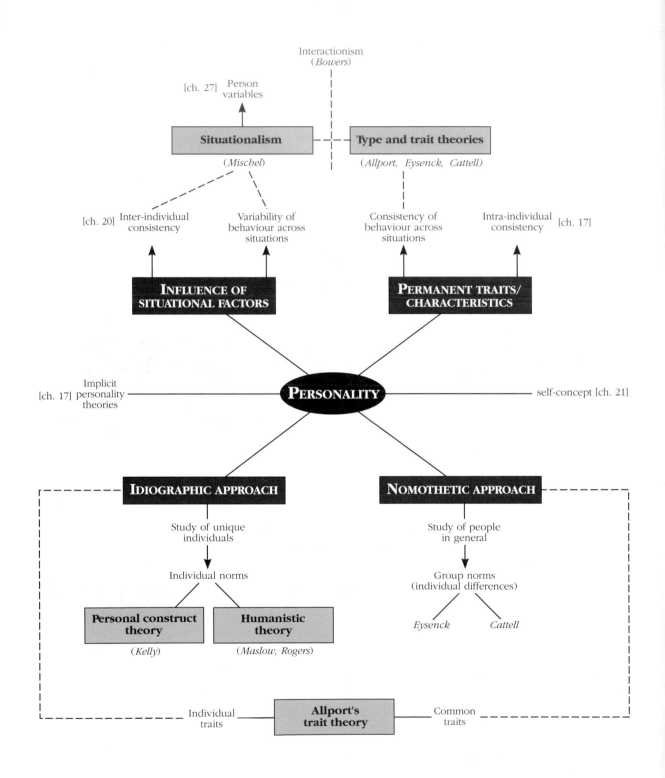

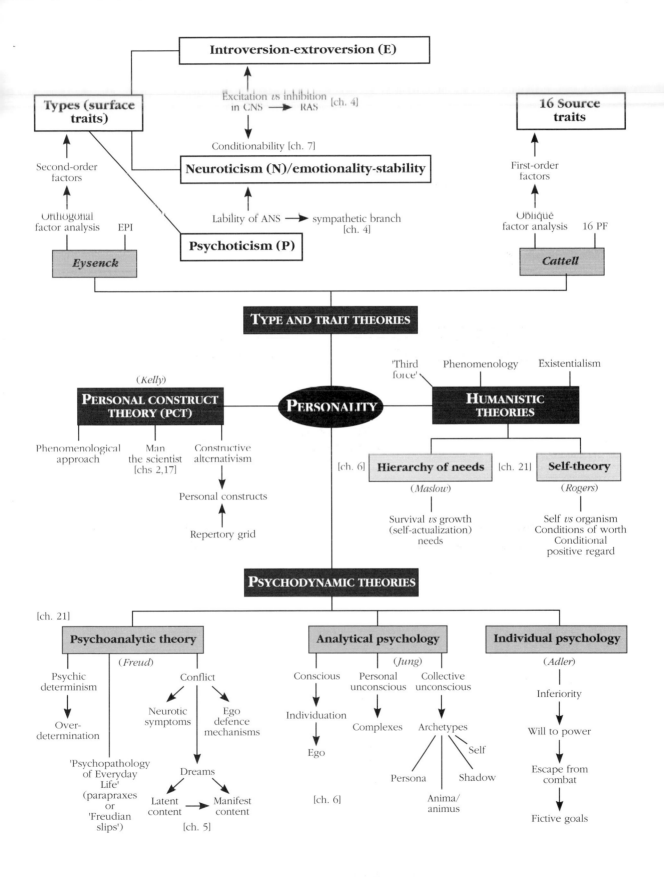

Introversion-extroversion (E)

Types (surface traits)

Excitation *vs* inhibition in CNS ⟶ RAS [ch. 4]

Conditionability [ch. 7]

16 Source traits

Second-order factors

Neuroticism (N)/emotionality-stability

First-order factors

Orthogonal factor analysis   EPI

Lability of ANS ⟶ sympathetic branch [ch. 4]

Oblique factor analysis   16 PF

Psychoticism (P)

Eysenck

Cattell

TYPE AND TRAIT THEORIES

'Third force'   Phenomenology   Existentialism

(*Kelly*)

PERSONAL CONSTRUCT THEORY (PCT)

PERSONALITY

HUMANISTIC THEORIES

Phenomenological approach   Man the scientist [chs 2,17]   Constructive alternativism

[ch. 6]   **Hierarchy of needs**   [ch. 21]   **Self-theory**

(*Maslow*)   (*Rogers*)

Personal constructs

Survival *vs* growth (self-actualization) needs

Self *vs* organism
Conditions of worth
Conditional positive regard

Repertory grid

PSYCHODYNAMIC THEORIES

[ch. 21]

Psychoanalytic theory

Analytical psychology

Individual psychology

(*Freud*)   (*Jung*)   (*Adler*)

Psychic determinism   Conflict

Conscious   Personal unconscious   Collective unconscious   Inferiority

Over-determination

Neurotic symptoms   Ego defence mechanisms

Individuation

Complexes   Archetypes   Will to power

'Psychopathology of Everyday Life' (parapraxes or 'Freudian slips')

Dreams

Ego   Self   Escape from combat

[ch. 6]

Persona   Shadow

Latent content   Manifest content   Anima/ animus   Fictive goals

[ch. 5]

30 PSYCHOPATHOLOGY

MULTIPLE-CHOICE QUESTIONS

1 The __ criterion defines as abnormal any behaviour which is infrequent or which deviates from the average.

a) deviation-from-the-norm
b) adequacy or mental health
c) statistical
d) mental illness

2 According to the deviation-from-the-norm criterion, __.

a) abnormal behaviour is a deviation from how one is expected to behave
b) abnormal behaviour is undesirable behaviour
c) certain kinds of behaviour are abnormal because they are unnatural
d) all of these

3 A problem with trying to identify characteristics which normal people should have is that __.

a) most people will simply not possess them and so will be judged abnormal or disordered
b) any such characteristics will involve value judgements
c) psychological normality and abnormality are relative to particular cultures and historical periods
d) all of these

4 The view of psychological abnormality as mental illness derives from the __ model.

a) psychoanalytic
b) behavioural
c) medical
d) humanistic

5 Regarding someone who is psychologically disturbed as sick __.

a) is based on the medical model
b) can be seen as more humane than regarding them as bad or morally defective
c) can be seen as removing the person's responsibility for his/her behaviour
d) all of these

6 According to Szasz, if mental illnesses are caused by disorders of the nervous system, then __.

a) we should call them mental illnesses
b) we should call them diseases of the brain or neurophysiological disorders
c) we need to distinguish between organic and non-organic causes of abnormal thinking and behaviour
d) b and c

7 Psychosis can be __ which means that __.

a) organic, there is a physical disease of the brain causing the abnormal thinking and behaviour
b) functional, something has gone wrong in the way the person functions in his/her social relationships
c) functional, it can actually be to the advantage of the patient
d) a and b

8 Blood tests, X-rays and other objective tests __.

a) provide signs of disease which aid diagnosis
b) are more important in general medicine than the patient's symptoms

c) are a much more reliable and valid source of information than the psychological tests used in psychiatry

d) all of these

9 Compared with medical diagnosis, psychiatric diagnosis __.

a) describes the whole person
b) confers a new and total identity on the patient
c) has implications for the legal and civil rights of the patient
d) all of these

10 DSM-III-R and ICD-10 are both __.

a) major systems for the classification of mental disorder
b) derived from Kraepelin's original designation of diseases or syndromes
c) multi-axial systems of classification
d) all of these

11 Both DSM-III-R and ICD-10 __.

a) have a separate category for organic mental disorders
b) use the term mental illness
c) continue to distinguish between neurosis and psychosis
d) have a single category for neurotic, stress-related and somatoform disorders

12 Although the traditional distinction between neurosis and psychosis is dropped from DSM-III-R and ICD-10, the terms __.

a) are still included in the two systems
b) are still used in everyday psychiatric practice
c) are still useful when a more precise diagnosis cannot be given
d) all of these

13 __ is defined as an extreme, irrational fear of some object or situation.

a) a phobia
b) anxiety neurosis
c) neurosis
d) psychosis

14 Agoraphobia __.

a) is the most common of all phobias
b) involves a primary fear of leaving the safety and security of home and being separated from familiar people
c) involves recurring irrational thoughts or ideas which are often associated with compulsive behaviour
d) a and b

15 Somatoform disorders __

a) represent a conversion of conflict and anxiety into physical symptoms in the absence of disease or injury
b) represent the model of neurosis on which Freud based his psychoanalytic theory
c) usually take the form of either sensory, motor or visceral symptoms
d) all of these

16 Somnambulism, amnesia, fugue and multiple personality are all forms of __.

a) conversion type hysterical neurosis
b) dissociative type hysterical neurosis
c) obsessive-compulsive neurosis
d) anxiety neurosis

17 Schizophrenia literally means __. Major symptoms include __.

a) split mind, primary delusions and auditory hallucinations
b) divided self, thought insertion, withdrawal and broadcasting
c) multiple personality, flattening of affect and psychomotor disorders
d) a and b

18 __ schizophrenics are more similar to each other than the other categories of schizophrenia and their major symptoms are __.

a) paranoid, delusions of persecution or grandeur
b) paranoid, hallucinations and disturbances of affect
c) hebephrenic, psychomotor disorders and negativism

d) catatonic, gradual social deterioration and increased apathy

19 In support of the genetic theory of schizophrenia, it has been found that __.

a) the average concordance rate for MZs reared together is five times higher than that for DZs reared together
b) the average concordance rates for MZs reared together and separately are very similar
c) adopted children who have a schizophrenic natural parent are much more likely to develop it themselves than other adopted children who don't have a schizophrenic natural parent
d) all of these

20 Genetic factors may play a greater role in the case of __ schizophrenia, in which __.

a) process, pathological symptoms have been evident for many years before the breakdown occurs
b) reactive, symptoms appear quite suddenly, often later in life
c) process, symptoms appear quite suddenly, often later in life
d) paranoid, delusions are the main symptom

21 The dopamine hypothesis is supported by __.

a) the finding that the limbic systems of schizophrenics contain unusually high levels of dopamine
b) the belief that anti-schizophrenic drugs, such as chlorpromazine, work by binding to dopamine receptor sites
c) the observation that high doses of amphetamines and L-dopa can produce schizophrenia-like symptoms
d) all of these

22 According to Laing's family interaction model, schizophrenia __.

a) is a severe form of mental illness which is made worse by certain kinds of family relationships
b) refers to an interpersonal ploy used by parents, doctors etc. in their interactions with the schizophrenic
c) can only be understood as something going on between people and not as happening within an individual
d) b and c

23 The __ personality is typically amoral, insensitive to others' feelings, impulsive, stimulus-seeking and unable to tolerate frustration.

a) antisocial
b) paranoid
c) schizoid
d) obsessive

24 Rosenhan's study of pseudo-patients __.

a) is meant to demonstrate the inability of psychiatrists to distinguish real from pretend patients
b) claims to show the unreliability of traditional psychiatric classification
c) almost certainly would have produced different results had it been conducted after the introduction of DSM-III
d) all of these

25 The reliability of psychiatric diagnosis has been increased by the use of __.

a) standardized interview schedules
b) explicit operational criteria
c) a multi-axial approach
d) all of these

26 Psychiatric classification is justifiable to the extent that psychiatric patients __.

a) have attributes in common with all other patients
b) have attributes in common with some other patients
c) have attributes which are unique to them
d) all of these

SELF-ASSESSMENT QUESTIONS

1 Describe and assess three criteria for distinguishing between psychological normality and abnormality

2 What is the medical model? Discuss the concept of mental illness as a way of explaining and dealing with psychological abnormality.

3 Present some arguments in favour of treating people with psychological problems as sick.

4 Present some arguments against treating people with psychological problems as sick.

5 Compare and contrast DSM-III-R and ICD-10.

6 Describe two types of neurotic, mood (affective) and personality disorder.

7 Describe some of the major symptoms of schizophrenia and show how these relate to different sub-types.

8 Assess the evidence relating to the genetic theory of schizophrenia.

9 Summarize the main features of any two theories of schizophrenia other than the genetic theory.

10 Discuss the advantages and disadvantages of classifying mental disorder.

11 How reliable and valid is psychiatric diagnosis?

KEY TERMS/CONCEPTS

adequacy (or mental health) criterion
agoraphobia
amnesia
anti-psychiatry (Laing)
antisocial (sociopathic/ psychopathic) personality
anxiety attacks
anxiety neurosis (generalized or free-floating anxiety)
bi-polar disorder (manic depression)
classification (of mental disorder)
conspiratorial model
depressive disorder
deviation-from-the-norm criterion
dissociative disorders
dopamine hypothesis
double-binds (Bateson)

DSM-III-R
environmental stressors
existential psychiatry
family interaction model
fugue
genetic theory (of schizophrenia)
ICD-10
maladaptiveness
manic disorder (mania)
medical model
mental illness criterion
multi-axial system
multiple personality
neurosis versus psychosis
nomothetic versus idiographic approach
normality/abnormality
obsessive-compulsive disorder
obsessive-compulsive personality

organic versus functional psychosis
panic attacks
paranoid personality
personal distress
phobias
physical capture
problems in living (Szasz)/ disorders of psychosocial or interpersonal functioning
interpersonal functioning
psychedelic model
psychopathology
psychosomatic (psychophysiological) disorders
reactive versus process schizophrenia
reliability and validity (of classification)
residual rules

responsibility
retardation
schizoid personality
schizophrenia: simple/ hebephrenic or disorganized/catatonic/ paranoid
seasonal affective disorder (SAD)
signs versus symptoms
social control
social drift versus social causation hypothesis
somatoform (conversion) disorders
somnambulism
statistical (deviation-from-the-average) criterion
stigmatizing labels
symbolic recapture
total institutions

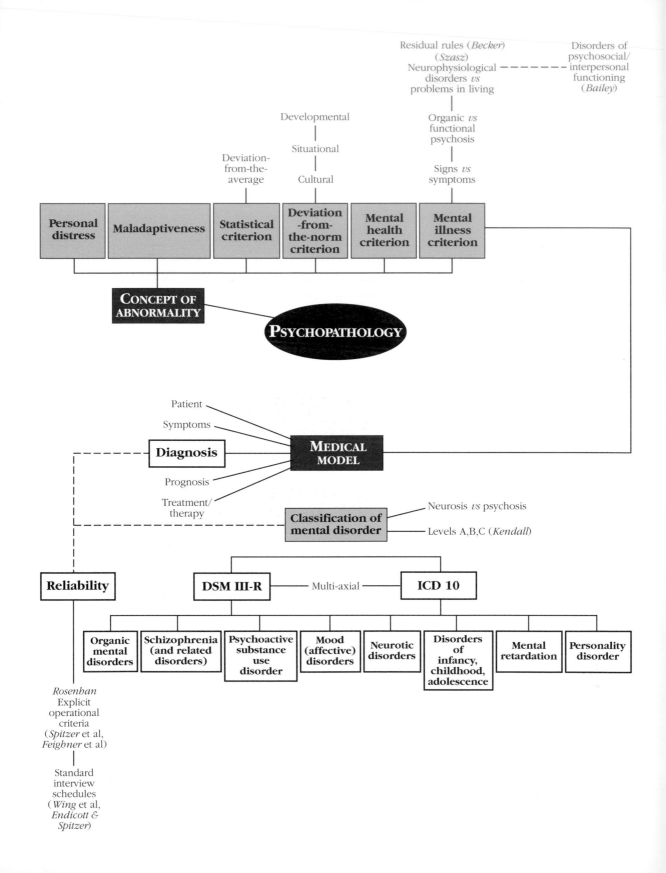

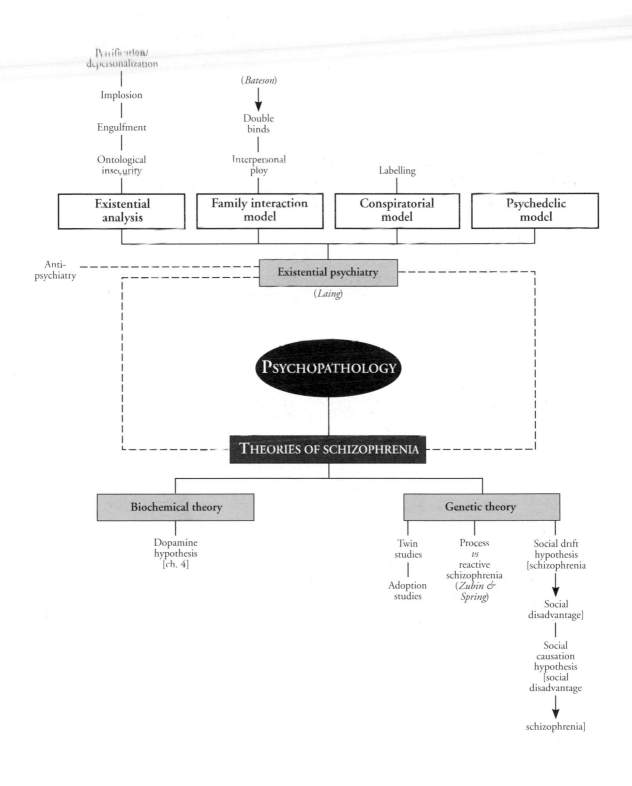

31 TREATMENTS AND THERAPIES

MULTIPLE-CHOICE QUESTIONS

1 A way of trying to classify different treatments and therapies is to distinguish between __.

a) physical (organic) and psychological treatments
b) directive and non-directive therapies
c) individual and group therapies
d) all of these

2 Directive therapies __.

a) focus on what is going on in the therapeutic relationship
b) involve the therapist making concrete suggestions to the client
c) are best illustrated by behaviour therapy, cognitive behaviour therapy, PCT and Gestalt therapy
d) b and c

3 Non-directive therapies are best illustrated by __.

a) psychoanalysis
b) client-centred therapy
c) cognitive behaviour therapy
d) a and b

4 Drugs used in the treatment of mental or psychological illness are called __.

a) psychodynamic
b) psychedelic
c) psychoactive
d) psychosomatic

5 Chlorpromazine is __.

a) a major tranquilliser widely used for the treatment of schizophrenia
b) an anti-psychotic drug known to have side-effects if used long term, including tardive dyskinesia
c) a minor tranquilliser which becomes concentrated in the brain stem and is released very slowly
d) a and b

6 ECT __.

a) is used mainly with severely depressed patients
b) is effective as measured by suicide rates among patients who have and have not received ECT
c) is a highly controversial treatment because of its side-effects and the issue of consent
d) all of these

7 Psychosurgery is used with patients suffering from __.

a) phobias
b) severe depression
c) abnormal aggression
d) b and c

8 When used with abnormally aggressive patients,__ leucotomies involve destruction of the __.

a) bimedial, tissue connecting the frontal lobes of the cortex with sub-cortical areas on both sides of the cortex
b) orbital, neural circuit connecting the amygdala and the hypothalamus
c) limbic, neural circuit connecting the amygdala and the hypothalamus
d) pre-frontal, dominant cerebral hemisphere

9 Phobias involve __.

a) the ego defence mechanisms of repression, projection and displacement
b) the ego defence mechanisms of repression, regression and sublimation
c) an object which in some way symbolizes the true, unconscious conflict
d) a and c

10 Psychoanalysis is intended to __.

a) change the client's behaviour
b) undo unsatisfactory defences
c) help the client to re-experience repressed childhood feelings and wishes
d) b and c

11 When the client displaces repressed feelings from childhood onto the analyst, including dependence, erotic attachment and anger, he/she is displaying __.

a) counter-transference
b) sublimation
c) transference
d) resistance

12 In psychoanalysis, the client's dreams, free associations, transference and resistance all need to be __.

a) investigated
b) interpreted
c) internalized
d) externalized

13 Behaviour __ refers to techniques based on __.

a) therapy, classical conditioning
b) modification, operant conditioning
c) therapy, social learning theory
d) a and b

14 Behavioural analysis refers to __.

a) study of the effectiveness of different techniques in relation to particular diagnostic groups
b) a nomothetic approach associated with Eysenck, Rachman and Marks
c) an idiographic approach which bases treatment on the stimuli and consequences found to be relevant in each

particular case of inappropriate behaviour
d) none of these

15 The classical conditioning explanation of phobias __.

a) sees the case of Little Hans as exemplifying how all abnormal fears are acquired
b) cannot account for the persistence of naturally-occurring phobias
c) assumes that all phobics will have had a traumatic experience involving the feared object as a conditioned stimulus
d) b and c

16 Gradually exposing patients to the object of their fear while they are relaxing is called __.

a) implosion
b) systematic desensitization
c) reciprocal inhibition
d) flooding

17 If a least-to-most frightening hierarchy is no more effective than a most-to-least or randomly presented hierarchy, then __.

a) a hierarchy of some kind is necessary but not sufficient
b) exposure to the feared object is the crucial ingredient
c) a hierarchy is not necessary
d) systematic desensitization is not a distinct form of behaviour therapy

18 __ involves removing some undesirable response to a particular stimulus by associating the stimulus with another __ stimulus, through a process of __ conditioning.

a) aversion therapy, aversive, operant
b) flooding, aversive, classical
c) aversion therapy, aversive, classical
d) systematic desensitization, incompatible, classical

19 When autistic children are given speech therapy, __.

a) a shaping technique is used
b) their first reinforcement is given for

producing single words
c) verbal approval is paired with food so that verbal approval eventually becomes a conditioned reinforcer
d) a and c

20 One technique used in behaviour modification with mentally handicapped and autistic people is __.

a) time out
b) to leave the person in a room on their own, so that undesirable behaviour cannot be reinforced
c) to leave the person in a room on their own as a punishment for undesirable behaviour
d) a and b

21 The token economy is based on the principle of __ and its introduction highlighted __.

a) reciprocal inhibition, the way that psychiatrists depended on major tranquillizers to treat psychotic patients
b) secondary reinforcement, how staff were inadvertently reinforcing psychotic behaviour
c) primary reinforcement, the need to make staff aware of the effect their behaviour has on patients
d) a and b

22 Cognitive behaviour therapy __.

a) regards most clinical problems as disorders of thought and feeling
b) attempts to change maladaptive behaviour by changing the maladaptive thinking underlying it
c) involves cognitive restructuring as an end in itself
d) a and b

23 According to __, emotional distress and neurotic behaviour are caused largely by __.

a) Ellis' rational emotive therapy, irrational thoughts
b) Meichenbaum's self-instructional

training, faulty internal dialogues
c) Beck, automatic thoughts
d) all of these

24 According to Bandura, __.

a) modelling is more effective than methods based on conditioning as a treatment for phobias
b) modelling is mainly effective in treating simple phobias in children
c) the central element in therapy is the cognitive change towards self-efficacy
d) all of these

25 The aim of personal construct therapy is to __.

a) bring the individual's personal constructs in line with his/her behaviour
b) change the client's way of construing the world in order to predict it more accurately
c) help the client to function more fully by loosening or tightening his/her constructs as required
d) b and c

26 According to Rogers' client-centred therapy, in order to bring about therapeutic change, the therapist must effectively communicate to the client __.

a) genuineness or authenticity
b) unconditional positive regard
c) empathic understanding
d) all of these

27 The question of the effectiveness of treatment and therapy is made more complex by __.

a) the fact that different approaches define 'cure' in different ways
b) the need to distinguish between research into outcome and research into process
c) the combined influence of factors related to the particular form of therapy and non-specific factors, such as relationship with the therapist and the expectation of improvement
d) all of these

SELF-ASSESSMENT QUESTIONS

1 Explain, giving examples, the difference between a) organic and psychological treatments and b) directive and non-directive therapies.

2 Discuss the use of psychoactive drugs in the treatment of psychological disorders.

3 Discuss the use of ECT in the treatment of psychological disorders.

4 Discuss the use of psychosurgery in the treatment of psychological disorders.

5 What, according to Freud, is neurosis?

6 Explain what is meant by: a) transference b) counter-transference c) dream interpretation d) free association e) resistance.

7 Summarize the major aims of psychoanalysis.

8 Explain the difference between a) behaviour therapy and modification and b) behavioural technology and behavioural analysis.

9 Compare and contrast the conditioning and psychoanalytic explanations of phobias.

10 Evaluate the use of either behaviour therapy or behaviour modification in the treatment of behaviour disorders.

11 Briefly explain the difference between behaviour therapy and cognitive-behaviour therapy. Outline the main features of two examples of cognitive-behaviour therapy.

12 Summarize the model of psychological disorder and therapeutic techniques involved in either Kelly's personal construct therapy or Rogers' client-centred therapy.

13 Does therapy work?

KEY TERMS/CONCEPTS

anti-depressants
aversion therapy
behaviour modification
behaviour therapy versus
    behaviour modification
behavioural analysis
    (functional analysis)
behavioural psychotherapy
behavioural technology
brief focal therapy
catastrophizing self-
    statements
client-centred therapy
    (Rogers)
cognitive behaviour
    therapy
cognitive restructuring
cognitive triad (of
    depression)
counselling
covert sensitization
directive versus non-
    directive
displacement
dream interpretation
drug therapy
    (chemotherapy)
effectiveness of treatment/
    therapy
electro-convulsive therapy

(ECT)
empathic understanding
encounter groups
Erhard seminars training
exposure
family interaction model
faulty internal dialogues
fixed role sketch/
    enactment
flooding
free association
frontal lobotomies
    (leucotomies)
genuineness (authenticity
    or congruence)
Gestalt therapy (Perls)
hierarchy (of fear)
implosive therapy
    (implosion)
in vivo exposure
individual versus group
irrational thoughts
loosening/tightening of
    constructs
major tranquillizers
minor tranquillizers
modelling (Bandura)
negative practice
neurotic paradox
neurotic versus moral

anxiety
nomothetic versus
    idiographic approach
personal construct therapy
    (Kelly)
physical (organic) versus
    psychological
preparedness
primal therapy (Janov)
projection
psychoanalytical first-aid
psychoanalytically-
    oriented psychotherapy
psychodrama (Moreno)
psychosurgery
Q-sort
quantitative versus
    qualitative (aspects of
    therapy)
range of convenience
rational emotive therapy
    (Ellis)
reciprocal inhibition
repertory grid
repression
research into outcomes
    versus process
resistance
safety signal hypothesis
secondary gain

secondary reinforcement
self-characterization
self-efficacy
self-instructional training
    (Meichenbaum)
social psychiatry
spontaneous remission
stimulus augmentation
stimulus satiation
symptom substitution
systematic desensitization
therapeutic atmosphere
therapeutic community
thought-stopping (Wolpe)
time out
token economy
    programme
transactional analysis
    (Berne)
transference/counter-
    transference
treatment of automatic
    thoughts (Beck)
two process/two factor
    model
unconditional positive
    regard

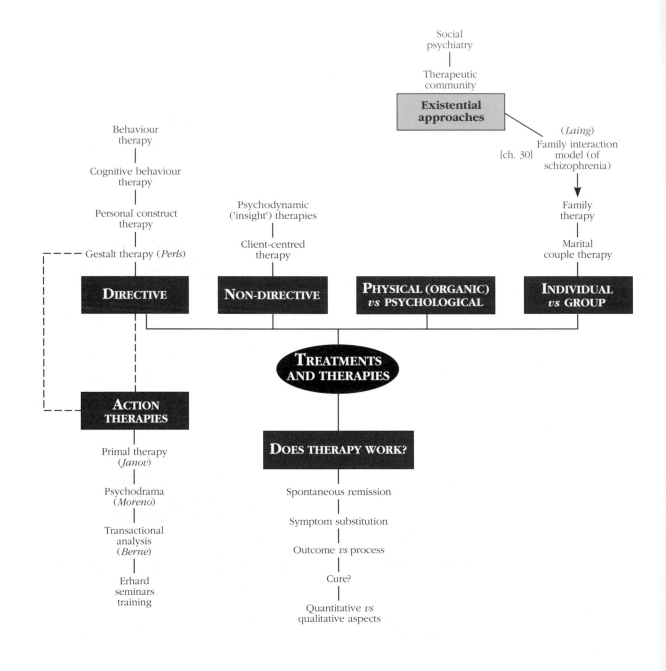

Social psychiatry

Therapeutic community

Existential approaches

(*Laing*)
Family interaction model (of schizophrenia)

[ch. 30]

Family therapy

Marital couple therapy

Behaviour therapy

Cognitive behaviour therapy

Personal construct therapy

Gestalt therapy (*Perls*)

Psychodynamic ('insight') therapies

Client-centred therapy

DIRECTIVE

NON-DIRECTIVE

PHYSICAL (ORGANIC) *vs* PSYCHOLOGICAL

INDIVIDUAL *vs* GROUP

TREATMENTS AND THERAPIES

ACTION THERAPIES

Primal therapy (*Janov*)

Psychodrama (*Moreno*)

Transactional analysis (*Berne*)

Erhard seminars training

DOES THERAPY WORK?

Spontaneous remission

Symptom substitution

Outcome *vs* process

Cure?

Quantitative *vs* qualitative aspects

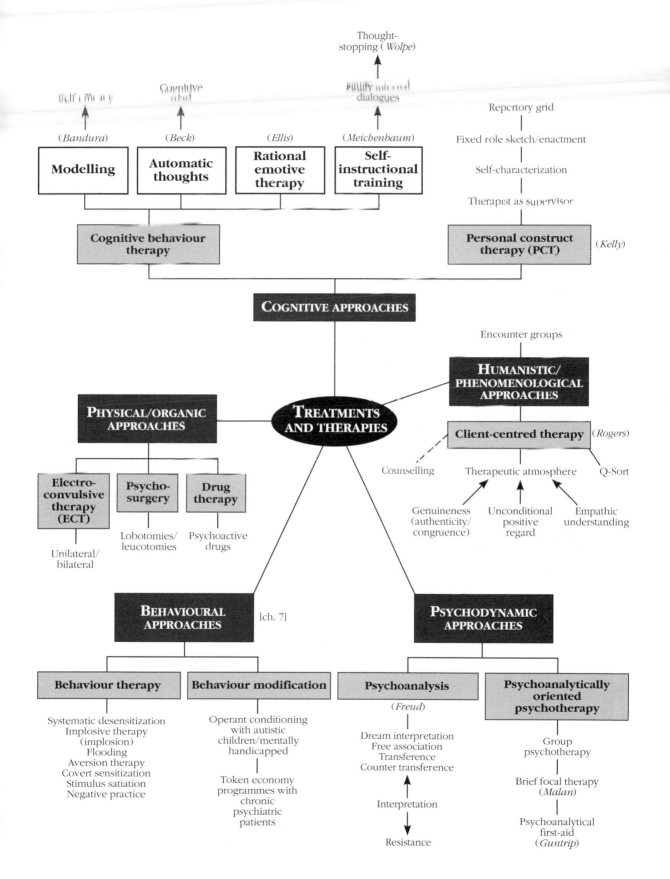

PART TWO

DEVELOPING ESSAY-WRITING SKILLS

So far this Study Guide has been concerned with helping you to work your way through the textbook, and to provide activities which will enable you to check your progress, your understanding and your retention.

Essay-writing may be regarded as a skill (or set of skills) in the same way that a person learns to drive a car or play a musical instrument. The same principles apply. We need to identify three components in the acquisition of all of these skills:

Skill
- Identification
- Rehearsal
- Feedback

In this chapter it will be possible only to deal with the first of these three components, the rest is up to you. You will need to practise (rehearse) the skills here identified in your future essays and read carefully (and act upon) the advice (feedback) given to you by the tutor who marks them.

Let us now consider exactly what skills are involved in writing essays. Let us tackle this through a short practical exercise.

> **Put the book to one side for a few moments and write down a list of what, in your opinion, makes a good essay.**

This is a very tough task, because it begs the question of what purpose the essay is to serve (for example, why is it being written, for whom and in what context?). But we shall return to these points shortly and it is a useful activity to identify some criteria which generally differentiate good and bad essays.

Obviously, the answer depends very much upon the level of the essay (e.g. GCSE, BTEC, 'A'/'AS', undergraduate, etc.) but the following characteristics will almost always be well rewarded:

1 Relevance (i.e. the essay actually answers the question)
2 Accuracy
3 Clarity of expression
4 Organization (there should be flow and shape to an essay)
5 Clear and logical line of argument
6 Demonstration of knowledge of psychology (e.g. studies, theories, methods)
7 Linking and contrasting different areas
8 Breadth and depth of coverage

9 Interpretation

10 Evaluation

This checklist of good practice is not arranged in order of importance (the factors will be weighted differently according to the level and nature of the essay).

It is important to note that some of the factors (for example, interpretation) are PROCESS factors and some (e.g. knowledge of psychology) are CONTENT factors. By process factors, we mean that they refer to skill performances (how you *use* what you know) whereas content factors refer to *what* you know. These are almost always interrelated. For instance, a student may *know* a great deal about a topic but *describe* it inaccurately in a particular essay.

> **Look again at the list just given. Which of the factors do you believe are process skills and which are content?***

These days almost all examinations in psychology have sets of *Aims and Objectives* which are available to students and teachers. You should familiarize yourself with these Aims and Objectives as early as possible in your course of study because they should spell out clearly and precisely what skills will be expected from you in that particular examination, how these skills will be assessed and the different weightings given to each of the skills.

The important point to make is that one of the easiest ways to produce poor or inappropriate essays in preparation for an examination, or as part of the examination itself, is to concentrate too heavily upon the content of the examination syllabus at the expense of developing the process skills. What you know is part of what will be assessed – it is vital to understand what you will be required to do with that knowledge.

The next important question we need to answer is *how* do examiners (or teachers in preparing students for examinations) judge the essays. This brings us to a consideration of the *marking scheme*. Most marking schemes tell examiners how to reward essays with reference to both content (the knowledge of psychology displayed) and process/skills.

The AEB Psychology 'A' level, by far the largest one in the country at the time of writing, instructs examiners to assess process in terms of two skills (imaginatively called Skill A and Skill B). These are schematically presented in Box 1.

Exactly how Skill A and Skill B apply to particular questions depends upon the exact wordings used. We shall return to this point later. But in essence Skill A is descriptive, Skill B is evaluative.

*Answer: factors 1, 3, 4, and 7 are process-only skills.

Box 1: Psychological content and skills

SKILL A	CONTENT	SKILL B
Description	Theories	Analysis
Knowledge	Concepts	Evaluation
Understanding	Evidence	Appraisal
Construction	Methods	Relevance/ appropriateness
Coherence	Application	Cogency
	Ethics	Relationships (e.g. theory and evidence

The 25 marks available for most of the essay questions set are then allocated as follows:

0–7 marks: both Skills A and B poorly presented
8–16 marks: EITHER
Skill A *or* Skill B well presented
OR
Skills A *and* B only partially well presented
17–25 marks: Skills A *and* B well presented.

Increasingly, psychology examinations are including more questions which break away from the traditional 'single sentence' format (for example, 'Discuss the evidence that gender roles are socially constructed'). But the principle still holds true: essays are judged by examiners on both content and process/skills.

> **Refresh your memory concerning the ten criteria of 'good practice' in essay-writing given on pp. 167–8. See how these fit into the AEB criteria.**

Remember it is criteria such as these that are used by examiners when assessing the quality of your examination essays.

You must ensure that you are totally familiar with the skills and abilities which are assessed by *your* examination. A knowledge of the Aims and Objectives (process/skills) and syllabus (subject content) will tell you *exactly* what your essays will be judged on. Remember that the development of a skill can be divided into three components:

● Identification
● Rehearsal
● Feedback

Having identified the factors and abilities assessed in your examination, you now need to rehearse them (in future essays) and learn from the feedback given on these practice-essays.

Undoubtedly, one of the most important features of a good essay is that of *relevance*. The 'blunderbuss' approach to essay-writing, in which the writer throws everything at the examiner and hopes that something hits the mark, is almost always doomed to failure. Remember that the essential purpose in writing an essay is to answer a particular question.

You should remember then, that when your lecturer or examiner sets a question for you s/he wishes you to actually answer it. One useful tip is for you to imagine that someone has asked you the same question face to face and is standing in front of you wanting an answer. Can you actually provide an answer to the person's question? Your lecturer and examiner do not want you to treat the questions s/he has set as Uri Geller treats spoons.

As well as relevance, *selectivity* is critical to good essay-writing. You will rarely be able to include *all* your material in an essay. Be selective and include that which will best answer your question.

Nevertheless, it is rare, in psychology at least, that any question will have a single correct answer. Your task is to use your knowledge of psychology and to display the skills assessed by your examination in a way that answers the question set to the very best of your ability.

Given that essay questions are set to be answered, it follows that the focus and emphasis of an essay should be largely determined by the exact wording.

Let us consider an example to illustrate this point.

> **Read the two following questions from past 'A' level papers carefully and make notes on a piece of paper of exactly what you think you would include in your answer if you attempted this question.**

EXAMPLE 1: Discuss theories that seek to account for human aggression and their implications for the control of human aggressive behaviour. (AEB, 1988)

EXAMPLE 2: Discuss social psychological factors which tend to elicit aggressive behaviour in people. (AEB, 1990)

How similar were the sets of notes that you produced for these two titles? What we need to ask is: what *exactly* are the similarities and differences between these questions?

The two questions have the same process/skill requirement: they both require you to 'discuss' something (but more of this skill requirement shortly). For the moment, let us concentrate on the content focuses of the questions. Below, the Example 2 question has been rewritten to indicate the parts in which it is similar (+) and different (−) to the Example 1 question.

DISCUSS (+)
SOCIAL PSYCHOLOGICAL FACTORS (−)
WHICH TEND TO ELICIT (−)
AGGRESSIVE BEHAVIOUR IN PEOPLE (1).

Note the following key differences between the two questions:

1 Example 1 specifies THEORIES instead of SOCIAL PSYCHOLOGICAL FACTORS.
2 It is concerned with SEEK(ING) TO ACCOUNT for human aggression, rather than being concerned with factors which TEND TO ELICIT (i.e. bring out) aggression rather than, for example, maintain aggression.
3 Example 1 requires you to consider the CONTROL OF HUMAN AGGRESSIVE BEHAVIOUR; there is no such requirement in Example 2.

Thus the two questions, which may appear very similar before careful 'unpacking' have only two points in common:

1 They are both 'Discuss' questions.
2 They are both concerned with human aggression.

We hope this analysis has clearly demonstrated the need to read every essay question slowly and analytically, word by word.

The above exercise has shown that it is necessary to read questions using two independent criteria: CONTENT *and* SKILL *requirements*. By this it is meant: what topic(s) does a question focus upon and what is it that you are being asked to do (for example, to describe, to evaluate, to contrast)? If you look back at the two questions we have just analyzed you will see that they both have a single skill requirement (to discuss), but that Example 1 has two requirements of content focus (theories or human aggression and reduction/control of human aggression), whereas Example 2 has only one content requirement (social psychological factors which tend to elicit aggressive behaviour in people).

This does not mean that Example 2 is an easier question than Example 1. You may recognize this as the old breadth versus depth issue. If examiners require students to deal with several issues or requirements there should be a corresponding reduction of expectation of depth.

An important part of this exercise is to show you what the precise words used in questions require you to do. We shall shortly deal explicitly with the process/skill words, but Box 2 overleaf gives you a typical set of content words which identify which aspects of your knowledge of psychology are required.

Consider the following examples of questions that vary by content and skill/process requirements:

SINGLE CONTENT/SINGLE SKILL:
'Normality is simply the absence of abnormality.' Discuss.

Box 2: Definitions of key content words

ONE OR MORE: The candidate may chose to focus on one in depth, or an increasing number in less detail. The candidate should bear in mind the requirements of Skills A and B. A very superficial review of many might result in failure to demonstrate Skill B.

APPLICATIONS: Actual or possible ways of using psychological knowledge in an applied/practical setting.

CONCEPTS: An idea or group of ideas. These are often the basic units of a model or theory.

EVIDENCE: Material (empirical or theoretical) which may be used in support or contradiction of an argument or theory.

FINDINGS: The outcome or product of research.

INSIGHTS: Perceptions which facilitate an understanding or conceptual reappraisal.

METHODS: Different ways in which empirical research is and may be carried out.

MODEL: Often used synonymously with 'theory' (see below) but, strictly, less complex/elaborate and often comprising a single idea or image meant as a metaphor. Explanation is often by analogy.

RESEARCH: The process of gaining knowledge and understanding via either theory construction examination or empirical data collection.

STUDIES: Empirical investigations providing evidence which, through reference to investigator's name and/or details of investigation/outcome, should be recognizable to the examiner.

THEORY: A (usually) complex set of interrelated ideas/assumptions/principles intended to explain or account for certain observed phenomena.

DUAL CONTENT/SINGLE SKILL:
Discuss trait and type approaches to personality.

SINGLE CONTENT/DUAL SKILL:
Describe and assess evidence from psychological research into the effects of media violence on children.

DUAL CONTENT/DUAL SKILL:
Describe one theory of personality and critically evaluate this theory in terms of its methods of assessment.

Finally, with reference to the structure of essay questions and how these should be read/interpreted, lecturers and examiners are increasingly setting structured (or parted) questions. In these questions separate marks are allocated to parts of questions. Two examples are given below:

1 (a) What do psychologists mean by 'motivation'?   (*3 marks*)

(b) Describe one physiological and one non-physiological explanation of motivation. (*10 marks*)

(c) Critically consider the evidence for and against either one of these explanations. (*12 marks*)

2 (a) Compare the experimental method with any one method used by psychologists. (*10 marks*)

(b) Critically contrast the relative strengths and weaknesses of these two methods. (*15 marks*)

You should read these questions analytically (as in the exercises above) by identifying their content and skill requirements. You should then ensure that the balance of your answer reflects the mark weightings given in the question. Don't spend 75% of your time answering a part of the question which will only earn you three marks!

Having worked through some exercises concerned with identifying the content and process/skill requirements, we need to turn our attention to a detailed consideration of exactly what the actual words used in the questions mean. Again, we need to distinguish between content and process/skill requirements. The words referring to content relate to the theories, concepts, evidence, methods, applications and ethical issues (see Box 2) which you will have learned about from your lectures and reading before the examination. Let us now deal with the skill requirements. What *exactly* is the difference between being asked to discuss and describe, for example? Box 3 is used by the examiners for AEB 'A' level psychology. It makes constant references to the Skills A and B described in Box 1 so you should refer back to that now to refresh your memory.

Box 3: Definitions of key skills words

ANALYZE/CRITICALLY ANALYZE*: These instructions require the candidate to demonstrate understanding through consideration of the components or elements of the stipulated topic area.
They are Skill B terms.

ASSESS/CRITICALLY ASSESS*: These instructions require the candidate to make an informed judgement about how good or effective something is based on an awareness of the strengths and limitations of the information and argument presented. The candidate is required to present a considered appraisal of the stipulated topic area.
They are Skill B terms.

COMPARE/CONTRAST: These instructions require the candidate to consider similarities and/or differences between the stipulated topic areas (e.g. psychological theories or concepts). This may involve critical consideration of points of similarity and differentiation.
They are Skill A and Skill B terms.

CONSIDER: This instruction requires the candidate to demonstrate knowledge and understanding of the stipulated topic area.
This is a Skill A term.

CRITICALLY CONSIDER: As 'CONSIDER' above, but in addition, the candidate is required to show an awareness of the strengths and limitations of the material presented.
This is a Skill A and Skill B term.

CRITICIZE: This instruction requires the candidate to critically appraise/evaluate the strengths/weaknesses of the topic areas.
This is a Skill B term.

DESCRIBE: This instruction requires the candidate to present evidence of his/her knowledge of the stipulated topic areas.
This is a Skill A term.

DEFINE: This is an instruction to the candidate to explain the meaning of a particular term such as one used to identify a particular concept.
This is a Skill A term.

DISCUSS: This instruction requires the candidate to both describe and evaluate by reference to different if not contrasting points of view. This may be done sequentially or concurrently. Questions may instruct the candidate to discuss with reference to particular criteria, for example by the use of the phrase '. . . in terms of . . .'.
This is a Skill A and Skill B term.

DISTINGUISH BETWEEN: This instruction requires the candidate to demonstrate his/her understanding of the differences between two stipulated topic areas (e.g. theories). Such a differentiation may be achieved at the levels of both descriptive and critical contrasting.
This is a Skill A and Skill B term.

EVALUATE/CRITICALLY EVALUATE*: This instruction requires the candidate to make an informed judgement regarding the value of the stipulated topic area, based on systematic analysis and examination.
This is a Skill B term.

EXAMINE: This instruction requires the candidate to present a detailed, descriptive consideration of the stipulated topic area.
This is a Skill A term.

EXPLAIN: This instruction requires the candidate to convey his/her understanding of a stipulated topic area and to make such an explanation coherent and intelligible.
This is a Skill A term.

JUSTIFY: This instructs the candidate to consider the grounds for a decision, for example by offering a supportive consideration of the logic behind a particular interpretation.
This is a Skill B term.

OUTLINE/STATE: This is an instruction to the candidate to offer a summary description of the stipulated topic area in brief form.
This is a Skill A term.

*These two terms are used interchangeably, with examiners being more likely to use the latter when they believe that it is useful to remind candidates of the need to be critical and evaluative.

PREPARATION

The time spent immediately before you write an essay is one of the most important parts of the process. We are now at the point where we can consider exactly how you should write your essay. The following is a summary of the key stages:

1 *Preparation* (e.g. acquiring the content knowledge and familiarity with the requirements of the task). All that we have considered so far in this chapter is intended to provide you with the appropriate preparation.
2 *Reading the questions.* Remember the importance of reading questions carefully and analytically, and 'unpacking' them to identify their skill and content requirements.
3 *Planning your answer.*
4 *Writing your answer.*
5 *Reading and reviewing at the end.*

Many students mistakenly believe that all that matters is point 4. In fact, it could be argued that if points 1–3 have been carried out properly the essay should almost write itself!

> **Write down on a piece of paper how *you* plan your essays and then compare it with the advice given here.**

Planning is one of the most important activities in constructing and writing an essay. One of the most frequent complaints made by examiners is that some essays appear to be of the 'Blue Peter' ('Here is one I made earlier') type. Pre-prepared essays which are reproduced irrespective of the wording of the actual question rarely earn much credit for the writer. Planning is the best way to ensure the most successful match between what you know and can do and what a specific question requires.

Because all of us have different strengths and weaknesses, and do things in different ways, there can be no *one* right way to create plans but the following works for most students.

Bear in mind throughout that what you are engaging in is a problem-solving exercise. The specific problem is the question you are about to answer. Your task is to decide exactly what the requirements of the question are and then try to use your knowledge of psychology and your skills to meet these demands to the best of your ability. It is often useful to think of this as a matching exercise: you are trying to achieve the best match possible between the *requirements* of the question and what you are able to *provide*.

Stages in planning

1 Read the question very carefully and analytically in the ways we have discussed above. Identify the content and skill requirements, and write these down.
2 Brainstorm what you feel you can contribute – i.e. write down (in the

briefest note form possible) all the items of knowledge that you possess that may be relevant to the question as set. Do not be critical at this stage or attempt any ordering/sequencing.

3 Re-read the question, and examine the relationship between the requirements of the question and your brainstormed list.

4 Go back to your brainstormed list, and delete items which are either irrelevant or only marginally relevant. Hopefully you will still have enough left for a good essay! This cutting process will make a substantial contribution to the quality of your essay. Remember a good essay will be to the point and answer the question as set. Content is only one part of the exercise – just as important is the use you make of your knowledge.

5 Structure the sequence of your essay. Aim for a beginning, middle and end. Try to organize the presentation of your evidence so that the essay will have shape and a coherent flow. For example, in answering a question which is focused on the nature-nurture debate you may wish to start with a broad statement which deals with what the debate is about (and perhaps provide some key definitions), then present theory and research findings relating to one side of the debate, and then repeat this for the other side. You may then highlight the points of difference between the two and provide some evaluation of their relative strengths and weaknesses. A conclusion may then sum up the main points of the essay and provide some (perhaps tentative) conclusions.

6 Re-read the question again, just to make sure you have not missed something crucial and look again at the fit between the requirements of the question and the answer you propose providing.

This activity will take quite a long time initially but with repeated and frequent practice it can be achieved in a matter of a few minutes. In an examination situation these few minutes will go a long way to determining how well you do.

> **On page 172 the following was given as an example of a dual content/dual skill question:**
>
> 'Describe one theory of personality and critically evaluate this theory in terms of its methods of assessment.'
>
> **Write out this question and produce an essay plan for the question. Allow yourself about 15 minutes to refamiliarize yourself with the materials in the textbook (see p. 907 for orientation), two or three minutes to check the skill requirements given in Box 3 of this chapter and a final 10 minutes for writing the plan following steps 1–6 above.**

Although, as has been said already, there is no one 'right' answer to any given question, a 'final-version' (i.e. stage 6) plan which meets the requirements of the question is given below. Note that for the purposes of clarity it is *not* written in shorthand.

PART 1: DESCRIPTION OF ONE THEORY OF PERSONALITY:
All Skill A (i.e. no evaluation), apart from introduction (first paragraph)

1 What is personality? Chosen theory: Freud's psychoanalytic theory.
2 Instincts: libido (*mention* of infantile sexuality) and death-wish. Psychic energy and need for release.
3 Structure of personality: id/ego/superego (*mention* of morality [conscience/ego-ideal] in superego).
4 Psychosexual stages of development: oral/anal/phallic (*mention* gender role determination as outcome of resolution of Oedipus/Electra Complexes)/(latency)/genital. *Mention*: fixation and regression.

PART 2: EVALUATION IN TERMS OF METHODS OF ASSESSMENT:
Skill B, but not *a* general *evaluation of Freud*

1 What is meant by methods of assessment? Actual techniques/ 'methodologies' used (i.e. not theory, but show links between the two if possible).
2 General characteristics of the methodology: e.g. idiographic, qualitative, retrospective. Issues of untestability/lack of 'science'.
3 Specific examples of 'methods of assessment':
   • analysis of neurotic symptoms;
   • analysis of defence mechanisms;
   • dreams;
   • parapraxes (Freudian slips); and
   • play (but not really Freud himself. Anna Freud, Melanie Kline, Virginia Axline).
4 Brief contrasting with other methods:
   e.g.   personality tests;
           humanistic self-awareness; and
           enhancement.

It will be clear to everyone that such a mammoth content load could not be delivered in the 40 minutes the examination permits (perhaps not even in the whole three hours!). Consequently, having constructed the above (which is intended to be pretty much all-inclusive), the next decision to be made is whether to go for **breadth** or **depth**: i.e. to try to skim as much of the above as possible or to be selective and concentrate upon various aspects. If you were to opt for the second approach it is advisable to try and *mention* the points (in passing) that you do not develop in detail. It should be clearly understood that neither approach is necessarily better than the other. It will depend upon your own strengths and weaknesses as much as anything else.

You will probably have noticed that the plan utilizes material from several parts of the textbook (at least four separate chapters), re-orders and integrates them. Notice particularly, that the plan does *not* give a *general* evaluation/critique of Freud or psychoanalytic theory, nor does it offer an evaluation of the various characteristics of the theory described in Part 1. The reason for this is very simple: the question does not ask for this. This reminds us of the vital maxim: *always answer the question set, not the one you prefer.*

WRITING THE ESSAY ITSELF

On p. 175 five key stages in writing an essay were identified. We have now reached stage 4.

Remember that many of the skills being measured in your examination are concerned with the quality of your delivery. For example, Skill A (Box 1) is partly concerned with the construction and coherence of answers. Skill B is partly concerned with relevance, clear and logical argument and linking different parts of the essay and topics/areas covered.

When writing your essays from your plans (especially those in exams) be sure to bear the following points in mind.

1 Try to be as clear and accurate as possible.
2 Make every word count. Your time is very limited and repetition will earn you no credit whatsoever. Don't waffle!
3 Write as if you were addressing an intelligent layperson – someone who can appreciate the construction of good argument, the ability to answer a question as set and a good display of specialist knowledge, but who does not possess this specialist knowledge, which is for you to convey.
4 Try to draw links between your sections, and remember to draw the whole thing together at the end.
5 Make references back to the question as often as possible; this will show the marker that you are making every effort to answer the question.
6 Try to be confident.

AN ILLUSTRATIVE ESSAY

Here is a sample 2000 word essay which would probably gain an 'A' grade at 'A' level.

Question

'If . . . the impression takes root that IQ tests really measure intelligence, that they constitute a sort of last judgement on the ability of the child's capacity, that they reveal scientifically his/her predestined ability, then it would be a thousand times better if all the intelligence testers and their questionnaires were sunk without warning' (Lippmann, 1922).

Discuss the above view in the light of the controversy surrounding the use of IQ tests.

PLAN

Introduction/outline of intent
Relationship between intelligence and IQ
3 different conceptualizations of intelligence
Brief history of IQ testing

Uses (Vernon)
g and s issue

Uses of tests (skill A – descriptive):
   measurement of ability
   norms of normality
   use as educational instrument
   developmental barometer
Uses (Skill B – evaluation)
   validity (e.g. Fontana; Heim; Ryan)
   culture and class biases (e.g. Vernon; Bruner; Kamin)
   labelling and self-fulfilling prophecy (e.g. Rosenthal and Jacobson)
   ethics

Conclusion: relate back to the quote:
              really measuring?
              last judgement (fluid/crystalized)
              (science)
              predestined ability
              sinking!

THE ESSAY

(Note: the paragraphs have been numbered only to make the following analysis easier. It is not normal practice to do this.)

1   The field of IQ testing has been one of the most controversial in all of psychology over the last two decades. It has included debates about, for example, the accuracy of psychometric measurement, the nature-nurture debate, issues relating to education, the social psychology of the testing situation and ethical issues relating to race and culture and to psychological labelling. This essay will begin with a consideration of the relationship between intelligence and IQ, and will examine three different views concerning the nature of intelligence. There will then be a brief account of the history of IQ testing, including a consideration of whether intelligence consists of a general factor or a series of specific ones. The essay will then examine four examples of the uses of IQ tests and evaluate these in the light of four different criteria. In conclusion, there will be a point-by-point analysis of the substance of the quotation given in the question.

2   The date of the quotation given in the question (1922) indicates that this statement was made in the relatively early days of IQ testing. Some of the phraseology used (such as the use of the word 'questionnaires') would be seen as a little peculiar in the 1990s. However, it is fair to say that there has been a very heated debate in more recent years concerning the use of IQ tests. In the late 1960s and early 1970s it centred on the issue of race and intelligence (e.g. between such figures as Jensen and H. J. Eysenck on one 'side' and Kamin, Ryan and Heather on the other). But the debate also concerned such wide issues as the role and responsibilities of the scientist in society.

3   One of the most vital questions in this debate concerns the relationship between IQ and intelligence. To put it crudely, does IQ actually measure

intelligence? Unfortunately, the only answer that can be given is, it depends. It depends essentially upon how one defines intelligence. More significantly, it depends upon the particular approach to intelligence – the issue concerns more than argument over fine detail.

4   Gross (1992) argues that there are within psychology three approaches to intelligence: the psychological approach which has concentrated heavily upon psychometric measurement; the bio-constructivist approach (e.g. Piaget) and the information-processing approach (e.g. Sternberg). It is probably fair to say the second two are more directly concerned with process-factors (e.g. what happens during intelligent activity? What processes are involved? What determines these factors?). Certainly, the concern of the psychometric approach is with measurement, and in particular quantitative measurement. Critics of the psychometric approach such as Heather (1976) have argued that there is an extent to which the tail is wagging the dog here. Parker (1992) has claimed that researchers define concepts in a way that suit their own purposes and then spend the rest of their professional lives 'researching their own fictions'. A classic illustration of this tendency is given by Boring's classic (1923) definition 'intelligence is what intelligence tests measure'. In essence the key problem here is that of validity. Two separate aspects of validity are relevant at this point: first, do the tests measure what they are supposed to measure (presumably intelligence), and second, is the validity criterion appropriate (i.e. are we defining intelligence in a way that enables us to measure it through IQ tests? Are we simply researching our own 'fictions'?).

5   We should note that these concerns are not exclusive to the IQ/intelligence debate. They affect most areas where psychologists are exploring and (especially) measuring concepts. Concepts such as attitudes, for example, are psychological constructions, not slices of 'real life'.

6   The history of IQ testing is generally taken as going back to Francis Galton in the 1860s, but his and other early tests (e.g. Cattell, 1895) were flawed because of the assumptions they made (e.g. that intelligence is a reflection of other forms of physical wellbeing). It is of interest to note that the first 'workable' IQ test was developed without reference to a justifying theory of intelligence. Binet and Simon's first test (1905) was developed as a practical response to the need to classify children whose mental development was not typical for their age. In these early days, the tests compared children's chronological age (CA) with their mental age (MA) which was defined by the level attained by most 'average' children of particular ages.

7   Later tests, such as those developed by Wechsler, were concerned with direct statistical measurement whereby it was assumed that intelligence is normally distributed within the general population and a person's score is compared with norms for his or her age group. In this way, the question of age is no longer of relevance.

8   Today, IQ tests are used extensively. Vernon (1977) has estimated that in excess of 2,000,000,000 tests of intelligence or achievement are administered in the USA alone every year. More recently, key-stage testing

in Britain has been introduced whereby all children are assessed at ages 7, 11 and 14. Many of these items assess intelligence and achievement.

9   Tests vary considerably according to the number of different aspects of intelligence that are taken to exist. Some tests measure verbal and non-verbal aspects of intelligence, whereas others measure only one or the other. In the last revision of the Stanford-Binet test (1986), four component scores were given instead of the single score which had been given previously.

10   This development was largely influenced by the debate concerning the component parts of intelligence and their interrelationship. This can be traced back historically to Spearman (1904) who factor-analyzed intelligence into two factors: (g) general and (s) specific. Thurstone (1937) developed a scale involving seven primary intellectual abilities whereas Guilford (1957) measured 120 outcomes. It should be noted in passing that there has been considerable debate within psychology about the uses and limitations of factor analysis.

11   Many uses have been made over the years of IQ tests. Essentially, of course, the prime function has been to measure, but it is the uses to which these measurements are put which has aroused most interest and concern amongst critics. Let us briefly consider four specific examples of the uses of IQ tests:
a) Use as an educational instrument. IQ scores may be used to place children in an appropriate class. They may indicate relative strengths and weaknesses in a particular child's abilities.
b) Establishing 'norms of normality'. Children may be classified as 'gifted' or having learning difficulties according to IQ test outcomes.
c) Use as a development scale. Children will often be tested at various times in their school lives (reference was made earlier to key-stage testing in British children). In doing this, a longitudinal measurement of a child's ability can be achieved. This may indicate a cause for concern if a child's scores markedly deteriorate over time.
d) Measurement of ability in non-school populations. Many job selection programmes include some form of IQ testing. People may take IQ tests for fun! Mensa uses IQ scores as its criterion for admission.

12   Let us evaluate the use of IQ tests (in any or all of the above examples) through four criteria: validity, bias, labelling and ethical concerns.

13   Many critics of IQ testing have questioned their validity. Fontana (1981) has said that whereas intelligence is a psychological concept, IQ is purely statistical. Ryan (1972) has argued that measurement in IQ tests is limited because it can never be absolute, only relative. In other words, an IQ component score cannot make sense on its own, only in comparison to other scores. Further, Rose (1984) has argued against the appropriateness of the assumption of the normal distribution of intelligence (Parker's 'fictions' again?) and Heather (1976) has claimed that general intelligence should really be called 'school intelligence'. Heim, although accepting the worth of IQ tests, contends that they constitute unacceptable reductionism: IQ should be viewed as simply one part of a whole person.

14   Critics claim that there are many biases inherent in IQ tests (and further biases in the way that they are administered) which operate against, for example, people of certain classes (Bernstein, 1961), races (Labov, 1970) and sex (Heather, 1976). Bruner has said 'the culture-free test is the intelligence-free test, for intelligence is a cultural concept'. Heather has demonstrated that if attempts are made to reduce these biases the ability of the tests to predict 'success' is reduced. This is because the biases in the tests are also usually found in the system itself (e.g. the educational system, job selection programmes). We may remove some of the 'isms' in the tests but they still live on in our cultural systems.

15   Work by researchers such as Rosenthal and Jacobson (1968) has shown the power of 'labelling'. Self-fulfilling prophecies occur when children live up (or down) to expectations held about them.

16   Recently, there has been great debate about the ethical responsibilities of psychologists. Much of this has derived from the status of psychologists as scientists. Following what has been said above, can psychologists really claim to be value-free and objective? Fairbairn and Fairbairn (1987) argue that the greater the 'scientific credibility' of research activity, the less likely it is to be challenged or debated. What are the consequences of psychologists showing that black people, working-class people or women do less well on IQ tests? It would certainly appear that this is of great concern to Lippmann in the quote given in the question.

17   Finally, let us put all of the above into the context of the Lippmann quotation. An analysis of the quotation would indicate that he identifies three areas of concern (and a rather drastic solution!). First, he asks if IQ tests really measure intelligence. We have seen that many psychologists and critics believe that they do not, and that even if they do, this may be because intelligence has been defined in such a way as to make this possible (e.g. Boring's definition). Second, that the scores represent a 'sort of last judgement on the child's capacity'. We have seen that because of the generally widespread scientific credibility of psychology, the products of its application are often not challenged, and furthermore because of self-fulfilling prophecies, outcomes are often created by our measurements. We make things true simply by stating them. It may simply be, however, that we need to think differently about intelligence. One way forward might be that given by Horn and Cattell (1982) who write about fluid and crystalized intelligence. Most IQ tests may be seen as drawing heavily upon the former.

18   Third, Lippmann is concerned that IQ tests may be thought to reveal predestined ability. This is largely concerned with the nature-nurture debate, which is beyond the scope of this essay, but many of the definitions of intelligence given by psychologists (e.g. Burt [1955] who defined intelligence as 'innate, general, cognitive ability') and many of the contributions (e.g. Jensen, 1969) to the 'race' debate do seem to encourage the view that intelligence is a given entity with a high heritability. Insofar as IQ tests produce an outcome which carries the impression of great accuracy and is often (perhaps inappropriately) assumed to be a relatively 'fixed' property of a person, they have served to reinforce this impression.

19   In the final analysis, Lippmann's solution may, however, be both too drastic and unwarranted. Flynn (1970) concluded that 'a reputable test is still the best single means of assessing an individual's intelligence, whatever definition is used. It is more objective, consistent and valid as a first approximation than any of the validatory criteria against which tests may be calibrated.'

ANALYSIS OF THE ESSAY

> Look back at Box 1 (p. 169) and make your own judgement about how well the essay meets all of the Skill A and Skill B requirements.

It is our view that the essay is excellent on almost all of the criteria. In terms of content, the only area of relative deficiency is that of methods – very little reference is made to the methodological concerns of IQ test construction, for example (although passing reference is made to factor analysis). It should be noted however, that that would appear to be legitimate since the essay question is primarily concerned with *uses* of IQ tests. It should be remembered that it is extremely rare for any one question to tap all of the Box 1 requirements equally.

It is our view that all of the Skill A requirements are satisfied.

With regard to Skill B, it would seem to us that, again, all of the requirements are satisfied. The 'critical' skills (analysis/evaluation/appraisal) are very apparent throughout the essay. The arguments presented are impressive and logical, and relationships between theory and evidence are well drawn. The essay scores particularly highly on relevance.

PARAGRAPH-BY-PARAGRAPH ANALYSIS

It is clear that it would be extraordinarily difficult to produce an essay such as this one under examination conditions. But it would be important to retain the high question-focus that it has and to try not to lose the overall shape and logic of the essay when 'pruning'. In the following analysis, we have indicated which parts might best be cut, and which should definitely be retained.

With regard to the question, note how the lengthy quotation gives the writer plenty 'to go for'; it is best used as a stimulus for the essay to follow. Note how this essay specifically addresses the content focus (uses of tests) and identifies both Skill A and Skill B modes of response – see plan.

PARAGRAPH 1: A very clear introduction. This would need to be shorter in an examination.

PARAGRAPH 2: Scene-setting and drawing links. This could be cut in an examination.

PARAGRAPHS 3 & 4: Relationship between intelligence and IQ. This is absolutely central to the answer. At the start of paragraph 4 a major temptation (to be drawn into a detailed consideration of different models of intelligence) was avoided. Note the critical tone in the second half of paragraph 4.

PARAGRAPH 5: Links and perspectives. Again, this could be cut in an examination.

PARAGRAPHS 6–8: A brief history of IQ testing. Again the temptation for over-elaboration was avoided. This could be reduced/cut in an examination.

PARAGRAPHS 9 & 10: Return to IQ and intelligence relationship. Note how it followed logically from what preceded it. Note the specific, orientating reference back to the question.

PARAGRAPH 11: Identification of specific uses of IQ tests. This was not 'sourced/referenced', showing the value of avoiding passive repetition of knowledge. This paragraph is central to the essay.

PARAGRAPH 12: Evaluation. Note the clear use of criteria.

PARAGRAPH 13: Again, appropriately selective. Note that there were other choices open to the writer (e.g. types of validity).

PARAGRAPH 14: Particularly sharp and concise. Note, again, the broader context of the discussion.

PARAGRAPHS 15 & 16: Less empirical evidence than in the immediately preceding paragraphs. Nevertheless, good, clear and relevant argument constructed.

PARAGRAPHS 17 & 18: This is excellent. Note how the writer unpacked the quotation. This showed a clear reading of the quote and attention to the question. It was also a way of giving a brief resumé of some of the main points of the essay. Note the reference to a topic not covered (the nature-nurture debate) demonstrating awareness of the limitations of the essay.

PARAGRAPH 19: A cheeky attempt at balance!

It is hoped that if you follow the advice given in this Study Guide the quality of your essay-writing will be significantly strengthened. We hope that it will have made you more secure in your knowledge of psychology and helped you acquire some useful analytical skills in reading questions and writing essays – both for your teacher/lecturer and your examiner. One final point: before handing in that essay or leaving the examination room, don't forget to re-read it and check for errors. A psychologist we have never heard of crops up every year — he appears to be called Fraud!

ANSWERS TO MULTIPLE-CHOICE QUESTIONS

Chapter 1
1b; 2c; 3c; 4c; 5b; 6c; 7d; 8a; 9c; 10d; 11b;
12d; 13b; 14c; 15d; 16d; 17d; 18d; 19a; 20c;
21d; 22d; 23d; 24a; 25d; 26b; 27d; 28d; 29b;
30c.

Chapter 2
1c; 2a; 3c; 4c; 5a; 6d; 7d; 8d; 9d; 10d; 11d;
12d; 13d; 14a; 15d; 16d; 17d; 18c; 19d; 20a;
21d; 22c; 23d; 24d; 25a; 26d.

Chapter 3
1d; 2c; 3d; 4b; 5d; 6b; 7d; 8d; 9d; 10d; 11d;
12a; 13b; 14d; 15a; 16d; 17c; 18a; 19d; 20d;
21d; 22d; 23a; 24d; 25d.

Chapter 4
1d; 2d; 3c; 4c; 5d; 6d; 7c; 8d; 9d; 10d; 11d;
12c; 13b; 14d; 15d; 16c; 17a; 18d; 19c; 20c;
21d; 22b; 23d; 24d; 25d; 26b; 27d; 28d; 29c;
30a.

Chapter 5
1c; 2a; 3b; 4a; 5d; 6d; 7c; 8b; 9c; 10c; 11c;
12d; 13d; 14d; 15d; 16a; 17d; 18c; 19d; 20d;
21d; 22d; 23d; 24d; 25d; 26c; 27d; 28c.

Chapter 6
1d; 2d; 3d; 4d; 5a; 6d; 7c; 8d; 9d; 10d; 11b;
12d; 13d; 14d; 15d; 16a; 17b; 18c; 19d; 20d;
21d; 22d; 23c; 24b.

Chapter 7
1d; 2a; 3a; 4d; 5d; 6c; 7d; 8a; 9d; 10d; 11c;
12d; 13b; 14d; 15d; 16d; 17d; 18d; 19c; 20d;
21d; 22a; 23a.

Chapter 8
1d; 2d; 3d; 4a; 5d; 6b; 7a; 8c; 9a; 10d; 11d;
12d; 13a; 14a; 15c; 16a; 17d; 18a; 19d; 20d;
21d; 22d; 23d; 24d; 25d; 26b.

Chapter 9
1b; 2d; 3d; 4d; 5d; 6d; 7d; 8a; 9d; 10d; 11d;
12d; 13d; 14d; 15d; 16d; 17b; 18d; 19c; 20a;
21d; 22b; 23d; 24a; 25b.

Chapter 10
1d; 2d; 3d; 4d; 5d; 6c; 7d; 8b; 9d; 10d; 11d;
12d; 13d; 14a; 15d; 16d; 17d; 18d; 19d; 20d;
21a; 22d.

Chapter 11
1d; 2a; 3d; 4d; 5c; 6d; 7d; 8d; 9d; 10d; 11d;
12d; 13d; 14d; 15d; 16d; 17d; 18d; 19d;
20d; 21d; 22d; 23d; 24d.

Chapter 12
1c; 2b; 3c; 4d; 5d; 6d; 7b; 8a; 9d; 10d; 11d;
12d; 13d; 14d; 15d; 16d; 17d; 18d; 19d;
20d; 21d; 22d; 23d; 24a.

Chapter 13
1d; 2c; 3d; 4d; 5a; 6d; 7d; 8d; 9d; 10c; 11d;
12d; 13d; 14d; 15d; 16d; 17c; 18d; 19a; 20a;
21d; 22d; 23d; 24a.

Chapter 14
1d; 2c; 3d; 4b; 5d; 6d; 7d; 8c; 9c; 10d; 11d;
12d; 13d; 14b; 15d; 16d; 17a; 18d; 19a; 20d;
21d; 22d; 23d.

Chapter 15
1a; 2d; 3d; 4a; 5d; 6d; 7a; 8c; 9d; 10d; 11d;
12b; 13d; 14d; 15a; 16d; 17b; 18d; 19c; 20d;
21b; 22d; 23d; 24d; 25b; 26b; 27d; 28a.

Chapter 16
1b; 2d; 3c; 4d; 5d; 6d; 7d; 8a; 9d; 10d; 11d;
12c; 13d; 14b; 15d; 16d; 17d; 18d; 19d; 20d;
21d; 22c; 23d; 24b; 25d; 26d.

Chapter 17
1d; 2a; 3d; 4d; 5d; 6d; 7c; 8d; 9c; 10d; 11d;
12d; 13c; 14a; 15a; 16d; 17d; 18d; 19c; 20d;
21d; 22d; 23c; 24a; 25d; 26d.

Chapter 18
1d; 2d; 3d; 4d; 5b; 6d; 7b; 8a; 9d; 10a; 11d; 12d; 13a; 14c; 15d; 16b; 17d; 18d; 19b; 20b; 21b; 22d; 23c; 24d; 25c.

Chapter 19
1a; 2b; 3d; 4c; 5b; 6b; 7d; 8d; 9d; 10b; 11d; 12d; 13d; 14d; 15d; 16d; 17c; 18d; 19d; 20d; 21d; 22d; 23b; 24d; 25d.

Chapter 20
1a; 2c; 3d; 4b; 5c; 6b; 7d; 8d; 9b; 10a; 11d; 12d; 13c; 14b; 15b; 16a; 17c; 18d; 19d; 20b; 21b; 22d; 23d; 24b; 25b; 26c; 27c; 28d; 29d; 30c.

Chapter 21
1a; 2d; 3b; 4c; 5b; 6d; 7a; 8b; 9d; 10d; 11c; 12d; 13d; 14d; 15b; 16b; 17d; 18d; 19d; 20b; 21d; 22d; 23b; 24d; 25d.

Chapter 22
1d; 2b; 3d; 4d; 5d; 6d; 7d; 8d; 9d; 10c; 11b; 12d; 13d; 14d; 15d; 16d; 17b; 18d; 19d; 20b; 21d; 22d; 23d.

Chapter 23
1d; 2a; 3b; 4b; 5d; 6d; 7d; 8b; 9d; 10b; 11c; 12d; 13c; 14c; 15d; 16a; 17d; 18d; 19d; 20a; 21b; 22b; 23d.

Chapter 24
1c; 2d; 3a; 4a; 5c; 6d; 7d; 8d; 9a; 10d: 11a; 12d; 13d; 14d; 15d; 16d; 17d; 18b; 19d; 20d; 21d; 22c; 23a; 24d.

Chapter 25
1c; 2d; 3d; 4a; 5a; 6d; 7d; 8d; 9d; 10d; 11d; 12d; 13d; 14d; 15d; 16c; 17d; 18b; 19d; 20d; 21b; 22d; 23d; 24d; 25d; 26d; 27d; 28d.

Chapter 26
1d; 2d; 3b; 4b; 5d; 6d; 7b; 8d; 9d; 10d; 11d; 12d; 13d; 14d; 15d; 16d; 17d; 18b; 19a; 20d; 21c; 22d; 23d; 24d; 25d; 26d; 27d.

Chapter 27
1d; 2d; 3c; 4d; 5c; 6d; 7d; 8b; 9d; 10d; 11d; 12d; 13d; 14d; 15d; 16d; 17d; 18d; 19d; 20d; 21c; 22d; 23c; 24b; 25d; 26d; 27d; 28b.

Chapter 28
1b; 2d; 3c; 4b; 5d; 6d; 7a; 8d; 9d; 10d; 11d; 12b; 13b; 14d; 15d; 16d; 17b; 18d; 19b; 20d; 21d; 22d; 23a; 24d; 25d; 26d.

Chapter 29
1b; 2a; 3d; 4b; 5d; 6a; 7d; 8a; 9d; 10d; 11d; 12d; 13d; 14d; 15d; 16c; 17a; 18d; 19d; 20b; 21d; 22d; 23b; 24d; 25d; 26d; 27a.

Chapter 30
1c; 2d; 3d; 4c; 5d; 6d; 7d; 8d; 9d; 10d; 11a; 12d; 13a; 14d; 15d; 16b; 17d; 18a; 19d; 20a; 21d; 22d; 23a; 24d; 25d; 26b.

Chapter 31
1d; 2d; 3d; 4c; 5d; 6d; 7d; 8c; 9d; 10d; 11c; 12b; 13d; 14c; 15d; 16b; 17c; 18c; 19d; 20d; 21b; 22d; 23d; 24d; 25d; 26d; 27d.